Constructing Dalit Identity

Constructing Dalit Identity

C. Joe Arun

RAWAT PUBLICATIONS

Jaipur • New Delhi • Bangalore • Guwahati • Kolkata

ISBN 978-81-316-0081-8

Reprinted, 2021

Published by
Prem Rawat for **Rawat Publications**
Satyam Apts, Sector 3, Jawahar Nagar, Jaipur 302 004 (India)
Phone: 0141–265 1748 / 265 7006
E-mail: info@rawatbooks.com
Website: www.rawatbooks.com

New Delhi Office
4858/24, Ansari Road, Daryaganj, New Delhi 110 002
Phone: 011-2326 3290

Also at *Bangalore, Guwahati* and *Kolkata*

Typeset by Rawat Computers, Jaipur
Printed and bound in India

Contents

Abbreviations

HRW	Human Rights Watch
NCDHR	National Campaign on Dalit Human Rights
BSP	Bhahujan Samajwadi Party
DMK	Dravida Munnetra Kazhagam
AIADMK	All India Anna Dravida Munnetra Kazhagam
DPI	Dalit Panthers of India
PT	Puthiya Thamilagam
BCs	Backward Castes
TTS	Tamil Nadu Theological Seminary
FRRC	Folklore Resources and Research Centre
PMK	Pattali Makkal Katchi
DRC	Dalit Resource Centre
ASSEFA	Association of Sarva Seva Farms
CRDS	Chengalpattu Rural Development Society
CFCA	Christian Foundation For Children and Aging
DCLM	Dalit Christian Liberation Movement
RDO	Revenue Divisional Officer

Key to Kinship Notation

M	Mother	S	Son
F	Father	W	Wife
Z	Sister	H	Husband
B	Brother	y	younger
D	Daughter	e	elder
P	Parent	C	Child

Note on Transliteration

Tamil

Short Vowels

a as in English *u*p
i as in English s*i*t
u as in English p*u*t
e as in English g*e*t
o as in English l*oo*k

Long Vowels

ā as in English p*a*lm
ī as in English s*e*al
ū as in English p*oo*l
ē as in English w*a*de
ō as in English r*o*be

Otherwise, in my transliteration, I generally follow the conventions of the Madras University Tamil Lexicon. Non-English words are italicised and given diacritical markings. Proper names are not italicised and diacritical markings are omitted from them.

Aknowledgements

This book is a modified version of my doctoral dissertation submitted at Oxford University in 2003. The main body of the content remains unchanged with some minor modifications. During my fieldwork and at the time of writing up my thesis I have benefited from interactions with many persons and institutions. I want to thank my mother, Mrs. Mariathal Chockalingam, who taught me to observe changes in society constantly and organise my life accordingly. I am grateful to her for instilling in me a sense of perception and discernment that helped me in this research indirectly. Directly, there were many people who in one way or other contributed constructively to my research in Oxford and in my fieldwork in Tamil Nadu. Among the many people to whom I owe a debt of gratitude, first and foremost I thank Reverend Father D. Jeyaraj SJ, who insisted that I should complete my D.Phil earlier than later. In similar way, Dr P. Francis Xavier SJ, who encouraged me at every stage of my research and gave me the freedom and the facility to do my fieldwork.

I am most grateful to Dr Marcus Banks, my supervisor, who with his perceptive critique guided my research at every stage. His generosity, patience, erudition, and attention to detail have never failed to amaze me. Both during my fieldwork in Tamil

Nadu and my writing up of my thesis in Oxford he guided me to ask the right questions at the right time with the right people. Professor Robert Barnes, with his wife Ruth Barnes, has been steadfast source of friendship and of support to my work at Oxford. With Professor Barnes I enjoyed a great range of conversations on the use of comparative method in anthropological research.

The study was made possible by Overseas Research Student Award at Campion Hall for three years. In the Hall, I owe a debt of gratitude to all the members of the Hall, especially to Dr Gerard J. Hughes SJ, Master, who supported me in every possible way and guided me in my life at the Hall. I am particularly indebted to Reverend Dr Clarence Gallagher SJ, tutor in Canon Law at Oxford and at the University of London, who read my thesis chapter by chapter to give me his sharp remarks on clarity of expression and presentation. His personal support and constant encouragement put me at ease in the midst of the stress of writing the thesis up.

This research would not have been possible without the generosity of the people of Pappanallur village who received me into their families and allowed me to study their life. I am particularly gratcful to Xavier, my research assistant and the key informant. His deep knowledge of the history of the village and performative social skills eased my interactions both with the Paraiyars and the Vanniyars in the village. My sincere thanks go to Reverend Father Jeyaraj Elankeswaran and the Jesuits of the Chengalpattu region who were helpful during my fieldwork. My thanks to the students of Loyola High School, Kuppayanallur, who helped me strengthen and sharpen my arguments in the thesis.

I also value the encounters and discussions I had with Manuel Alphonse SJ, Thirumavalavan, leader of Dalit Panthers of India (DPI); Dr Mohan Larbeer at Dalit Resource Centre in Madurai; Aloysious Irudayam SJ, Ms. Pama, Dalit Novelist, Dr Gopal Guru, in Pune; Yesumarian SJ, Dr Vivek Kumar, Dr Eleanor Zelliot, Antony of Kuppayanallur. P. Arockiadoss SJ. I am thankful to the librarians at Dalit Resource Centre in Madurai, the Indian Social Institutes in Bangalore and New Delhi, the Connemera Library in Chennai, and the Taylor Library of the Institute of Social and Cultural Anthropology, Oxford.

My special thanks go to Dr Michael Amaladoss SJ, who persuaded me to persevere in my application to Oxford when I was almost losing hope and had started looking for a university in the United States. I am personally most grateful to Arul Sivan SJ and Joe Antony SJ, Michael Alosanai SJ, Leema Rosario, whose love and companionship was a source of energy and inspiration during my research. Hélène Neveu, Morten Kringelbach, George Stroup, Loradana, Consy Valentine, and Vasanth Don Bosco were as unstinting in their encouragement to my research as they have been generous in their friendship.

I

Introduction

1

Constructing Dalit Ethnicity: Arguments and Theories

On July 17th, 1997, K.R. Narayanan, a member of Dalit community, was elected President of India. This was the first time in the fifty-year history of India that a Dalit had been elevated to such a high position, supported by the traditional political parties. Nevertheless, a few days earlier, on June 30th, a gang of high caste men attacked nine Dalits who were travelling on a bus in the district of Madurai, Tamil Nadu, South India. Six were killed on the spot; one of them, K. Murugesan, who had just become President of the village council of Melavalavu, was beheaded and his head was thrown into a nearby well.[1]

These two events exemplify the reality of the condition of the Dalits in India in general, and of those of Tamil Nadu in particular. On the one hand, the Dalits, in an attempt to get rid of their centuries-old humiliation of untouchability, assert their identity and demand a respectable position in social life, while on the other, they face violent reaction of the higher castes against these assertions. The Dalits' assertions and the higher castes' resistance are the two sides of life in India today.

The present study focuses on the side of the Dalit assertions and describes the process in and by which the Paraiyars, one of the Dalit groups of Pappanallur village, Tamil Nadu, South India, attempt to construct their identity by reversing the symbols of pollution,[2] that defined them as low and polluted, into symbols of their culture and positive identity.[3] Specifically, it considers, first, how conflicts between the Paraiyars and the Vanniyars, the dominant high caste group in the village, remain the source and driving force that makes the Paraiyars become conscious of their low identity, and persuades them to form a new positive self-identity.[4] Secondly, the thesis focuses on the symbols and myths, which were used by the higher castes to define the identity of the Paraiyars as polluted and segregated, and it explains also how the Paraiyars are now using these same symbols and myths to re-form their identity. Thirdly, the study examines the view of the elites – the higher castes – who are resisting the rise and mobility of the Paraiyars, and who continue to produce new forms of domination.

The three key phases of this process of identity formation are conflict, symbolic reversal, and identification. By 'conflict', I mean a struggle in which a group of people competes with one or more groups with a view to achieving objectives either by violent or non-violent means, or by both.[5] The competition in this study focuses on the cultural resources by which peoples are defined, for instance, the symbolic resources that are used to define different castes. This need not always involve violence, although violence can help to sharpen the objectives of the competition. Apart from this, the concept of conflict is here understood as a combination of three approaches to the study of conflict and violence in anthropology: operational, cognitive, and experiential (Schröder and Schmidt 2001: 1-2, 16-18; see also Tambiah 1996: 20-35). The operational approach focuses on the expressive material and political aspects of conflict as to how this is carried out – the 'etics of conflict'. What are the actors doing in constructing conflicts and why are they doing this? The meaning they give to conflicts is called the cognitive approach – 'emics of conflict'. The experiential approach concentrates on what the actors in the conflicts experience personally during and after their participation in the conflict; conflict is more contingent on the

Map 1
India showing Tamil Nadu

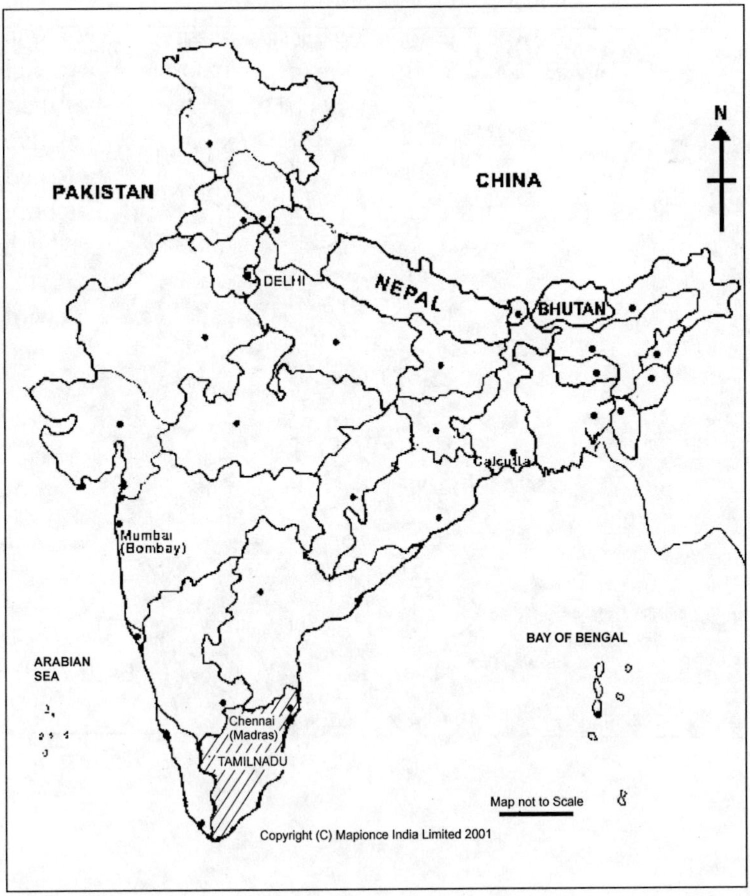

Map 2

Tamil Nadu showing Districts

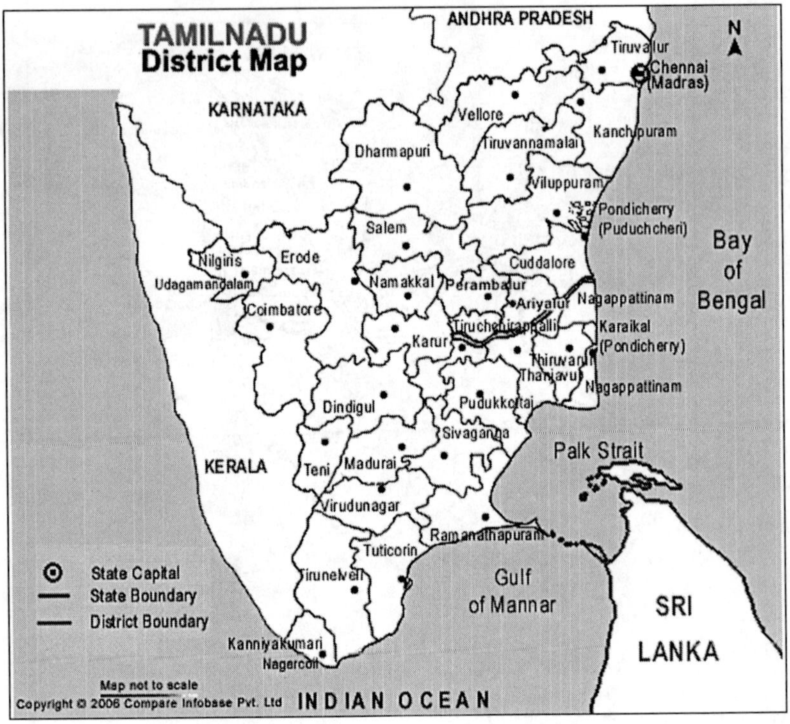

Map 3

Kanchipuram District showing Pappanallur Village

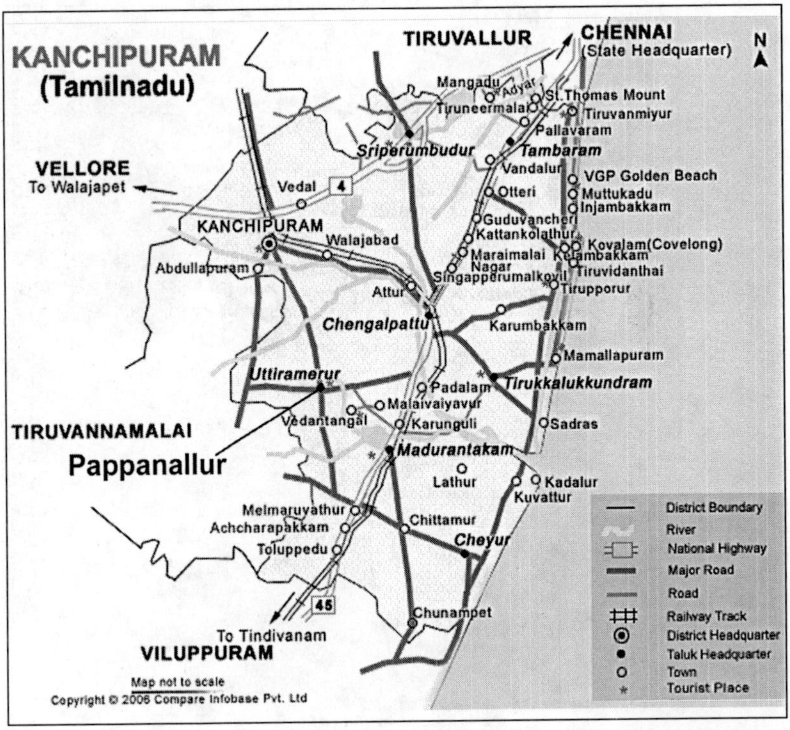

Map 4
Pappanallur Village

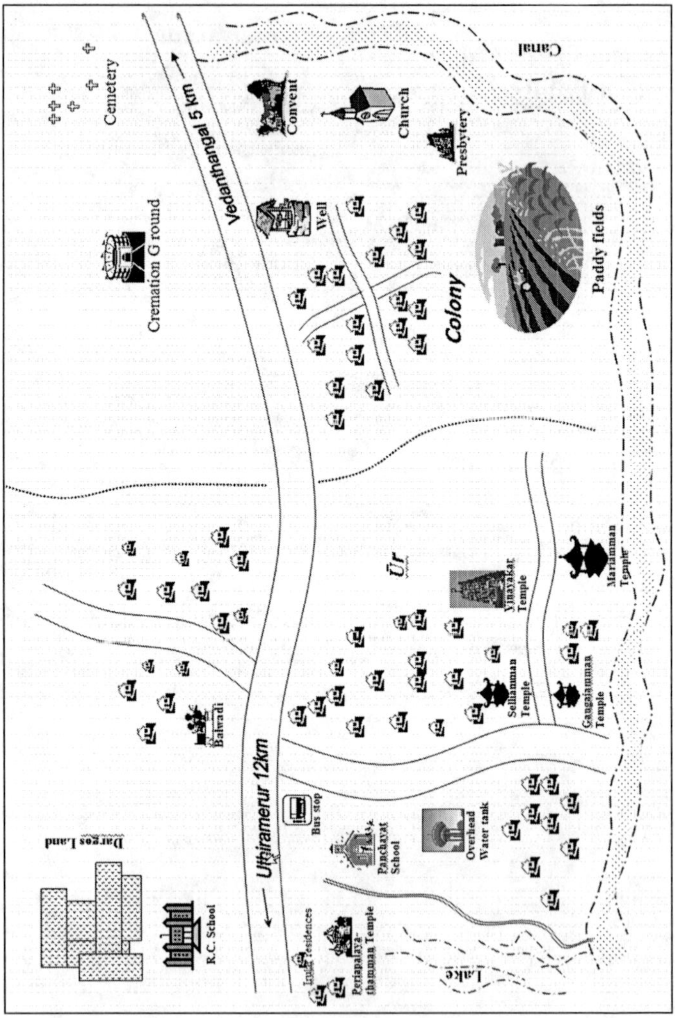

Map 5

Villages around Pappanallur Village

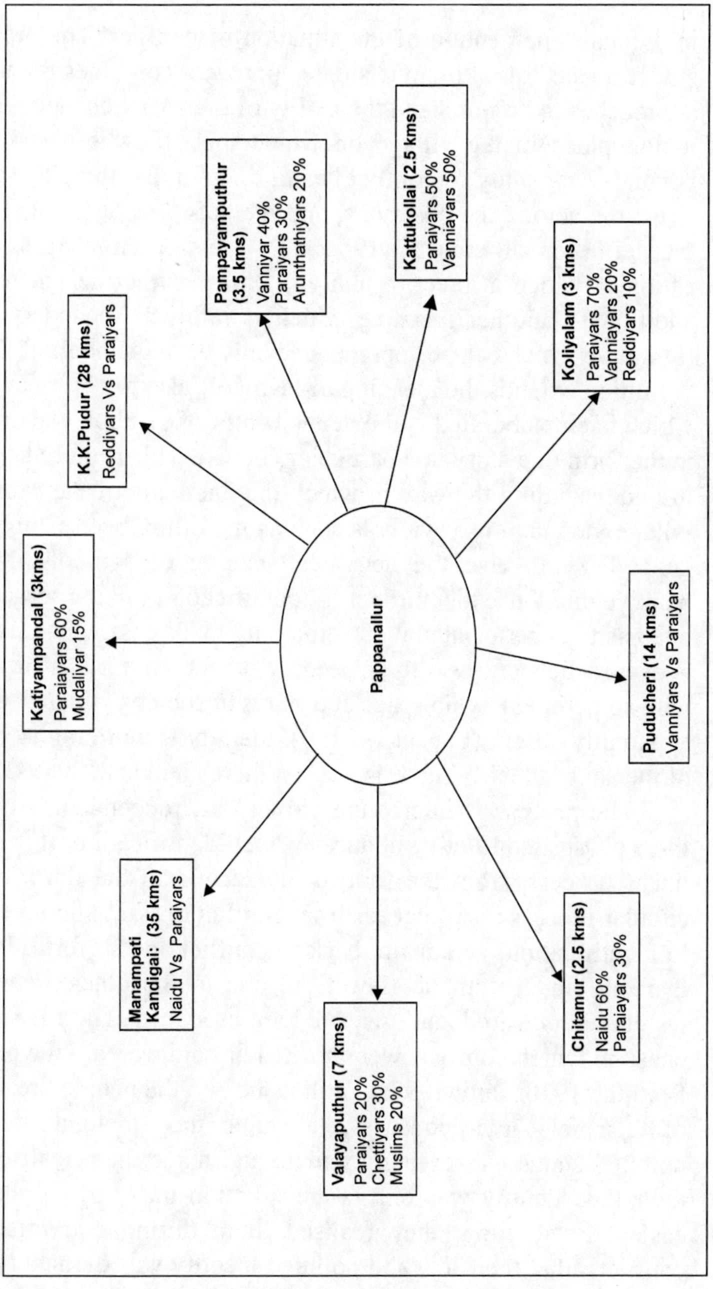

individuals' perception of the situation of conflict. The present study, instead of taking one single approach, combines the three approaches to comprehend the reality of the social change that is taking place in the village on which this study is based and beyond. Any study of conflict has to draw on the three perspectives: the actors, the observers, and the acts. For 'symbol' I use the definition of Ricoeur (1986: 12): "any structure of signification in which a direct, primary, literal meaning designates in addition to another meaning which is indirect, secondary and figurative which can be apprehended only through the first". This definition extends the meaning of 'symbol' also to cover 'myth', which is an elaborated and extended form of symbol, elaborated in the form of a story in a particular context. This is more helpful in understanding the way in which the Paraiyars of Pappanallur village view and use symbols such as the drum, beef eating and land. They reverse the negative meaning of symbols into a positive one. I use the third term 'identification', in the sense that one has to be associated with something to express whom he/she is or how he/she wants to be seen by others. One has to identify with something to gain space and status in society, which is often apparently absent (Laclau 1994: 3). Identity is more in the sense of the act of identifying; it is not just there (Jenkins 1996: 4).

The process is interconnected and interdependent between three phases: conflict-symbolic reversal-identification. It is not a linear process, from the first to the second to the third, but a circular process that proceeds from conflict to symbolic reversals to identification, and again, back to conflict and so forth. It is a dynamic and automatic flow from one to the other, in which results both desired and undesired are produced. The first is the phase in which conflicts were created or engineered – the period from the 1930s until 1997. Conflicts helped the people break out of their false consciousness, in which they thought of their polluted status was divinely willed, and made them realise that their low identity was only a construction made by the higher castes. In addition, they realised, both during and after the conflicts, that their low and polluted identity was defined by the symbols and symbolic practices in the form of their traditional and polluting services to the higher castes, and it was constructed on the myths attached to the symbols such as the drum (*parai*), beef eating and land. Therefore, after the conflicts they gradually came to abandon all the village institutions – the Hindu religion, the village council, the village school – and all the symbolic practices that had defined them as low and polluted, and distanced themselves from the higher castes of the *Ūr*.[6] Put simply, conflict is the starting point that gives the Paraiyars the self-consciousness that makes them *re-imagine* their life as independent of the *Ūr* and different from the life they lived before. This leads to the second phase of the process of identity formation in which they focus on the symbols of the drum, beef eating and land, which I call the foundational and identity symbols. They deconstruct the polluting and negative meaning of these symbols, and construct a new meaning for them by evolving counter myths that portray them positively, and by which they can 'de-pollute' themselves. Their realisation that the meaning of symbols is a crucial factor in the definition of their identity persuades them to change the meaning in order to have a new identity. More precisely, the very fact that they gain the ability to change the meaning of symbols manifests that they have recovered their agency to define themselves. In this sense, the core of the present study is about problems of meaning.

In the final phase, the Paraiyars try to identify themselves with the re-formed symbols in order to have an identity of their own. The three phases do not occur one after the other, step-by-step, but all take place simultaneously. The process of conflict-symbolic reversal-identification is an interconnected process in which the three acts happen at once to effect a change in the life of the Paraiyars, who had been making efforts since the 1930s to reimagine their life. This does not mean that they have completed the process and achieved their new identity. Nor were they themselves clear about the process of forming identity. Instead, what the present study attempts to do is to recognise a process and a pattern in the way the Paraiyars of Pappanallur, from the 1930s to 2003, have been making efforts to challenge the way they used to be treated, and to remove the stigma of untouchability. To this extent, the present study traces the process of identity – formation, working backwards from the outcome – the present state of the Paraiyars in the village – and asking what led to what, which factors contributed to what. This kind of process tracing can give us a history or a biography of identity formation better than causality (Varshney 2002: 14). In brief, this thesis examines the ways in which the Paraiyars attempt to form a new identity from being Dalits to becoming a *caste*. I recognise this process as the 'ethnicisation' of the Paraiyar identity, and this will be one of the main conclusions of my study.

My research falls within two theoretical traditions of enquiry: symbolic interactionism and constructivism. Symbolic interactionism stresses the fact that people interact with their environment (human beings and objects) based on the meaning they attribute to it, because meaning is not intrinsic to objects, neither is it a manifestation of one's mind, but it emanates from the tendency with which an individual acts towards it (Blumer 1986; see also Baert 1998: 66-74). In this way, meaning, which is a social product, formed in and through interactions between people, gives an individual or a society/group an identity. This is crucial in the way in which the Paraiyars of Pappanallur interacted with the *Ūr*, and were defined by others previously, and the way they define themselves now. Similarly, the way in which the Paraiyars are trying to form themselves as a caste group, with its own history and culture, could be seen as an attempt to turn themselves into an ethnic community for which, and with which, they continue to create conflicts with the higher castes in order to strengthen and sustain their new identity.

To understand the kind of ethnic community into which the Paraiyars are forming themselves, we need to locate this within the theoretical tradition of constructivism, which views identities as constructed. This is in some respects different from three other theoretical traditions of ethnicity: essentialism, instrumentalism, and institutionalism (Tambiah 1996: 20-24; Varshney 2002:

27-39; Banks 1997: 11-48; Eriksen 1993: 1-17). Essentialism speaks of ethnic identity as intrinsic or ethnicity as something inhering in human beings. Instrumentalism focuses on the use and manipulation of ethnicity for political ends. Institutionalism relates ethnic identity to the socio-political institutions that provide space for groups to define and sustain their identity. Although these three traditions of enquiry do explain in some respects Paraiyar ethnicity, they are inadequate in terms of explaining the central dynamics involved. Constructivism, on the other hand, informs us much more emphatically about the kind of social change that the Paraiyars are making. Kenneth Gergen defines constructivism as an anti-foundational theory arising out of "the social-discursive matrix from which knowledge claims to emerge and from which its justification is derived; the values/ideology implicit within knowledge posits this; the modes of informal and institutional life sustained and replenished by ontological and epistemological commitments; and the distribution of power and privilege favoured by disciplinary beliefs" (quoted in Williams and Velody 1998: 2). Locating Paraiyar ethnicity within the theoretical tradition of constructivism, the low identity of the Paraiyars in the past was a constructed one, not one ordained by God, nor was it naturally given to them from the beginning, but rather it was defined by others, such as the higher castes, through mythico-symbolic discursive formulations, to maintain their domination. Therefore, it follows that a new identity is possible and can be constructed in the way they desire. This study places greater emphasis on the idea that mythico-symbolic discourse and the 'regime' of practices that this discourse effects are the fundamental and constitutive factors in the formation of identity. For it was not the institutions nor the laws that formed their identity, rather the traditional occupations and practices in the village which the Paraiyars once did, and which they are now trying to alter. These not only have regularity and their own logic and strategy but they also define who they are (Foucault 1991; see also Dean 1998). The set of traditional services performed by the Paraiyars were born out of mythico-symbolic discourses that constructed ways of seeing, ways of knowing, ways of understanding self and society, and ways of understanding themselves and their identity. Therefore, this study is mainly concerned with the questions, who constructs (the Paraiyars), what means they use (mainly symbolic discourse), and ultimately, what is being constructed (a new identity and culture), rather than the use of economic and political resources in their efforts to improve their position, although the present study recognises the contribution these have in the production of culture by the Paraiyars.

This should, therefore, be understood along with the 'separation' model in the theories of untouchability (Berreman 1963, 1979; Mencher 1974; Lynch 1969; Gough 1960, 1973; Khare 1984; Charsley and Karanth 1998; Shah 2001; Micahel 1999; Mendelsohn and Vicziany 1998; Jaffrelot 2003; Kumar 2002) that discuss the Dalits who oppose the caste system and try in many ways to assert their identity in moving away from it. But it should be distinguished from the 'unity' or consensus model (Dumont 1980; Moffatt 1979). Moffatt (1979: 98), basing himself on his field study of a group of Paraiyars in a village in the Chengalpattu district of Tamil Nadu, argues that the Dalits do not have and are not capable of having their own distinctive culture, and more importantly, that they replicate the hierarchy found among the higher castes in terms of "highness and lowness, purity and impurity, superordination and subordination", and thus, he concludes, they are culturally part of the caste system. On the contrary, the present study will show that the Paraiyars are forming their own community, culturally distinct from the Hindu higher castes. This study will be an addition to the studies that have recognised the assertiveness of the Dalits. But many studies (Michael 1999; Kumar 2002; Jaffrelot 2003; Shah 2001a; Illaiah 2001; Guru 2001; Rao 2001; Pai 2001; Pushpendra 2001) have only focused on economic mobility through the reservation of jobs and in education and political participation. Very few studies have positively looked at the question of how the Dalits use cultural resources for their mobility (Charsley and Karanth 1998;

Osella and Osella 2000; Zelliot 1996; Michael 1999) and studied the question of identity of the Dalits (Shah 2001b; Punalekar 2001). However, there are hardly any studies that have focused the identity formation of the Dalits from the perspective of symbol and conflict. This is the novel and positive contribution of present investigation into the study of the Dalits in India.

This study is about one part, not the whole system of hierarchy, in which the focus is on the ways in which the Paraiyars, a part outside the whole, try to reject the caste hierarchy, and construct and imagine a new world. It is concerned with what happens within a part of the whole of caste system – the Paraiyars (Dalits) – and explores how they are struggling to free themselves from the inequality of the system, the means they use to gain their freedom, their discontents about what they were and their images of what they want to become. It examines how they are trying to change the terms and values under which they used to live and construct a kind of 'episteme' of practices that will perhaps provide them with a new life, independent of the caste system. The focus is on the construction of *personhood* from *objecthood*. It tries to look at the ways in which the people, who were merely objects that removed pollution for and from the higher castes and worked in their lands to produce food for the masters, are now becoming *persons* who have their own independent knowledge, culture, history and land. In Fanon's words, it is a transformation from the state in which they were 'sealed into that crushing objecthood' to a state in which they are the agents of their own life (quoted in Young 2003: 21). The core dynamics at work here is the discursive formulation that helps define identity. The recovery of agency and the rejection of the hegemony of the higher castes is achieved mainly through the use of mythical discourse that changes the meanings of symbols from pollution to culture and identity. In brief, this study is about the Paraiyars' attempt to produce their own distinctive culture that demonstrates the idea of the Paraiyars, namely, that in the past 'we' were defined by 'them' (higher castes), and made us live up to their expectations, but now 'we' define 'us' in the ways that are meaningful to us: our self-identity.

However, this study does not pretend to provide a neat and clean picture of the new reality that the Paraiyars have completed in the formation of a new identity, that the Dalits have eradicated and ended untouchability successfully. It does expose the quandaries and ambivalences that the Paraiyars are going through in their transitional phase, from the state of being Dalits to the state of being a community with their own positive identity. The people, who have endured all kinds of suffering to escape from the locus of stigmatisation and of being dominated may want to go back to it when they face the insecurity of their new existence. Sometimes the fact that they are liberated from untouchability gives them a deep sense of relief, yet at other times, they may regret that they have lost the advantages of being Dalits. They shift their stand and often fall into utter confusion. But what remains at the end is the feeling among the Paraiyars of Pappanallur that they will never go back to the *Ūr* and serve its residents as Dalits. This is what the present study intends to highlight, while not ignoring of course the ambivalences that result from the process of social change.

Multi-sited Contrastive Approach: Methodology

Although my principal focus was on Pappanallur village and the Paraiyars in the village, I have studied and collected data from different locations and sources that were directly or indirectly related to the Paraiyars of Pappanallur village. This has strengthened my study and sharpened my understanding of the people. In fact, I did not set out to do multi-sited ethnography, rather I was led into this by the circumstances of the field. The motivation came from the ways in which the Paraiyars of Pappanallur have drawn inspiration for their assertive efforts from sites and sources outside their village. Therefore, I needed to study these sites in addition to that of the Paraiyars. Accordingly, besides my field study of the Paraiyars, which has been my primary focus, I chose three sites. The first was the *Ūr*, the residential area of the higher castes; particularly the Vanniyars with whom the Paraiyars were in direct conflict. I lived there with the higher castes – the elites – for three months to investigate their perspective towards the Paraiyars and their recent moves to assert themselves. Apart from studying them in their own right, in my interactions with the high caste men and women and children, I put them the questions that I had framed on the basis of the data collected during my stay with the Paraiyars. This clarified some details about which I had been in doubts while I stayed with the Paraiyars. Later I took the questions that arose during my stay with the higher castes back to the Paraiyars, and made a comparison of the data from each side. Most of my findings from the *Ūr* I have used in Chapter 6 in which I discuss the view of the elites. The second site was the nearby villages (see Map 5), with which Paraiyars of Pappanallur constantly frequent in so many ways. More importantly, I came to realise that it was from these villages that the Paraiyars have drawn inspiration for their conflicts with the Vanniyars. In four of the villages, the Dalits have had conflicts with the higher castes, quite similar to those I found in Pappanallur. I spent my time mainly with the Paraiyars in these villages who had been directly involved in the conflicts with the higher castes, and listened to their account of conflicts. Although every village had its own unique nature and dynamics in the conflicts, my study of these villages helped me greatly understand better the reality in Pappanallur. During my stay with the Paraiyars of Pappanallur twice a week I visited these villages, and more regularly three villages where I noticed similarities with Pappanallur – Ettucheri, Kattukollai and Thiruvenkadapuram.

The third site of study, outside my primary location – Pappanallur – was four Christian villages – Thatchur, Manambathi Kandigai, R.N. Kandigai, K.K. Pudur – to which the Paraiyars of Pappanallur relate more than in their relationship with the second site, in the sense that they had married women from, and had given brides to these villages. In addition, the Paraiyars of the four Christian villages are Christians and they too are in conflict with the higher castes (Naidus, and Reddiyars) of these villages to the extent that the churches had remained closed for the last four or five years, as the Paraiyars objected to practice of untouchability in church services.

The concept of multi-sited ethnography, according to Marcus (1995, 1999), has arisen in response to empirical changes in the world. Anthropologists have traditionally studied people linked by shared relationship in terms of the way they organise themselves and make sense of life together in a single place/space. But the empirical reality today is different. This is now governed by trans-national mobility and virtual communications, and the changing social, territorial and cultural emergence of group identity by migration. They regroup in new locations and reconstruct their histories leading finally to the construction of their identity. Any reality, or any social institution, is closely linked with another reality or institution in some other space and time, and its nature can be appreciated only by an intersubjective approach. So studying only a single site would hardly provide us with a complete understanding of the subject we want to explore. Instead we have to locate our study in more than one site, and to see the reality from one to the other. The underlying ideology in this is that the subject of anthropology is 'a field of sociality, not a specific place' (Henry 1999: 1-5) and present day's field of sociality between groups is spread out in many places/sites, a multi-ethnoscape which calls for a change in perception and perspective from traditional ethnography (Appadurai, 1991). Now, the method is largely used to study the movements of migrants, transnationally in the diaspora and in exile, and involves studying the history of the circulation of objects and techniques. In addition, it is used to study the relationships of dispersed communities and networks that define the processes at macro level of the free flow of capital and expertise. Some anthropologists argue that multi-sited ethnography is not that new; it is simply the logical extension of the traditional modality in studying peoples, who are now in motion. So, in this case, some minor changes are required in the traditionally regulated fieldwork, but no radical change is warranted. Another criticism of the concept of multi-sited ethnography is that academic interest in social relations, processes, structures, systems, and institutions is slowly waning, and attention is now being shifted to subjectivity, discursive analysis, and the micro-cultural project of identity construction. The debate is between two camps – one insisting on traditional ethnography and the other in support of multi-sited ethnography (Bolton and Weiner 1991). There is no need to enter into the debate in the present study. Nor do I personally feel confident to do so, instead I use some of the techniques suggested by the new developments in anthropological fieldwork. More precisely, I have made use of the suggestions made by Marcus (1998: 89-97), who recommends the following techniques in multi-sited research: follow the people, follow the thing, follow the metaphor, follow the plot, story, or allegory, follow the life, and follow the conflict. In the context of the complexity and multifaceted life of the Paraiyars, they cannot be studied unless we place our observatory lens focussed on those different locations with which they are constantly interacting. So after having done a single-site intense observation of and participation with the Paraiyars of Pappanallur, I followed the objects such as the drum, beef eating and the land. I followed the conflicts at Pappanallur between the Paraiyars and the Vanniyars who literally travelled from village to village provoking similar conflicts along the way, and in return, strengthened and modified the conflicts at Pappanallur. I followed the myths I heard in Pappanallur which were also told by others in the nearby villages and beyond with some variations. The myths that I will discuss in Chapter 5 associated with symbols are the outcome of such a method. Further, I followed the lives of the drummers from the time when they had been performing their traditional services to the *Ūr* to the present when they are reconstructing the meaning of the drum and drumming. Similarly, I followed the biography of the cremation assistant and tried to elucidate his state of being from the time when he buried or burnt the dead bodies of the higher caste people to the present when he is trying to live by taking up different jobs in nearby towns. In all this, I tried to focus on the implications of what was going on in the sites mentioned above for the primary site of my research for the present study and vice versa. The key question I asked in all this was: what among the Paraiyars is parallel to the identifiably similar phenomenon in the sites that are in some sense related to my primary site? The articulations of the Paraiyars of Pappanallur are not merely the outcome of their own self-consciousness, it is also the result of their interactions with what goes on outside their village, such as their participation in the Pancahmi land struggle and their participation in Dalit cultural festivals in Tamil Nadu. In all this I have attempted to construct a relationship of the local to the trans-local, and thereby to identify the primary site of study along with other variously situated sites and subjects. This is what is called 'strategically situated ethnography' (Marcus 1998: 97; sec also Willis 1981).

On Sources of Data

For the data on the situation at national and state levels, I collected my material mainly from newspaper reports and published works such as the *National Campaign On Dalit Human Rights* (2000), *Human Rights Watch* (1999), *Legal Resources for Social Action* (1998), *Komathinayagam Commission Report* (1999) Jacob (2000), Alm (1996). Besides these documents, I visited the Indian Social Institutes in Bangalore and Delhi to hold interviews with groups who are working with the Dalits all over the country to learn the nature and dynamics of the conflicts they had seen among the Dalits in other parts of India, and how they view the approach of the Paraiyars of Pappanallur. For the data on the caste conflicts in Tamil Nadu, I visited the Dalit Resource Centre (DRC) in Madurai and Folklore Resources and Research Centre (FRRC), Palayamkottai, where I interviewed the three groups who had involvement in the caste conflicts in the southern districts of Tamil Nadu. I interviewed two categories of informants – elite (politicians, religious leaders, business etc. – players of conflicts) and subaltern (victims and participants in the conflicts). To get a more intimate feel of the places and the people of the conflicts I visited Melavalavu, a Dalit village in the Madurai district and Rengappanaikkanpatti in the Virudhunagar district, where a major conflict had taken place between the Pallars, (one of the Dalit groups, dominant in the south as the Paraiyars are in the north of Tamil Nadu), and the Thevars, a dominant high caste group in the south. In northern Tamil Nadu the conflict is mostly between Vanniyars and Paraiyars and in the south it is between Thevars and Pallars. By looking at the conflict situation in the south I compared and contrasted it with the conflicts in the north, particularly in Pappanallur.

To understand the conflict situation of Pappanallur more clearly I also visited nine villages around Pappanallur. I learnt that in the past thirty years, there had been many conflicts between the Paraiyars and Vanniyars/Telugu Reddiyars/ Mudaliyars, quite similar to the conflicts in Pappanallur (see Map 5). I chose five key informants in each village – two women, (over 20 and another over 40), one school boy and two men (over 25 and another over 45), although in general, I also talked briefly to others to clarify any doubts I had about the data collected from others. With these persons I shared what was happening in Pappanallur village. Immediately they started telling me about similar conflicts they had in their villages with the high caste groups. In this fashion, I collected narratives of conflicts, and it became clear to me why and how conflicts erupted and what the Paraiyars in these villages achieved through their conflicts with the higher castes. I hoped that this would cast light on the situation of Pappanallur village, which is the main concern of the present study.

The data on the conflicts of Pappanallur were based on my field study from October 2000 to August 2001, and later from October 2002 to January 2003. Since there were no official records or written accounts about the conflicts, I turned to collecting oral histories narrated by both Paraiyars and Vanniyars and others in the village and beyond. At the beginning I talked mainly to men and women over the age of sixty. From these I tried to get them to recall their memories of the conflicts that occurred before the 1960s, in which either they themselves had taken part or of which they had been eyewitnesses. To strengthen this data, I listened to the Paraiyars and the Vanniyars who had not witnessed the conflicts but had heard about them from older generations. I talked to a total of one hundred and thirty three people consisting of school children, youths, middle-aged men and women. From all of these I was able to collect enough information for my purpose. Moreover, I spent some more time with a number of persons from within each group, who I thought would be able to provide key information. I went over and over the topic with them in order to clarify my doubts on the data and contrast and compare what they told me with the data I collected from others.

For the conflicts that had occurred after 1960s, I talked to persons, from both the Colony and the *Ūr*, who had played an active part in them and could give me first-hand reports. It was very useful to have multiple versions: from the Vanniyars and the Paraiyars, and in these two groups, from the older generations. All this helped me to make an informed choice from amongst the facts that were put forward by my informants. The Vanniyar men and women agreed that conflicts had taken place between them and the Paraiyars, but they did not agree with the details of the Paraiyars' version. As explained earlier, the method I used was that I first stayed with the Paraiyars who gave me their account of the conflicts and what happened afterwards. Later when I went to stay with the Vanniyars, I put forward the Paraiyars' version of the conflicts without mentioning that the Paraiyars had given this to me, but the Vanniyars were quick to recognise the source. The Vanniyars rejected the version of the Paraiyars. To resolve this difficulty I turned to two further sources: four Catholic priests who had been the parish priests from 1985 until 2001, and who were there in person during the conflicts, and the Vanniyars of the nearby villages – Pampayamputhur, Kattukollai, Katyambandal and Koliyalam – some of whom were the main movers in the conflicts. Although the parish priests and the Vanniyars of these villages had a bias towards the Pappanallur Paraiyars and the Vanniyars respectively, their accounts were in fact useful in providing details that gave quite a comprehensive picture of the conflict situation. To some extent I could see certain objectivity in their explanation of what happened during and after the conflicts, since they themselves were not part of the two groups directly involved. Apart from all these, I also talked to shopkeepers in Uthiramerur town (14 km from Pappanallur) who interacted everyday with the people of Pappanallur. They told me how they understood the conflicts from information picked up in course of their conversations with both the Paraiyars and the Vanniyars who regularly visited their shops to buy their groceries and vegetables. The reason for including the shopkeepers' account of the Pappanallur conflicts is that in their interactions and transactions in Uthiramerur, I found that the people of Pappanallur were spontaneous and, without being self-conscious, talked to outsiders like the shopkeepers freely about life in their village. For instance, it was only through a shopkeeper that I came to know that most of the conflicts in Pappanallur had been 'engineered' by the Paraiyars in order to assert their identity. Earlier, I had thought that this was a spontaneous reaction between the two groups in a particular context. Later when I clarified this with the Paraiyars, they confirmed it, and said that they did not want to reveal their strategies so easily fearing that this would jeopardise their efforts. Another source from which I was able to collect a substantial amount of data were the party members of the Dalit Panthers (*viduthalai siruthaigal*), a Paraiyar dominated political party, who have been instrumental in making the Pappanallur Paraiyars politically aware of their rights and had been eyewitnesses of most of the conflicts. Their account was more articulate than most of the accounts I had collected in the villages. This helped me to finalise my reconstruction of the conflict narrative, in which I give more weight to the Paraiyars' account than to that of the others. The latter I use only to make a contrast with the Paraiyars' account.

This multi-locale study helped me demonstrate not only how the situation in Pappanallur had effects on other locales such as the Vanniyars of the nearby villages but also what impact the other locales had on the situation in Pappanallur. For instance, the situation in Manampathi Kandigai village (see Map 5), where the parish church has been closed for the last three years due to the conflict between the higher castes and the Dalits in the village, had a definite influence on the Paraiyars of Pappanallur in the sense that it gave them the confidence to challenge the Vanniyars more emphatically.

To understand how the Paraiyars imagine their life after severing all links the *Ūr*, which I discuss in Chapter 5, I found that the drummers were able to provide me with the key to understanding other realities in the Colony and the *Ūr*. Listening to the stories of their life before and after they abandoned their services to the *Ūr* provided me an entry into their world in which the Paraiyars construct a new world-view. My stay with one of the drummers in his house and having them as my key informants throughout the fieldwork, helped me greatly to gain a better understanding of the change in the lives of the Paraiyars. To understand their efforts towards the reformulation of drum music, I went to three Dalit cultural festivals in Tamil Nadu (in the cities of Madurai, Thanjavur and Palayamkottai) from which the Paraiyars of Pappanallur have drawn inspiration and guidance. For the symbolic change in the practice of beef-eating, apart from my observation in the Colony and beyond, I focused on the attitude of the Paraiyar children who study in different schools, and I interviewed them individually. This gave me a picture of what kind of change is taking place in terms of the attitude to beef-eating being transformed from being a polluting act into a Paraiyar social custom. That took me to Dalit leaders and Dalit scholars in Tamil Nadu and two Indian Social Institutes in Bangalore and Delhi to discuss and clarify my conclusions reached so far. This helped me to construct the central idea for the section on the symbol of beef-eating. For the question of land, my key informant was a former village watchman (*kambukūṭṭi*) and his family who did the services of cremating the dead for the higher castes, rituals of pollution in Mariamman festival and guarding the village and the paddy fields. In the process of my study of the three symbols, I clearly realised that the Paraiyars have evolved new myths to counter the conventional myths in order to change the meaning of the symbols that had defined them as low and polluted. So I spent a substantial amount of time in collecting the new myths from Pappanallur, nearby villages and from Dalit scholars such as Parattai at the Dalit Resource Centre in Madurai and Pama, a Dalit novelist and schoolteacher, who lived in Uthiramerur, twelve kilometres away from Pappanallur.

In all this, I tried largely to be gender sensitive: fifty per cent of my interviewees were men, thirty per cent were women, and twenty youths aged between fifteen and twenty-five. In addition, I also talked to a hundred and fourteen Paraiyar children (59 boys and 55 girls) at Loyola School (a school exclusively for the Dalits) in Kuppayanallur and in the evening schools called Senthalir Evening schools (*Senthalir Mālaipalli*), which were run in twenty-five villages exclusively for Paraiyar children. The attitude of these children I considered very important if the initiatives that are now being taken are to yield desired results in future. This is why the Paraiyars are very particular to spread the new ideas about the practices for the construction of their new identity among their children. At the same time, I should note here that as a male researcher, I have hardly addressed the question of identity formation from the point of view of the Paraiyar women, although I did talk to women with regard to the organisation of their association (*sangam*) and have included their observations. The nuns of a Pondicherry Roman Catholic religious order and women from different Non-Governmental Organisations (NGOs) who work among the Paraiyars were helpful in obtaining the views of the Paraiyar women to a certain extent. In fact, the Paraiyar women were much more free to share their views with me than the Vanniyar women.

On the Mode of Narration

There are two biases in the way in which my narrative has been constructed: the subjectivity of the Paraiyars and my own subjectivity. Reconstructing their history on the basis of what the Paraiyars of Pappanallur now remember about the past has to be done also in the light of their present efforts to form their identity. For them the details of the past have to be recalled because these are the resource for the formation of their new identity, and because of this, I found that they often exaggerated their story and the way in which they were treated by the higher castes in the past. This bias in their narration has made them focus only on the conflicts and what the conflicts did to them or what they expected to happen after the conflicts. They are selective about the details of the past in that they highlighted the suffering and oppression they experienced under the higher castes, and disguised the positive elements in their past. Because, according to them, that is what is giving them a background against which they try to imagine their new life. In doing this, they constantly struggled as much as they could in their conversations with me, to obscure the ambivalences and contradictions they faced in the present reconstructive efforts to imagine their life. For instance, some of the Paraiyars in the Colony and in the *Ūr* often shifted their perceptions about their life and activities; sometimes the Paraiyars would tell me that they should go back to the ways in which they served their higher castes, because that had given them some security, yet the same people would at other times, strongly express the view that they were happy now that they had abandoned their services to the *Ūr*, and should now focus on forming a new identity. I have made a point as much as possible of recording and documenting these variant and contradictory voices that I heard in various parts of the present study wherever and whenever they were needed. However, I have tried to a certain extent to play these voices down in order to highlight the positive side of the social change that is taking place in the village. Therefore, sometimes my mode of narration might appear to be triumphalist and it might look as if I had not been objective in looking at the reality from an effective distance.

In fact, I quite deliberately did not want to do this. For I was a higher caste among the Dalits, trying to observe the social change that they were trying to bring about without letting my observation with my 'high caste attitudes'.[7] So I needed to involve deliberately in their life emotionally and to speak from their perspective, which is what Kearney calls 'representative thinking' (2002: 62, 63). I did not want to make this thesis a study of the subaltern by an elite scholar from the elite's perspective; instead I tried as much as I could to construct a thesis about the subaltern from the subaltern's perspective. I do not know for sure whether I have been successful in this. But I can candidly assert that I have tried in this regard consciously, with a sense of reflexivity. Although I did 'step out of the field and into the field' to comprehend the diverse reality of the field data, I wanted to be careful not to obscure their voices by my 'objective' theories and analysis. To make the voice of the people we study heard in theses such as this is, I think, the moral responsibility of a researcher. To this extent, in my case, the term 'objective' meant being involved sufficiently with the Paraiyars and at the same time trying to be conscious of their subjectivity. However, I also realised in the process that it would be very difficult to be completely detached from my personal history and the socio-cultural circumstances under which I work and write "have a profound effect on which topics and peoples are selected for study" (Davies 1999: 5). Such reflexivity is and should be a part of any social research and it should be acknowledged openly so that we can be intellectually honest about what we write (Okely 1992; Kuper 1988; Fabian 1983; Clifford and Marcus 1986). Therefore, my representation of the Paraiyars of Pappanallur village should be understood against this background.

Keeping my subjectivity in mind and using the above mentioned multi-levelled sources of information, in the following chapters, I will trace the processes in which the Paraiyars are forming their new identity: it is a process-tracing study. Varshney

(2002: 14) says that process-tracing runs backwards from the results of conflict, looking for the facts about what contributed to what and how it did this. Such a process-tracing method gives us a history of the conflicts from which I came to learn that the Paraiyars have found the conflicts as the defining moments of their new life and this has led them to focus on symbols as the locus of the definition of their identity.

How the Book is Organised

The present study is organised into seven chapters including this introduction and the brief concluding remarks. In Chapter 2, I present a descriptive account of the place, the people and their life on which the study is based. This ethnographic chapter is intended to provide a picture of the life of the Paraiyars and of the life in the whole village, both as it was in the past when the Paraiyars were part of the *Ūr* and at the moment of my fieldwork in 2001-02. In this chapter, I have focused only on those areas in the lives of the people in Pappanallur that I considered relevant to the main emphasis of the present study.

In Chapter 3, I present the core theoretical framework of my study. Here I discuss the theory around which the whole study revolves. This is not to suggest that the theoretical framework was preconceived before the fieldwork, as if I already had a theory into which I fitted the field data. Instead, it is the theory that grew out of my field research and was further confirmed when I was going through the data collected during the fieldwork. More precisely, this chapter carves out the essence of the whole thesis and stands as the guide map for the reader throughout the work. With very little reference to the ethnographic setting in this chapter I try to set out the idea of how the Paraiyars of Pappanallur village are working out their identity: the process of identity formation from conflict to symbolic reversal and then to identification. In a sense, this chapter opens possibilities for the universal applicability of the theory well beyond the context of the village from which the theory sprang.

Although it has been my intention to keep the whole study as descriptive, analytical and interpretive at the same time and in equal measure, I have kept Chapter 3 analytical only. This chapter could be read either after having read all the other chapters or even before reading them; if read after the other chapters the reader would get the basic idea of what had been central to the other chapters, and if read before the other chapters the reader will have a clear picture of what is going to be the central idea in the study.

In the next three chapters I embody the theory in substantiations and their empirical context. In Chapter 4, I provide the history of the conflicts that the Paraiyars have had with the *Ūr* higher castes from the 1930s till 2003. For this I have chosen six major conflicts out of more than thirty that I studied during my fieldwork. The choice of these six has been dictated by the change they have brought about in the life of the Paraiyars and in the whole village, although one cannot deny the contribution made by all other minor conflicts to the six major conflicts, and to the changes in the village. Therefore, after presenting each conflict, I have explained the changes that the conflict brought in the village. At the end of the chapter I sought to highlight the important characteristics that are embedded in the conflicts.

Chapters 5, 6 and 7 discuss the question of what the Paraiyars did and are doing after having distanced themselves from the *Ūr*. More precisely, I examine the ways in which the Paraiyars have tried to reverse the meaning of the three symbols – the drum, beef-eating and the land – from the meaning of pollution that gave them a negative identity as 'Dalits', marginalised outside the village, into the meaning of the culture and social practices unique to the Paraiyars, and which is intended to provide a positive identity. The three symbols have characterised their polluted identity and they now use these same symbols to characterise their new and positive identity by transvalueing their meaning.

Chapter 8 deals with re-symbolising and identification with these symbols. The gist of the chapter is the identification with symbols of a positive meaning and the de-identification with the symbols of a negative meaning. This chapter can be seen as central to the present study in terms of providing a grammar by which we can try to understand the social change that is taking place in Pappanallur and beyond in the lives of the Dalits.

I look at the Paraiyars' construction of identity from the point of view of the higher castes, mainly the Vanniyars, what I call the view of the elites. By considering the views of the higher castes in the village, I explain how and why the elites refuse to recognise the new identity of the Paraiyars and the ways in which they continue to forge new forms of domination to resist the change in the life of the Paraiyars.

Finally, in Chapter 9, in the form of conclusion to the study, I try to indicate the direction the Paraiyars' ways of forming identity may be said to be taking. I observe that the Paraiyars are making an attempt at rising up to the status of an ethnic community of their own from 'Dalit to caste'. This, I argue, characterises the life the Paraiyars are trying to imagine being outside the caste hierarchy of the *Ūr* and the village.

Notes

1. See *The Hindu*, 11, April 1999, an article by P. Sainath on Melavalavu Murder. Visit also http://www.ambedkar.org under the title 'Crimes against Dalits' for a catalogue of atrocities against the Dalits in India (visited on 07 July 2003).
2. The term 'pollution' is used here more in the political sense than in the sense of ritual. In that sense, purity and pollution are viewed as superordination and subordination respectively. The Paraiyars are subordinated by their polluting services such as scavenging cattle, drumming, cremating the dead and chasing the demons away in festival rituals. For a detailed discussion on purity and pollution, see Fuller (1992: 12-16).
3. In Tamil Nadu, there are three dominant Dalit groups: the Paraiyars, the Pallars, the Arunthathiyars (earlier called Sakkiliars). I will say more about the three groups in Chapter 2.
4. For the Paraiyars of Pappanallur village, the term higher castes mean Brahmins, Reddiyars, Vanniyars. The Brahmins and Reddiyars from the 1970s had started leaving the village to settle in nearby towns and Chennai city. At the time of my fieldwork (2001-3), only the Vanniyars

were the dominant high caste group with which the Paraiyars were directly in conflict, although in the 1940s the Paraiyars had conflicts with the Brahmins and Reddiyars as well. The Vanniyars in the *Varna* system is included under varna of the Shudras (Brahmins-Kshatriyas-Vaishyas-Shudras), in other words the Vanniyars should be called a low caste. But from the point of view of the Paraiyars the Vanniyars are a high caste group, in a sense, considered equal to the Brahmins. In fact, in the state of Tamil Nadu, the dominant low castes (shudras) such as the Thevars, the Vellalars, the Udayars, the Chettiyars are seen as higher castes by the Dalits.

5. For a similar approach see also Coser (1956: 8) and Horowitz (2000: 95).
6. The village is divided into *Ūr*, which is the residential area of the higher castes, and the Colony, which is the residential area of the Paraiyars. The a village is the one that includes all the castes and it is more in the sense of geographical boundary. Valentine Daniel (1987) defines '*Ūr*' as the sacred geographical space marked by the temples of a village and *kirāmam* as the administrative boundary of the village, pp. 63-94. Significantly, the term '*Ūr*' is defined in a person-centred manner: a place is named and referred to according to the people who populate in it. In that sense, *Ūr* is where higher castes live and therefore it is pure and respectable in contrast to '*Colony*' or *Cheri* that refers to the place in which the Dalits live, who by their services to the *Ūr* – burying or burning the dead and clearing away dead cattle, beef-eating and drumming – are viewed as impure, marginal and least respected. See also Moffatt (1979: 64-7); David Mosse (1985: 56).
7. At this point I should give an autobiographical note to the reader in order that he/she can put the present study in a proper perspective. I was born in a high caste Hindu family and later converted to Christianity and became a Catholic priest in the Jesuit Religious order. In my field research and in writing the thesis I needed to be constantly aware of this self-image. For example, once during my stay when I was offered a beef dish by a Paraiyar woman something deep within me revolted against it. It took me quite some time to eat it. The woman said, "Oh, if you find it difficult to eat what we eat then how will you study and write about us?" Then later on another day one of my Jesuit priests who by birth was an Dalit said to me that it would be difficult for me to understand the emotions of his people. All this remained deep within me as a guiding point in my research and in representing the people properly whom I studied. In fact, initially I thought of writing a section on reflexivity but it is beyond the scope of this thesis. Perhaps, on another occasion, I could elaborate on this.

2

The Setting

In this ethnographic chapter I intend to provide a picture of the life of the Paraiyars of Pappanallur by juxtaposing their past and the present. Until 1941, they had been part of the *Ūr*, performing their traditional services (thoḷil) such as drumming (koṭṭuatital), cattle scavenging (thōṭṭi), cremating the dead (veṭṭiyān), and guarding the village (kambukūṭṭi). But from 1941 when they converted to Christianity till the time of my fieldwork (2000-2002), in and through conflicts they have made a series of attempts to construct their own identity of what they say is their unique culture. To understand and explain the process by which they are forming their new identity, about which I will be concerned in the later chapters, we need to have an idea of how their life used to be in the past. This comparison is deliberately done at this point so as to show the two ends of the spectrum of life in the village.

The Place: Landscape

The village of Pappanallur lies in the northern part of Tamil Nadu, in the Maduranthagam *taluk* of the Kanchipuram district, about 90 kilometres south of Chennai (Madras) (see Map 1, 2, 3). Historically the northern region of Tamil Nadu had been under a series of regimes starting with the Pallavas in the seventh century and ending with the Nawab of Arcot, during the early part of the nineteenth century, when it came under British rule.

Kanchipuram district, earlier known as Chengalpattu in the 1991 census, has been recently bifurcated into Thiruvallur and Kanchipuram districts. The present Kancheepuram district has eight *taluks*, one hundred and eighty seven revenue villages, thirteen revenue blocks and five municipalities. The village of Pappanallur comes under the Achirapakkam legislative constituency of the state assembly, Madurantagam *taluk*, Achirapakkam union and Endathur *pirkā*. Within a radius of three kilometres, the village is surrounded by nine villages (see Map 5) in which the high caste groups are much stronger in terms of population and wealth than the Dalits. We should not fail to note here that the Paraiyars of the villages have been a great support to the Paraiyars of Pappanallur in their resistance to the Vanniyars and other higher castes.

The village is linked to the town of Uthiramerur, twelve kilometres to the west, and the town of Chengalpattu, thirty five kilometres to the north, where the people often travel either by bicycle or on buses run by the state government and mini-buses[1] operated by private parties, for shopping or to go for movies. Palmyra trees and thorn bushes surround the village to such an extent that it cannot be seen from the outside. On arrival at the village the first thing that can be noticed is the spatial division between the Paraiyars and the Vanniyars: '*Ūr*'and '*Colony*'. If you come into the village from Vedanthangal, that is from the east, the first things that one sees are two burial grounds – cremation ground (*suṭukāṭu*) for the Vanniyars, and cemetery (*kaḷḷarai*) for the Paraiyars (see Map 4). In between the burial grounds in the north and paddy fields in the south the Paraiyars' Colony (residential area) is situated. Since it is a low-lying area in the village, in the rainy seasons, the whole Colony is often submerged, even though there is usually no serious flooding. But the Paraiyars still have vivid memories of a major flood in 1964 when all their huts were washed out and they had to live on food given by the Vanniyars, who also confirmed the incident. When asked about this the Paraiyar youth told me that it was one of the ways by which the Vanniyars have excluded them as polluted people from the main village. They further added that this was the reason for the Paraiyars area being called a 'Colony' and the Vanniyars as '*Ūr*' (the real village). In this way, even the geographical location of the residence of the two groups is taken by the Paraiyars as a reason for conflict with the Vanniyars. Another group of the Dalits are the *Irulars, Vettaikarans, Karumrs, Kuruvikkarans,* who live like the Paraiyars on the periphery of the village (see Map 4).

The second division between the two groups is the physical form of the dwellings. Most of the houses of the Paraiyars are huts, which have roofs of dried palmyra leaves. The huts have neither doors nor windows. Very recently, they have built fourteen *pakkā* (solid) houses with the help of the state government and the Archdiocese of Madras-Mylapore. Most of the houses in the Vanniyar area are *pakkā* houses. The house of Elumalai Gounder is the biggest house in the Vanniyar area, where there are a few huts but these are different from the Paraiyars' huts.[2] They are higher and larger, and have three living spaces: a veranda in front, the main living space in the middle and a back veranda where many articles like utensils and paddy bags are stored. Most of the houses have a separate hut for cooking meals.

There are five temples in the Vanniyar residential area. The Mariamman temple and the Periapalayathamman temple mark the boundary of the village (*kirāmam*), the former on the southern boundary and the latter on the western side. Temples for Selliamman, Draupadi and Vinayagar are built within the village. Since the Paraiyars are Christians they have their church of St Theresa of the Child Jesus at the eastern tip of the village. The village has two schools, one run by Roman Catholic nuns (The reign Missionary Sisters of Pondicherry), which is situated away from the village on the right of the road that goes to Uthiramerur, and another run by the state government that is near the main bus stop.

The village has a distinct oral tradition. Although we do not have written records of it, the accounts of the people in the village and a careful examination of a variety of studies of South Asian history provide us with good evidence concerning the origin of the village. The name 'Pāppānallur' – *Pāpāns* (Brahmins)+ *nall* + *ūr* (good village) – means a good village of Brahmins. In other words, since the Brahmins are the owners of the village it ought to be a good village. Many scholars on South Asian history enlighten us on this point that during the Chola period, the rulers presented many villages to Brahmins that were called *brahmadēya* (Nilakanda Sastri 1975; Champakalakshmi, 2001). The Brahmins administered the villages by forming an assembly named *sabhā*. Although there were non-brahmadeya villages too, which were called *Ūr,* the brahmadeyas were the backbone of and "indispensable for the understanding of the power structure of the Chola rule" (Karashima 2001: 3). In the seventeenth and eighteenth centuries, and later, during the British period these villages were transformed into *mirāsidār* villages. Probably, Pappanallur would have been one of these villages owned by the Brahmins.

The People: Ethnoscape

The Paraiyars

The Paraiyars of Pappanallur are one of seventy-seven Dalit sub-groups in Tamil Nadu.[3] The Paraiyars, the Pallars and the Arunthathiyars[4] are considered to be the main three Dalit groups in Tamil Nadu. The Pallars are concentrated in the southern districts such as Madurai, Ramanathapuram, Thirunelveli, and Thiruchirappali whereas the Arunthathiyars live more in the west, in places like Salem, Coimbatore, and Madurai. The Paraiyars are concentrated mainly in the northeastern districts of Kanchipuram, Thiruvannāmalai, Vellore, Dharmapuri, Cuddalore and Viḷuppuram. Of the three Dalit groups, the Paraiyars have the highest population in Tamil Nadu.

A conservative estimate puts the figure at 6.32 million and the Kanchipuram district (see Table 1) itself has 94 per cent Dalits who are Paraiyars (Sathianathan 1998: 65; Moffatt 1979: 60-65). It is difficult to establish with precision the historical origins of the Paraiyars since there are many contradictory accounts and theories.[5]

Paraiyars of Pappanallur were originally Hindu Dalits until 1941 when they converted to Christianity following a conflict with the higher castes of the village at that time.

Table 1

Population (1991 Census)

Category	*Total*	*Dalits*
India	84,63,02,688 (2001 Census: 1,02,70,15,247)	13,82,23,277
Tamil Nadu	5,58,58,946 (2001 Census: 6,21,10,839)	1,07,12,266
Kanchipuram District	46,53,593 (2001 Census: 28,69,920)	12,08,417
Madurantagam Taluk	2,41,703	95,103
Pappanallur	1,135	433 (Paraiyars)

Although they became Roman Catholic Christians in 1941 they have been performing all the services (*thoḷil*) – drumming, cattle scavenging (*veṭṭiyāṉ*), burning the dead and acting as the village watchman (*kambukūṭṭi*) – for the higher castes of the village until 1997, when they stopped doing all those jobs in course of a major conflict with the Vanniyars. In cultural identification the Paraiyars acquire their 'Dalitness' or their polluted nature, by performing these services. Most of these services require handling dead – dead cows, dead humans, and blood – that pollute them and get them excluded from the village castes in general, and from the Vanniyars in particular, who are the dominant high caste group in the village. As we have seen earlier, the four services done for the *Ūr* castes make the Paraiyars low and untouchable. To be a Paraiyar is to deal with dead objects and thereby be polluted. Such a state of pollutedness was at the core of their identity.

As Moffatt (1979) explains, the definition of the Pappanallur Paraiyar identity in the past could be perceived through the services they did for the higher castes, and the myths of their origin they had and the higher castes had, are still alive. Here, I must not forget to note that the Paraiyars in Pappanallur have a different version and understanding of those myths, which I will discuss as I go along.

Table 2

The Dalit Population in Rural and Urban areas of Tamil Nadu

Area	*Males*	*Females*	*Total*	*%*
Rural	42,59,370	41,68,670	84,28,040	78.68
Urban	11,55,229	11,28,997	22,84,226	21.32
Total	54,14,599	52,97,667	1,07,12,266	100.00

Source: 1991 Census and Tamil Nadu Social Development Report 2000.

Since we will be considering the services provided by the Pariyar later in this chapter, I will restrict my description in this section to the question of what and how the people of the village, both the *Ūr* castes and the Paraiyars, feel about what it is to be and live as a human person in the village. In a sense, I am more concerned with their mental attitudes towards human life. This will be very significant in the present study of identity formation.

If we look at the Paraiyars, we have two types of them in Pappanallur. The first type is the people, mostly among the older age group, who are the repository of past lives of the village, more importantly, of their experience of untouchability and discrimination first, at the hands of the Brahmins and later the Reddiyars, and lastly, the Vanniyars, about which they have many stories to tell. One of the stories gives us a fair idea of the history of the Paraiyars of Pappanallur. They were the original inhabitants of the village. Athimulam, the eldest Paraiyar in his 90s recalled: "when I was six years old my father used to tell me that we cultivated paddy three times a year (*pōkams*) on the lands on the southern side of the village. In the month of *thai*[6] [January] they harvested 100 bags of paddy in a three-acre field. When my father told me this, his eyes were filled with tears. The whole village were organised peacefully by our leaders from four *Vagaiyarās* [lineage]. What happened afterwards was not known to anybody. What everybody remembered was that one-day suddenly four families of Brahmins arrived at our village and asked us to work for them. From that time onwards we have been agricultural slave labourers (*paṭiyāl veḷai*)".[7]

We have no evidence to confirm the details of the story. But what is true is that irrespective of the authenticity of the story, the Paraiyars, particularly the youth, now contend that they were the original possessors of the lands in the village and the higher castes came from somewhere and usurped their lands and power.

However, although the older Paraiyars do remember the time when they lived as landowners they do not want to put up a fight with the higher castes of the village. They want to hold on to their life as slaves of the Higher castes. Indication of this is found in the way they dress and the way they behave in front of a high caste member of the village. They still do not wear shirts and when they meet the higher castes of the village, they remove their towel from the shoulder in respect.

In the same way, the older Paraiyar women do not wear blouse and sandals, and they still hold the high caste leaders in high respect. One of the women, the wife of Athimulam, told me that it would be difficult to see another leader like Elumalai Gounder who was a popular Vanniyar caste leader in the 1950s. When I asked her whether she approved the leader's treatment of the Paraiyars, she answered without any hesitation that 'we are paraiyans who should be treated that way, it is written in our forehead by God (Brahma)'. What they did as *paṭiyāl* work (bonded labour) for the Vanniyars, they feel, gave them a peaceful life. Each Paraiyar family was attached to a high caste family and worked for the higher castes on their lands. Whenever they needed money or any other assistance, the higher castes provided them. The Paraiyars do not see these things as something unusual against human freedom and equality. In this connection, Barnabas, another elderly Paraiyar told me, "show me where is real equality; even in my hand there is no equality between the fingers. Take for example, I have taken my midday meal but you have not had yours. Does this mean you are lower than me? Did the Goundans decide where I should be born? No, it is Bhagavan [God] who decides my birth as Paraiyar. God gives each one his place in life. We should accept it and live accordingly." Paraiyars of this type accept their lowly status as ordained by God and think that protesting against it would mean going against the law of God. They do not approve of the younger generations' violent approach to the caste system of the village. Nevertheless, they feel happy to see their sons and daughters freed from servitude to which they were subjugated in their lifetime.

The second type of Paraiyars are of the younger generation who are assertive and articulate, decently dressed and educated. In fact, they have been successful in persuading the middle-aged Paraiyars to abandon the demeaning services like drumming at the higher castes' funeral, clearing the dead cattle, burying or burning the dead. These Paraiyars want to form a different identity from that which their forefathers have had for centuries. They try in every possible means to get away from their polluted status by taking over the symbols – the land, drumming, beef-eating and the festival – by which their ancestors were excluded, exploited and subjugated, and changing them into symbols of a new identity. This will be the central concern of the present study.

The younger women are more assertive and articulate than the men of the second type. Pushpa, one of the leaders in the women's association (*Māthar Saṇgam*), told me "if any Goundan calls me a *paracci* [the feminine form of *paraiyar* that is used to address a Paraiyar woman contemptuously], I will slap him and his thirty-six teeth will fall out. One day when I was travelling by bus, a woman from the *Ūr* asked me to give up my seat. I asked her: don't I have buttocks just as you have? She murmured something that hurt me. Immediately I shouted "*pōṭi nāyē*" (you are a dog)".

In a sense, when meeting these two types of Paraiyars, one can easily get an idea of what they were 'then' and what they want to be 'now'. The two types of people produce also two kinds of discourse: conformative and constructive. Not contradictory, but necessary ambiguity, I think, is needed in the process of identity construction. When I shared myths of Paraiyars' origin with the Paraiyars of Pappanallur they were furious about it and told me that it was the design of the higher castes to keep them as untouchables and powerless. They have decided not to allow such

Table 3

Caste Composition of Pappanallur Village

Caste Name	*Number of Households*	*Population*
Ūr Castes		
Vanniyar	90	620
Idaiyar (Yadava)	20	26
Chettiyār	1	4
Reddy	1	5
Āsāri	1	5
Dalits		
Vettaikāran	6	17
Karumār	5	13
Kuruvikkāran	1	5
Ambattan	1	4
Vannān	1	3
Sub-total	125	702
Paraiyars	110	433 (Male 199 + Female 234)
Total	235	1135

designs to succeed any longer. The High Caste people were able to get away with this, they said, because of the ignorance of their grandparents (*pāṭṭans*), but not any more. Now they produce new myths of origin that are quite different from those they have heard about so far. These explain how they originally lived a life of high status and how they were cheated by the higher castes.

By creating new myths and reinterpreting the symbols of pollution and transforming them into positive symbols of identity, (which will become clearer as we go along,) they want to form a new Paraiyar identity or a new Paraiyar personhood, which they think is, and should be different from the Vanniyars'. In their manner of speaking and behaving, they make serious efforts not to look like the Dalits of yester year. Now they are much more politically conscious of their place in the society they live in and have become increasingly assertive of their rights as human persons. They refuse to be considered any longer as people who are exploited, polluted, discriminated against and dependent.

Instead, they want to be persons who do not belong to the bottom of the caste hierarchy. During my conversation with them, Arul, one of the youth leaders, told me, "we are as human beings as the Vanniyars; in no way are we lower than them. Look at them how ugly they are; they take always porridge (*ragi* millet, *kūl*) but we rarely take that. Go to our houses you will find only rice" (taking porridge as a meal is treated as low but rice is a meal taken by high caste people). To demonstrate this, they use different means. One of the means is that they take special care to look neatly dressed even while they are at home, and make serious efforts to send their children to schools. The Paraiyar youth prefer to wear trousers and shirt rather than white dhoti (white loin cloth). To dress themselves in trousers and shirts is to belong to a high class/caste group. Among the Tamil Nadu politicians Krishnaswamy of Puthiya Thamilagam (PT) and Thirumavalavan of Dalit Panthers of India (DPI), and Dalit political party leaders, always appear in public in trousers and shirt, whereas most of the Tamil Nadu politicians have a tradition of wearing white dhoti and a towel on their shoulders. When asked about it, Father

Yesumarian, who is a lawyer as well as a Jesuit priest, coming from a Dalit family, thinks that dress is a very important symbol by which they would like to show their superiority over the higher castes. He referred to it as a reversal of history. Earlier in the district and elsewhere in Tamil Nadu both the Paraiyar women and men were not allowed to cover their chest, particularly the men should not wear the turban, and their loincloth was not allowed to reach below their knees. The Paraiyar women in the village for a long time were not allowed to wear precious clothes like silk. They were forced to wear what they receive as a gifts from their *jajmān* (landlord) at festival time. This made them "dirty, foul-smelling and generally repulsive" (Deliege 1999: 107-8). The Paraiyars are making every effort to change this picture of themselves. At times, it goes to the extent of buying costly materials beyond their means. When there was a celebration of the birthday of a seven-year-old boy in one of the Paraiyar houses, the father of the boy, who earns Rs. 40 as his daily wage, gave the boy the gift of a pair of shoes which cost Rs.178. He does not see this as wrong. He told me, "nobody should think my son as *parappayal*" ('Paraiyan'). Also, they now tend to be more explicitly violent when they are ill treated for being Paraiyars. Education and political action only, they think, will give them a proper place in society and will provide them the needed power and imagination to form their own self-identity. The second type of Paraiyars, mostly the youth, is deeply conscious of what the drum, land, and beef-eating meant so far and what should mean to them now. What was polluting them, they insist, should give them the strength to fight for equality: "the ones that made us shameful gives us power".[8] They have pride in calling themselves as 'Paraiyars', which they once disguised in public since it betrayed their low status.

The Vanniyars

The Vanniyars in Tamil Nadu constitute a significant number (12%) in proportion to the total population as well as to the non-Dalit population in the northern districts of Vellore,

Dharmapuri, Thiruvannāmalai, Salem, Cuddalore, Viḷuppuram, Perambalūr, and Kanchipuram (Jacob: 2000: 37-8). According to Vidyasagar (1988), in the undivided districts of Chengalpattu, North Arcot, South Arcot and Salem the Vanniyars are the powerful caste group (see Table 3). Although the Vanniyars are called by different names, like *Padaiyācci, Naikkar, Nayagar,* and *Gounder*, they are an endogamous caste group in Tamil Nadu and the biggest group among the backward castes (BCs).

In terms of education, landholding and urbanisation the Vanniyars are no better than the Paraiyars. In some villages during my field study, I found the Vanniyars living in much more abject poverty than the Paraiyars. Many of them are marginal and landless agricultural labourers. We find an illuminating point on this from the Census Report of 1881 that refers to the *paḷḷi* or the Vanniyars as slaves of Brahmins (quoted in Kumar 1965: 99). Even the Vanniyars who migrated to cities like Chennai work as casual labourers in hotels and in road works. However, their sense of caste identity is very strong. In 1871, the Vanniyars petitioned the government authorities to include them among the *Kshatriyas*, the warrior caste in the four-fold Varna system. By imagining a higher identity in the caste system, they began to organise the group politically forming an association called *the Chennai Vanniyakula Kshatriya Maha Sangam* in 1888. Later, the Vanniyar leaders like N.A. Manickavelu and S.S. Ramasamy Padaychi, formed a political party called Tamil Nadu Toilers Party in 1951, which split and formed another party named Common Weal Party in 1952. In the assembly elections during that year, the party won 25 assembly seats and formed an alliance with the National Congress Party. Nevertheless, later, for various reasons, especially inner party conflicts and splits, the party was dissolved. After a long absence, the Vanniyars once again entered emphatically the political scene in Tamil Nadu with the formation of the *Vanniyar Sangam* (The Vanniyar Association) under the leadership of Dr. Ramadoss in 1980. It became popular among the Vanniyars by its regular agitations, rallies and protests against the state government, representing the causes of the Vanniyar caste.

In 1987-8 the Vanniyars fought with the state government for twenty per cent reservation in the state employment and two per cent in the central government employment. The party claims to have more than ten thousand units in almost all the villages of Tamil Nadu and there are more than four hundred thousand official members of the party.

In the road blockade war (*sāḷai mariyal pōr*) from September 17 to 23, 1987, which is also called by the Vanniyars the 'September Revolution', 25 Vanniyars were shot dead by the state police. Although it was against the state government it also led to communal riots all over the state in which the houses and properties of the Paraiyars of the northern districts were razed to the ground.

Table 4

Comparative population between the Dalits and the Vanniyars in the northern districts of Tamil Nadu

District	*Vanniyars (%)*	*The Dalits (%)*[9]
Chengalpattu	26.94	26.21
North Arcot	31.43	19.89
South Arcot	49.88	25.97
Salem	22.88	15.07

Source: R. Vidyasagar (1988) and G. Jacob (2000)

As many as ten thousand Vanniyars were arrested all over the state and many Paraiyars were injured. The reason for the Vanniyars' animosity against the Paraiyars is from the fact that although both have a common mode of living in terms of poverty and backwardness, the Vanniyars think that they are the immediate superior upper caste to the Paraiyars. The result of the struggle was that the Vanniyars began to be viewed as a force to reckon with. The Vanniyar Sangam was changed into Pattali Makkal Katchi (PMK – The Toilers Party). In the beginning the party vehemently opposed parliamentary democracy and Mr Ramadoss went to the extent of asking the Vanniyars of Tamil Nadu to 'beat the politicians who might come to Vanniyar villages asking for votes with torn slippers', but later on for various reasons the party took part in the Assembly as well as Parliament elections. By doing so the Vanniyars further consolidated their political platform in Tamil Nadu. Now the PMK is a party that cannot be ignored in Tamil Nadu politics.

This background is necessary if we are to understand the Vanniyars of Pappanallur. The seventy-five families of the Vanniyars often identify themselves with the PMK party. Even when I wanted to talk to them they immediately wanted to know whether I had any authorisation from the local leaders of the political party. Power for the Vanniyars here is viewed in two forms. One is their political participation in the State, and the other is their ability to wield power over the Paraiyars in Pappanallur. Elumalai Goundar, who has been their eldest leader since 1930s, (although there is an elected Panchayat leader) insists on the latter form of power. For him, the caste hierarchy, they at the top and the Paraiyars at the bottom, is very important for the social order in the village. Whenever this system is disturbed, the Vanniyars feel that their identity has been challenged. Before 1965 there were four *paṇṇaikārars* (land lords) who were the main Vanniyar leaders. The whole village obeyed them whenever they needed to take decisions on important issues, and looked up to them for counsel even for family disputes.

Among the four *paṇṇaikārars*, Eḻumalai Goundar is an impressive man in his nineties, known for his talent for argument and sharp articulation of problems. There had been a time when everything functioned in the village according to his say-so. It is interesting to note that he was more powerful even though there were Brahmins and Reddiyars who were higher caste people than the Vanniyars to which Elumalai belonged. Many Vanniyars feel that this was due to his organisational capacity, to which no caste hierarchy could be considered comparable in terms of power and authority.

The Vanniyars also organised themselves in terms of *Vagaiyarā* (lineages). The term '*Vagaiyarā*' literally means *'etcetera'*, but connotatively, a 'division' within a caste group; it could also mean 'lineage' (*kulam*), since they consider all *Vagaiyarā* members to have come from a single original family (see also Moffatt 1979: 157). The five *Vagaiyarās* of the Vanniyars are *goundan vīṭṭu, āsām vīṭṭu, aithar vīṭtu, ellām vīṭṭu* and *yādavā vīṭṭu.* Among these *Vagaiyarās*, the *goundan vittu Vagaiyarā* is very powerful and wealthy. Jodipillai Goundar who belongs to this *Vagaiyarā* owns 25 acres of wetland. He told the story about how he had to fight with the Brahmins and later the Reddiyars of the village in the 1950s to buy these lands. But other Vanniyars say that four Brahmin families sold all their land on a lower price to him, since they decided to leave for Chennai city. Apart from rice, they cultivate ragi, millet, and groundnuts during the off-season. In fact, the Vanniyars prefer to invest more in cereal varieties than in rice cultivation. The main reason is, according to a Vanniyar woman, that with one kilogram of ragi (millet) five in a family will be able to feed themselves for three days, whereas one kilo of rice is adequate for three persons for a day only.

Apart from owning land, the Vanniyars also have a large number of livestock – goats, sheep and milch cows. Subrahmanian of *ellām vīttu Vagaiyarā* owns 170 sheep worth more than 17000 rupees. In fact, the Vanniyars there value livestock more than land, since this can easily fail them when there is a failure of the monsoon.

Although there are more powerful people in terms of wealth, the Vanniyar leadership comes from the Goundan *Vagaiyarā*, since this has been the tradition even at a time when Brahmins and Reddiyars lived in the village. In the 2001 Panchayat elections Karpagam Pakkiri who became the president of the Panchayat belonged to this *Vagaiyarā*. Without exception all the *Ūr* castes believe that they follow a good tradition in voting the leaders of the Goundan *Vagaiyarā* to power. It was only once in 1985 that when the families of the Goundan *Vagaiyarā* were divided in a family dispute, Venuppillai, from another high caste group in the village called *Idaiyar*, became the Panchayat president. But on all other occasions the leadership had come from the Goundan *Vagaiyarā*.

It is important to understand this phenomenon, which will be pivotal to our understanding of the conflicts between the Paraiyars and the Vanniyars later. The fourteen families of the Goundan *Vagaiyarā* are the protectors of tradition and system. Every one of them insists that the village should be organised based on caste hierarchy and there should be higher castes who are pure and the Dalits who are impure. If this is not acceptable for anybody in the village, they say, he should leave the village. According to them, every tradition is basically good in every sense. Otherwise, they argue, their ancestors would not have planned it so for them. And such an ideology is again and again repeated in many ways. One of the ways is by celebrating the annual Mariamman festival in which the caste hierarchy is dramatised in front of a big crowd, and the place for each caste in the village is indicated and reinforced. More importantly, the Dalit drummers are made to realise their polluted character more vividly than at other times of the year. In such festivals the leaders from the Goundan *Vagaiyarā*, in particular Elumalai Goundar commands enormous power in giving orders to each participant in the rituals. Many Vanniyars as well as other higher caste people believe that if the leadership had not been left with the Goundan *Vagaiyarā* the village would have been split into so many factions. In brief, the Vanniyars of Pappanallur want to hold on to their high position in the village and expect the Dalits to perform their appointed services to them.

Other Ūr Castes

This group includes non-Dalits apart from the Vanniyars (see Table 2). To understand the Vanniyars' dominance in the village we must consider the role and power of other *Ūr* castes in the village. Most of the *Ūr* castes prefer to side with the Vanniyars in everything concerning village life. They do not have any individual opinions on any issue. Even if they some times seem to have any point of dissent, they prefer to keep quiet about it. It is not easy to understand this lack of influence of the non-Vanniyar castes in the village. The one Reddiyar family of the village, which seemed to have had great influence and power in the 1940s, is now least concerned about village affairs. The Reddiyars are often absent from the village. They are to be seen in Chennai or in Uthiramerur town where they run different businesses, and it is there most of their close relatives live. They do not find any reason for active involvement in the village affairs, since their concern is with their businesses beyond the village. The reason why they want to keep their house in the village seems to be for overseeing the cultivation of their five-acre wetland. I met some members of the family who told me that they would soon be selling off their land and the house, and settle down either in Uthiramerur or in Chengalpattu. The Chetty family is not very different from the Reddiyars. Their traditional profession being commerce, they prefer to travel throughout the year selling cloth and saris. So they do not want to become too involved in the village affairs. The Idaiyars (herdsmen) are prosperous in terms of their cattle and other livestock. For some reasons or other, they live a life quite away from the village, more sharply, from the Vanniyars. For them the rearing of livestock and selling it in the market are their main preoccupation. To participate in the politics of the village, they think, will affect their livestock business adversely and thereby their whole livelihood. Yet whenever there had been a conflict between the *Ūr* castes and the Paraiyars, the youth of the Idaiyar families had actively participated in the conflict and supported the Vanniyars. But their involvement in the ordinary affairs of the village is very little. Some Vanniyars see the lack of interest of other caste groups in the village matters as an opportunity for them to take the lead in the village.

The other Dalits – Vannan, Kuruvikaran, Vettaikaran, Ambattan and Karumar – are different from the Paraiyars in terms of their opposition to the higher castes. Although they do not accept their lower status in the caste system of the village and want to be freed from untouchability, they hesitate to oppose the higher castes openly, particularly the Vanniyars, because of their continuing dependence on the *Ūr*. Moreover, these Dalit groups feel that they are treated in a better way than the Paraiyars. The Vannans are the washermen for the *Ūr* higher castes and they are called *Ūr* Vannans. They wash the clothes of the higher castes and in particular, the clothes soiled by menstruating women. During life-cycle rituals, they assist by providing cloth spread used for the guests to sit on and collect all the soiled ones at the end of rituals. Most of the services of the Vannans are related to cloth and especially washing its dirt, more accurately, its 'pollution'. At funerals, the Vannans lead the mourners, and when the body is taken to the cremation ground, on its way it is stopped to perform a ritual, in which the Vannan leads the eldest son of the dead person in circumambulating the dead body three times with an earthen pot filled with water. At the end of every round the Vannan makes a hole in the pot. Later, on the sixteenth day, he plays an important part in the funeral ceremony (*karumāti*). However, it is important to note here that this service is not done for the other Dalits. More importantly, the Vannans refuse their services to the Paraiyars. In the same way, the Ambattans who are barbers serve only the higher castes. As found in the village of Endavur studied by Moffatt (1979), the Ambattans do not act as funeral priests but an Ambattan from Thiruvenkadapuram, a nearby village, comes for such services. Nowadays the Vannans and the Ambattans prefer to work in the town, where they will get ready cash instead of waiting for the share (*paṇku*) of paddy during the harvest seasons. Other castes, Vettaikarans and Karumars have very little do with the village. Even the Vettaikarans, who used to make baskets for the village, have abandoned the job and gone to other places for different kinds of work.

The detachment from the life of the village of all the other castes makes the conflict between the Vanniyars and the Paraiyars much more perceptible and exhibits itself often as the only thing that happens in the village. In everything, from festivals to daily rituals, this conflict becomes the main focus of village life.

The Life of the Paraiyars: Socioscape

We need to look at the life of the Paraiyars from two vantage points. First, there is the period from 1939 to 1996, during which the Paraiyars were part of the *Ūr* and continued to perform all the Dalit services (*thoḷil*) to the *Ūr* and especially to the Vanniyars, though they had converted to Christianity in 1941. Second, there is the period since 1997, when they no longer performed the services, and instead started asserting themselves by transforming the symbols of pollution into symbols of their identity. To paint an authentic picture of the social life of the Paraiyars in particular, and the life in Pappanallur in general, we need to juxtapose the 'then' and the 'now' life of the Paraiyars. More accurately, the dialectical play between the past and the present is a necessary basis for understanding the Paraiyars' construction of identity, which is the central concern of the present study. For, constant recreation of their life in the past brings them to self-consciousness and leads them to the future where they deconstruct the past.

Social Relations: Equal Before the Enemy

Each Paraiyar identifies with his/her *Vagaiyarā* more than with any other social institutions in the Colony. The whole hundred and ten Paraiyar households are organised in four *Vagaiyarās* – *Talaiyari, Theradi, Sanar,* and *Thoti*. These four *Vagaiyarās* trace their genealogy to a common ancestor. But, the extent of the genealogy is only four generations. The men and women of the Talaiyari *Vagaiyarā* come from the original family of *Kodungayur*. Similarly, the Sanar is from the *Nachanathur* family; the Theradi from *Anaithangal;* the Thoti *Vagaiyarā* from the *Milapur* family. Although all these family names look like village names, the Paraiyars insist that they indicate family names of their original lineage. In all probability, the Paraiyars of Pappanallur should be a local segment of a larger endogamous subcaste that lives in surrounding villages about thirty kilometres away from Pappanallur. Within each *Vagaiyarā* there are two units such as lineage or sublineage (*koṭṭu*) and family (*kuṭumbam*). Each *Vagaiyarā* is composed of a number of lineal units and each of these lineal units is composed of a number of families.

The *Vagaiyarās* were formally differentiated by their *Ūr* services (*thoḷil*) – drumming, scavenging, village watchman, and cremation attendant – they did for the *Ūr* higher castes. Not every member of a *Vagaiyarā* has to perform a service. But being a member of a *Vagaiyarā* that is responsible for such services is enough to be defined as belonging to that particular group. The Paraiyars told me that before their conversion to Christianity Talaiyari, Thoti and Theradi *Vagaiyarās* had done those services. Sanar *Vagaiyarā* never performed any services to the *Ūr* but they were available as a labour force in the fields of higher castes. Talaiyari *Vagaiyarā* families assisted the village policeman (*munisif*) in collecting tax (*vari*) and maintaining law and order in the village. Since this was a non-polluting service *Vagaiyarā* was considered high in the ranking of the *Vagaiyarās*. Theradi *Vagaiyarā* did the service of announcing (*vāriyan*) message of death to appropriate relatives of the deceased. In addition, they were labourers on the land of the *Ūr* castes. Thoti *Vagaiyarā* did all other services such as drumming, cremating the dead, cattle scavenging and being the village watchman (*kambukūṭṭi*). Theradi and Thoti *Vagaiyarās* were considered low since they did polluting services. But this division of the *Ūr* services, and the ranking they acquired according to their services, were abandoned after their conversion to Christianity in 1941. Instead, except in the Sanar *Vagaiyarā*, all the other *Vagaiyarās* shared the services among themselves.

Five families performed the services to the *Ūr* castes, chiefly the Vanniyars until 1997, after which they stopped all the services after a major conflict. They are the families of Ambrose (Taliayari *Vagaiyarā*), Selvaraj (Theradi *Vagaiyarā*), Meiyappan (Thoti *Vagaiyarā*), Michael (Theradi *Vagaiyarā*) and Uthariyam

(Talaiyari *Vagaiyarā*). Selvaraj, Michael, and Uthariyam are mainly the drummers; on rare occasions any member of the Meiyappan family is asked to substitute for one of the three. Michael is the person in charge of drumming during the village festivals and at the funerals of the Vanniyar households. Meiyappan, worked as *kambukūṭṭi*, this literally means a heavy wooden stick, which he carries when he guards the fields at harvest time and when he is in the *Ūr* during festivals, and when he goes to the *suṭṭukāṭu* to cremate dead bodies. Meiyappan also has another duty of announcing the death of any member of the *Ūr* higher castes in other villages on behalf the families of the deceased. All these polluting services make the Talaiyari Paraiyars very low among the Paraiyars. The Thoti *Vagaiyarā* Paraiyars mainly involved themselves in scavenging dead cattle, before they became Christians but later, until 1997, this was also done by the *kambukūṭṭi*. The Sanar and the Theradi *Vagaiyarā* Paraiyars were earlier the main labour force for the Vanniyars and other *Ūr* higher castes. Most of them now, particularly the Sanar Paraiyars, go for different jobs to Chennai city and to other places in the district.

The Paraiyars of Pappanallur, as in the Dravidian kinship relations, divide all kinship into two main categories: parallel relations and cross relations. The former are related as 'brother' or 'sister' and the latter are relations of and in marriage. Apart from this, there is a next category called relative age that divides relations into elder and younger. They make their marriages with any Paraiyar family that is in marriageable relationship (*mōrai*) calculated in terms of their previous marriages. The Talaiyari *Vagaiyarā* are the wife-givers (*māmānmaccān* or *konṭan kuṭuthan Vagaiyarā* [cross relations]) to other three *Vagaiyarās*, who are cousins (*aṇṇanthambi Vagaiyarā*), or *pankālis* (literally 'sharers', it should be understood here as 'brotherhood' [parallel relations]).[10] There are three possible choices of proper marriageable girls (*urimai pen*): MBDy (Mother's Brother's Younger Daughter), FZDy (Father's Sister's younger daughter), and eZDy (Elder Sister's Daughter). The Paraiyars of Pappanallur prefer MBDy and FZDy marriages. Very rarely they have had eZDy marriages (see Appendix I for the figures of MBD, FZD, and eZD marriages and related kinship terms).[11]

For 78 families of *aṇṇantambi Vagaiyarā* families in the Colony (*aṇṇiyam*), 32 families had to provide brides, which often led to a strain in social relations. But these days, the Paraiyars told me that they were not strict about it, and mostly they marry brides from outside the Colony. If they had brides within the Colony it was always from the Talaiyāri *Vagaiyarā*. Now, there are only four surviving families who have taken wives from the Talaiyâri *Vagaiyarā*. All the others have gone over to places such as K.K. Pudur, Vedapalayam, R.N. Kandigai, and Viluppuram to get brides and have given grooms to these places. In the last six years (1997-2003) there was no bride taken from Talaiyari *Vagaiyarā*, instead they have taken brides from outside.

There are many reasons of why the Paraiyars take brides from outside the Talaiyāri *Vagaiyarā*. Arockiasamy of Theradi *Vagaiyarā* told me that the three *aṇṇanthambi Vagaiyarās* favoured educated brides and bridegrooms, which they could not find in Talaiyāri *Vagaiyarā*.

Table 5

The Vagaiyarā Structure in the Colony

Vagaiyarā	*Number of Households*
Talaiyāri	32
Thoti	18
Sanar	33
Theradi	27
Total	110

Particularly, men from Thoti *Vagaiyarā* told me that they were angry with a family of Talaiyari *Vagaiyarā* who refused to give a bride to their man in 1991 and that led to continuous conflict between Talaiyari *Vagaiyarā* and the other three *Vagaiyarā* families. Secondly, from the 1940s the marriage has been blessed in the church, parish priests have discouraged close kin and cross cousin marriages and persuaded them to look for brides outside the Colony.

In addition, more and more many young Paraiyars, who have begun to take jobs outside the village in places like Chennai city and nearby towns, prefer brides and bridegrooms from those places and these marriages mostly have been love matches. These gave rise to non-kin marriages that led to the collapse of close kin and cross cousin marriages. Most of the Paraiyars told me that they did not want to get stuck within the Colony and wanted go beyond the Colony, that they think would bring some change in their life.

Economic Relations: Expending Labourers

Although now many Paraiyars own land (see Table 7), before the 1950s the Paraiyars started their life as landless labourers. The Paraiyars who did the traditional services to the *Ūr* castes lived on the *paṇku* (share) of paddy given to them after the harvest. At other times they survived on the food they collected from the high caste houses everyday. All other Paraiyars worked either as *patiyāl or pativelai* (semi-bonded labourers) on the lands of the higher castes. The daily wage was one measure of *marakkāl* (more or less one and a half kilograms).

Table 6

Landholdings by Dalits in Tamil Nadu (1991 Census)

(in acres)

Size Class	*Dalits*	*Higher castes*
Marginal (below 1 acre)	7,54,526	50,56,867
Small (below 2 acres)	1,07,578	11,49,567
Medium (below 10 acres)	6,958	2,17,688
Large (above 10 acres)	480	30,402

Source: Statistical Handbook of Tamil Nadu 1998.

Everyday they had to collect this and cook their meal. Barnabas, one of the elder Paraiyars, recounted that often they had to go to bed hungry. And the next day when he failed to turn up for work due on account of ill health, he was given a beating by *Peria* Reddy (literally big/the eldest Reddiyar man).

Abject poverty, dependence on the *Ūr* higher castes and the enormous amount of debt seemed to have been general characteristics of their life before the 1960s (Deliege 1999: 117). These terrible conditions were graphically illustrated by Abbé Dubois who described how he could not bear the 'sickening smell' of the Dalits who were 'dying of cold and hunger' (1906: 59), when the Pappanallur Paraiyars had an existence that was entirely at the mercy of the *Ūr* higher castes under whom they were bonded labourers, *padiyāl*.

At the time of my fieldwork, only a few Paraiyars worked on the land of the *Ūr* castes, since they have their own land that they have acquired slowly year after year in many different ways. The Paraiyars who worked as coconut tree tappers have bought lands with the money they earned, and if they did not have ready cash in their hands they received loans from rural banks. Parish priests supported their applications for loans from the banks. Apart from this, the Catholic Archdiocese of Madras-Mylapore has stood by the Paraiyars financially through the parish priests of Pappanallur to purchase lands and build houses. In addition, a number of Paraiyars have occupied the public lands (*purambōkku*) illegally.

The chief crops in the wetlands are paddy, ragi, and lentils; and on the dry lands they cultivate subsistence crops like millets and pulses. Although the Paraiyars have the right to get a quantity of water from the tank (*ēri*) for their wetlands, the Vanniyars have always prevented them from getting their proper share. Every year a solution of the problem is reached only following a major fight between them.

Often the Paraiyars are forced to depend on the tank water since many Vanniyars have irrigation wells (*kinaru*) that are used to irrigate both dry land and wet land cultivations. Despite such difficulties the Paraiyars work hard on their lands when there is no monsoon failure. Michael, who owns eight acres of land, harvested thirty bags of paddy in 2001, which is quite a lot higher than the amount of paddy some individual Vanniyars harvest.

Nevertheless, not all have lands to live on, and one or two acres that some Paraiyars possess are highly dry lands that entirely depend on the monsoon. Even if there is sufficient rain, some Paraiyars find it difficult to hire bullocks for ploughing. So most of the time almost sixty per cent of the Paraiyar lands is left uncultivated.

Another important source of income comes from the coconut palm tree-climbing in the suburban centres of Chennai – Thambaram, Crompettai. Every week on Friday, about forty men leave the Colony for this kind of work. Since Saturday and Sunday are weekly holidays in the state, the house owners are usually at home and able to let the Paraiyars climb their coconut palm trees.

Table 7

Landownership by the Paraiyars and the Ūr higher castes[12]

Size of Landholding (in acres)	*The Paraiyar Households*	*The Ūr higher castes*
0-0	30	11
0-1	58	43
1-2	10	30
2-3	3	13
3-5	5	15
5- above	4	13

Source: Village Panchayat Board

Many Brahmins, who live in the suburban centres of Chennai, grow coconut trees from which they get coconuts for their own use. Since they know nothing about trees, the Paraiyars are asked to look after them. The Paraiyars climb the trees to collect the coconuts, to prune the leaves and to spray them with insecticide where necessary. There are different wages for these jobs. For plucking coconuts they are paid 20 rupees, for spraying the tree with insecticide 35 rupees, for cutting and clearing dried leaves 15 rupees. On Tuesday they return to the Colony after having done some shopping with the wages they received. In normal circumstances, each one earns 150 rupees every week.

There had been times in which the Brahmins refused to allow the Paraiyars to work on the coconut trees if the trees were located close to the main structure of the house in which the Brahmins usually have a small shrine, since the Paraiyars would pollute the Brahmin house. Arul, one of the tree climbers, told me, "in the last month itself at least in two Brahmin houses I was refused work on their coconut trees by the housewives (*māmīs*). One day I told a Brahmin woman that her coconut tree needed treatment since it was dying. She told me that as I was a Paraiyar she did not like to allow me into her house, and she said that she was looking for a Nadar man [another caste group that specialises on tree tapping]." At such times the Paraiyars would get some insects that eat up the palm flowers and put these in the coconut trees without the knowledge of the Brahmins. This ensured that the next time the house owners would need their help urgently to look after the trees. This is the way in which the Paraiyars react to the Brahmins in Chennai city who treat them as untouchables. However, some of the climbers feel that this is unfair and that it is immoral to cheat people.

The other Paraiyar families look down on the coconut palm tree climbers partly due to their act of cheating in the city. They are also, to a certain extent, jealous of the climbers' economic stability, because the income others in the Colony get by doing agricultural work is considerably less than the income the climbers bring home in ready cash every week. There is always a division between the Paraiyars who get jobs that are not agricultural and those who stay in the Colony working on the land. Seventy families depend on the land and on the wages they get from working as daily labourers. Also there is one of the Paraiyars who is a secondary grade teacher and works in the state school in Padalam, 12 kilometres from Pappanallur. But he is not interested in the affairs of the Colony and keeps well away from the conflicts between the Paraiyars and the Vanniyars. The other

Paraiyars do not have much to do with his family either. Another Paraiyar works as an assistant to the Village Officer (VO), who is the representative of the state government. For this work, which is mostly going on errands, he receives 700 rupees per month. The Paraiyar assistant is called 'Talaiyari' that does not mean exactly one of the conventional Dalit services. And one Paraiyar is a school teacher in a union school. More than twenty young boys and girls work in factories run by multinational companies that produce textile, leather products, and plastic utensils for export. Excepting these people, who have a regular income, all the other families work as daily labourers.

Political Networks: Forming Self-Consciousness

The elections are one of the moments in which the Paraiyars have come to realise their power to conduct their lives as they wish. They used the last two elections in 2001 – the Panchayat and State Assembly – to assert their identity. In the Panchayat elections the Paraiyars fielded their own candidate for the post of Panchayat president although they could not win it. In the run up to the Assembly elections, twice they threatened to boycott the elections unless the candidates promised them proper drinking water facility, employment for their youth and regular transport to nearby cities. This was impossible in the past when they were subservient to the *Ūr* higher castes. Being poor, dependent, ritually polluted and socially excluded, they were powerless people; they had no power or role in the decision-making procedures of the village. The *Ūr* higher castes' council or *Ūr* Panchayat decided what they should do and should not. Be it a village festival or a dispute, they were supposed simply to follow what the *Ūr* high caste leaders told them. Eḷumalai Goundar was the supreme leader in the 1940s, for whom every member of the village had deep respect. His sharp intellect, his ability to take quick decisions and his powerful persuasive skills were, and are still today, highly appreciated. Theft, murder or disputes between families were all handled and settled very efficiently by him single-handed. The older Paraiyars narrated many stories that highlight his enormous influence in the village for more than four decades. He stands as a symbol of what the power-relations in the village were in the past. Though Eḷumalai is unable, due to his old age of 98 plus, to have any say now in the affairs of the village, he still exerts influence because of his knowledge of village traditions.

The Paraiyars today refer to him as the personification of high caste contempt for the Dalits. They remember even today how he used to beat them with leather sandals and metal nails. The reasons were mostly because they did not remove their towel as a mark of respect when they happened to meet him in the street, or for not going to work on time when the Paraiyar families worked for his *pannaiyāl*.

Another similar story that many Paraiyars remember is the one about how they were not allowed to fish in the village tank (*ēri*). One day in 1963, Megalai, 67 years old Paraiyar woman went to the tank to collect firewood. While she was searching for firewood, she found that plenty of fish were swimming near the shore of the tank, something quite unusual. She collected them by using her sari as a net and was happy that she would not need to struggle to search for her food that day. But some Vanniyars boys who were grazing their cattle went and told the village leaders about it. Immediately, Eḷumalai Goundar sent three men to bring her to his house. Then the Goundar, after beating her with the cane used to chase cattle, fined her 20 rupees for fishing in the tank, which the Paraiyars were forbidden to do. The fine money was a huge amount at that time, when the daily wage was only 4 rupees for women. So she had offered to work in the Goundar's fields for a week, which the Gounder allowed her to do. In this way the Paraiyars did not have any rights over public resources. Public lands, tamarind tree products, Palmyra tree produce and fish from the *eri* were all used only by the higher castes. Only the left over was given to them by the higher castes.

Another event that Barnabas, the eldest Paraiyar in the Colony, recalled, will help us to understand just how powerless they used to be. He related how he had to go to plough a field of

Elumalai Goundar, for planting paddy, on his wedding day. Two days after his marriage, he threw himself on the ground at the feet of the Goundar and begged to be allowed to be with his wife for a few days as he was a newly-married person. The Goundar said, "how dare you, paraiyans want to have sexual pleasure".[13] By implication, only the higher castes could enjoy such pleasures. When Barnabas begged the Goundar at least to allow him work off for half a day, the Goundar said 'if you want a holiday, send your newly-married wife (*pudupondātti*) to sleep with me for a day, then you can take a day off' and 'you, paraiyans should not eat anything fresh, you should eat only our leftover (*ecci sōru*).' When Barnabas finished telling this story his eyes became red suddenly and filled with helpless but tears of anger and his lips were trembling, his body shook with rage. His son, Xavier who was sitting beside him, held his right hand and stroked the back of his head to calm him down. A little later, composing himself once more, he said quietly 'I am happy. At least my children do not have to go through this *asingam* (dirt)'.

Now, however, the situation is quite different, especially since 1997, the Paraiyars have become politically more powerful in many ways. I could indicate a few areas in and through which they empower themselves and assert their identity. They are the parish council, the *Mātharsangam* (women's association), the village Panchayat board, and from outside sources of power there are the two Non Governmental Organisations (NGOs) – the Chengalpattu Rural Development Society (CRDS) and the Association for Sarva Seva Farms (ASSEFA) – and the Dalit Panthers of India (DPI), the Dalit political party. In addition, the priests who have been in charge of Pappanallur parish had consistently supported the Paraiyars in terms of providing them with finance to acquire lands and build decent houses, and more importantly, they had been instrumental in making the Paraiyars become politically conscious of their rights. Particularly, the Jesuit priests who were parish priests in Pappanallur helped them to realise the importance of getting rid of the polluting services, and whenever the Paraiyars were worse affected by their conflicts with the Vanniyars the parish priests stood by them in terms of employing lawyers to argue for the Paraiyars. All these have made the Paraiyars politically powerful. In Chapter 4, I will discuss in detail the contribution of the NGOs, the Dalit political parties, and the church to bringing about the change in the lives the Paraiyars.

Religion: Security from Subordination

The Paraiyars until 1941 were Hindus. They were part of the village performing all the traditional services (*thoḷil*); working on the land of the *Ūr* higher castes as semi-bonded labourers (*padiyāl*); and living on the cooked food given them by the higher castes and a share of paddy given to them by the landlord as *mānyam*.[14] In 1940, there was a conflict with the Vanniyars over a piece of land, in which many Paraiyars were arrested and imprisoned in Achirapakkam jail, though they themselves considered that they were innocent. They felt that the higher castes, besides beating them, bribed the police to imprison them unjustly. The police refused to release them till they agreed to give the land back to the higher castes. But the Paraiyars refused to do so. In such a situation where there was no one to help them, they went to ask Father Paul, the parish priest of Cheyur, for assistance. The priest arranged to get them released from jail by using his rapport with the police of the British colonial time. That made the Paraiyars realise that the only way to be freed from the domination of the *Ūr* higher castes was to convert to Christianity to live a more secure life. On 19 June 1941, according to the baptismal records kept in Cheyur parish church, forty-nine Paraiyars converted to Christianity and later, on the 8th of August in that same year, another twenty-eight Paraiyars were baptised as Christians by Father S. Paul Puthanangady, called '*paul sāmmiyār*. Other Paraiyars were gradually baptised in the next two years, and in 1949 eighty per cent of the Paraiyars had become Christians.

Although they had changed their religion until 1997, they continued rendering the services that they had traditionally been doing for the Vanniyars. The five distinct roles or tasks – *parai* drummer, cattle scavenger, cremation ground attendant, death announcer (*variyān*), and village watchman (*kambukūṭṭi*), were now being done by different *Vagaiyarā*, as opposed to the strict role allocation to a particular *Vagaiyarā* of a particular service, which had been the case before their conversion to Christianity. All this defined their identity as being of low and impure social status in the village.[15] In every way, either explicitly or implicitly, all these roles were involved with death, either of – human beings and cows – and evil spirits – *pēy pisāsu* – of the malevolent dead persons. Thus from the point of view of the *Ūr* higher castes, the Paraiyars were looked down as persons polluted and culturally of a low social status. In fact, such a status was considered more in terms of religious practice rather than of social behaviour, because of their job of clearing impurities that makes them seem intermediaries between higher beings, human as well as divine, and lower divine beings such as evil spirits and demons. This was the way the higher castes of the *Ūr* thought of and looked upon the Paraiyars. Sammanasu, who has an experience of forty-two years of drumming, said, 'we drummed in order to chase away the *pēy* and prevent them from entering the holy places'.

More specifically, their role as drummers was always required in the village festivals, such as Marriamman and Pongal in which the drumming was very important, and without it no ceremony would be complete. So the Paraiyars continued to perform the five traditional roles to the *Ūr* higher castes from the time they converted to Christianity until 1997. Not only that, they also continued to worship their *ista deivam* (the chosen god/goddess), *vīṭṭu ṭēivam* (household god/goddess), *kula ṭēivam* (lineage deities) discreetly, but without the knowledge of the parish priests and the nuns.

For more than half a century, while being Christians they continued to perform their roles in the Hindu rituals, and for quite a long time they had held on to their Hindu pantheon. My observation in the field convinced me that since the services they did to the Vanniyars were fundamental to their identity, abandoning them all of a sudden demanded strong will and conviction. This they have managed to do through many conflicts, and they have at last stopped providing the services and formed a new identity. To focus our attention on the religious aspect, it may be mentioned that they considered the act of drumming as an organising principle in their life in general and their religious life in particular, even though this gives them a negative identity as the cleaners of impurities, from which they are now trying to recover and form their own positive status.

Therefore, it is important to discuss the role of drumming in festivals and funerals, with which all the other three services, except the service of village watchman (*kambukuṭṭi*), – cattle scavenging, cremating human bodies, *vāriyan* announcing – are interconnected. More precisely, the festivals and death rituals are the times when the polluting roles of the Paraiyars are dramatised or displayed openly in the gaze of the village, which reminds them as well as the other castes of their social status. By this ritual inclusion their social exclusion is determined, or as Fuller puts it, they "are included precisely so that they can be portrayed as excluded" (1992: 139). In an important sense, the Paraiyars' identity is predicated on this ritual exclusion. This point will help us understand why the Paraiyars have abandoned these roles in the festivals and funerals in order to make the same roles, especially the drumming, more positive, and in a way it can be treated as their unique culture and that will be the central concern of the present study.

Hindu Festivals and the Role of the Christian Paraiyars[16]

The Vanniyars hold five annual festivals in the village: the Vinayaka festival, the Periapalayathamman festival, the Selliamman festival, the Mariamman festival and the Pongal festival. The Vinayaka festival is celebrated by the Vanniyars with the help of Uthiramerur, a Brahmin priest, in which the Paraiyars have no role except that of collecting *prasadam,* leftover food that had been offered to the god. The Paraiyars take an active part in the Marriamman and Pongal festivals, though their role has been low and impure, but it was necessary for the rituals to be complete.[17]

Marriamman Festival

In the month of *Ādi* (between 15 July to 15 August) the festival for Mariamman is celebrated in Pappanallur as elsewhere in Tamil Nadu. According to the Vanniyar elders, the festival, which the people in Pappanallur call *kūḷūṭura ṭiruviḷā* (porridge festival), used to be celebrated for eight days, the actual celebration runs through five phases.[18] But these days, the festival in Pappanallur is celebrated only for three days, condensing many rituals and omitting others for a variety of reasons.

On the first day, the village decides the ways in which they are going to celebrate the festival and how much tax each household will be asked to pay. On the second day, the main part of the festival is held. In this there are three principal movements in which the goddess Mariamman is worshipped. In the first movement, following the myth of Mariamman who acquired an untouchable body and a Brahmin head, the goddess is installed in two forms; the higher form is at the temple where only the head of the goddess is kept and the lower form at a well outside the village where a stone that symbolises the untouchable body of the goddess is established. The higher form is accomplished by a Valluvar priest who performs a puja while the Vavunian (also called Valluvar Pandaram), invited from a nearby village, plays *bambai* and *uṭukkai*, which are considered auspicious. When the puja is stopped the five Paraiyar drummers – three drummers from Talaiyari *Vagaiyarā* and two from Theradiyan *Vagaiyarā* – play the drums standing at a distance away from the temple. The sound of the drums indicates that the festival is about to begin, and, more importantly, it is meant to drive away evil spirits from the place where the ritual is being performed, since the drummers and the drumming are associated with malevolent spirits. After this ceremony the Valluvar priest ties a sacred thread (*kāppu*) to the *kambukuṭṭi* Paraiyar. The Vannan priest (*pūsāri*), assisted by the *kambukuṭṭi* Paraiyar, installs the lower form of the goddess by making three *karakam* pots: mud pots are filled with milk and lime and decorated in a conical shape with sandalwood paste and saffron paste. Then the *karakams* are taken in a procession to the temple where the higher form of the goddess is kept. The drummers lead the procession by announcing loudly the coming of the goddess and drive away demons and evils spirits (*pēi pisāsu*) along the route of the procession. Followed by the drummers, the *kambukuṭṭi* Paraiyar runs holding a knife in his right hand and shouting, 'go away demon' (*oh, haiya, oh haiya*). On arrival of the *karakams* a goat sacrifice is offered at the temple.

In the second principal movement of the festival the *drummers* and the *kambukūṭṭi* Paraiyar take the *karakams* from household to household in the *Ūr* where offerings are made to the goddess. This helps the whole *Ūr* get purified from all evil spirits. The final movement is that the higher form of the goddess is taken in a car procession throughout the *Ūr*. This is elaborate and complex ceremony involving many rituals.

At the end of the procession the *karakams* are taken to the Vannan house where the *kambukūṭṭi* Paraiyar safeguards the goddess from pollution, while the drummers keep drumming at intervals only in order to heat up the *parai* drums and maintain its tension. One of the Vanniyar thread persons said that if the drumming was not done, the goddess would become angry and would assume her fierce form, and that would be ominous for the village. This is why the drummers are forbidden to take much time off for their meals, for which their women go around the village collecting cooked food from the *Ūr* high caste houses.

On the third day of the festival, all the *karakams* are taken in a procession to a well outside the village, and drown the *karakams* to signify that curse of the goddess is cleared from the village. With this the festival comes to a close.

In 2001, during my fieldwork, the Paraiyars did not participate in the festival, since 1997 they had stopped all their traditional services. In the last three years, no one has been willing to take up the Paraiyar roles in the festival for they are seen as roles only meant for the Paraiyars who are supposed to perform polluting services. In playing the roles one would pollute anybody, as the roles are primarily meant to drive away malevolent spirits, and, on account of this, the drummers and the *kambukūṭṭi* Paraiyar are distanced and excluded even though they are needed for the festival to be complete. In 1998, I was told that the Vanniyars invited Paraiyars of Vedanthangal village to perform these services, but anticipating the opposition of the Pappanallur Paraiyars, they declined the invitation.

The Pongal Festival

Pongal festival is celebrated in Tamil Nadu, in the Tamil month of *Thai* (January-February) every year. Pongal means a "ritual cooking of milk-rice" (Dumont 1986: 412; Good 1983: 226). The Tamils celebrate the festival by boiling raw rice and offering it to the gods for blessings on their land and livestock to enable them to have a plentiful harvest. There are three kinds of Pongal: the *pōki pongal* in which all the old clothes and materials are burnt; the *vīṭṭu pongal* in which Pongal is celebrated inside each house or in a lineage temple; the *māṭṭu pongal*, which is a Pongal for bullocks. The third kind is a major festival in Pappanallur.

In the morning of the festival, the livestock are washed and painted with colour; the horns of the bulls are decorated with red and white spots; balloons and *manji* (a rope made with the bark of what Dumont (1986: 423) calls, *Sanseveria Zeilanica*) are tied around the necks of the bulls. Before noon on the day of *māttu pongal*, the people start preparing Pongal in two new mud pots – one plain and another sweet Pongal – outside every house, or more accurately inside the shed/enclosure where the livestock are kept. Once the Pongal is prepared, the men fill many vessels with turmeric water mixed with mango and margosa/neem leaves and sprinkle the water on the livestock. In some houses, the sprinkling of the turmeric water is done to the accompaniment of singing. At the time of my field study in 2001, in Ramakannappa Goundar's house the head of the family sang a song, praising the gods who had given them healthy and hard-working bulls and goats and for giving them unfailing monsoons; his two sons with their families repeated this along with him, shouting '*pōngalō pongal*'.

After this, the people have their festive meals, mostly vegetarian, and share pongal with other houses with which they have a close relationship. At this time, the other *Ūr* Dalits – Vannan, Ambattan, Kuruvikaran – go to every house to collect their food.

From the point of view of the Paraiyars, what happens later in the day is very important. Around four o' clock, the livestock, especially the bullocks are taken for racing the bulls (*mādukalaital*), for which the Paraiyar drummers go to every house in the *Ūr* drumming and gathering the livestock into one place.[19] Once all the livestock are gathered at a strategic place in the village the drummers beat the drum in a fast rhythm, and from there the livestock are taken in a procession to the lake, which is at the time of the festival dry, for a final game. There the livestock are assembled in the centre and around them the village people wait to see the spectacle. The drummers start their drumming in a fast rhythm that makes the livestock run aimlessly all around the village and into the fields. The men who hold the bulls by ropes release them one by one to allow the bull fighters to snatch the decorative articles tied around the bulls' horns, which is a mark of bravery enjoyed by the people who are gathered around. The livestock that has raced is left that day to wander around the fields where paddy and millets are grown. It is the custom that on Pongal day no one can complain if the bulls destroy their fields. Using this, as we will see later, the Vanniyars every year destroy the paddy and millet fields intentionally. This causes conflicts every year, interestingly from 1939 onwards until 1996, between the Paraiyars and the *Ūr* higher castes and later, from the 1960s between the Paraiyars and the Vanniyars. As we will discuss these conflicts later, I shall not describe these conflicts here in this section except noting in passing that the festival was the time when the Paraiyars and the Vanniyars used to show their strength and settle their scores every year. Moreover, this is why I will argue later that the festivals, both the Mariamman and the Pongal, are symbols of the conflict in which the Paraiyars become conscious of their low social status and their powerlessness in actualising their roles. It is such a consciousness that has indeed led the Paraiyars to reject their low status and look for a new identity.

In a similar vain, the Paraiyars realise their polluting status and identity, but much more forcefully, while they act out their roles at the funerals of the higher castes.

Funeral Rituals and the Paraiyars

Although the Paraiyars no longer perform their funeral services to the *Ūr* higher castes, I am giving a brief description of the services that the Paraiyars used to do before 1997 in order to project an idea about their past life against which their present efforts can be understood.

Death rituals in Pappanallur, as elsewhere in Tamil Nadu, documented by Good (1991), involve three stages: the disposal of the corpse; rituals in the cremation ground; the purificatory rites. These are observed by all the *Ūr* castes though there are variations, except for the Paraiyars who follow Christian burial rites. When a person dies the first group to be informed are the Paraiyars. After they have received the news of the death, the drummer Paraiyars go to the house of the deceased and start drumming; in this way the whole village comes to know of the death. Also a *kambukūṭṭi* Paraiyar is sent as a messenger to different places in the district and beyond to inform the relatives of the deceased. The *Ūr* Dalits – Ambattan, Vannan – are asked to go to the house of the dead, where the former blows his conch at important passages from one ritual to another, and the latter provides clothes for the purpose of removing death pollution from the house of the dead. The drummers have an important role in terms of the removal of the impurity caused by death. When a person dies his or her 'spirit' leaves the body, and if it is not driven away, it might enter into persons in the village. Not only that, even by touching the dead body one can be defiled substantially, and require a ritual of purification. As elsewhere in India (Mines 1990),[20] a death in Pappanallur for the *Ūr* castes involves a series of ceremonies, which I do not intend to discuss. What I shall focus here is the role of the Paraiyars in funerals to set the stage for my discussion of identity construction.

From the time a high caste person dies until the body is cremated the drummers have to go on playing the drum. At the beginning, they play in the shed built in front of the house, where the corpse is kept in a chair in a sitting posture. Later, when the relatives of the deceased arrive the drummers accompany them. When the women in the house do their bewailing rite (*māradital*), the drumming is suspended. After the village elders have decided that main rituals can begin, the drummers lead the close relatives of the deceased to a nearby well for the ceremony of taking the water garland (*nīrmālai edutal*). The ritual consists of putting on a white thread belt as worn by Brahmins from the right shoulder to the left. Moreover, the sons of the deceased collect water in small brass vessels and the women, closely related to the deceased, collect water in pots after bathing and return home. With the water brought from the well, the corpse is bathed, if the dead person is a woman, women do it and if it is man, men do the bathing. The *kambukūṭṭi* Paraiyar ties the limbs and the head with white stripes and rubs sacred ash and sandal wood paste all over the dead body; the mouth is covered with kumkum (red powder used ritually) paste.[21] Later the corpse is laid on a wooden platform. At this time, a group of selected women depending on their kinship relationship to the deceased – Brothers' Wife (BW), Brothers' Daughter (BD), Sisters Daughters (ZD) – with the dead man's wife stand around the corpse and start ritually to bewail for some time. When they have finished this, they circle round the body three times and at the end of the circling each one puts, yellow rice on the mouth of the dead person (*vāikkarisi*). At this time, the wife of the dead person is given a new sari by one of the dead person's brothers. When this is being done the drumming is suspended, for this ritual is considered to have a semi-auspicious value, though some say that it is to allow the mourners concentrate on the rituals.

Meanwhile, the Vannan and *kambukūṭṭi* prepare a wooden bier (*pādai*), with fresh logs cut from the trees on the bank of the lake. Then to the sound of loud drumming the body is placed on the bier and carried fast by the pall-bearers towards the cremation ground, while they shout '*Arohara*, *Arohara*' (oh, God). In front of the bier the drummers run, keeping pace without losing the rhythm of the drumming. At the cremation ground where *kambukūṭṭi* Paraiyar had already piled logs of wood for the cremation, the bier is put down for the final ceremony of pot-breaking (*kuṭam uṭaiṭal*). The elder son of the dead person circles around the bier carrying an earthen pot with water falling from a small hole punched in it by the Ambattan. At the end of every circle, there are three circles, the pot is punched and after the last hole the pot is thrown down to the west of the bier. The close relatives put on the mouth of the body yellow rice as the women at the house had done and place a few coins on the body. When this is over, the *kambukūṭṭi* Paraiyar removes the money and the new dress from the body, which is considered to be his right. Then, with the help of his men he takes the body and places it on the funeral pyre. The elder son lights the pyre and leaves the cremation ground, leaving *kambukūṭṭi* Paraiyar to cremate the body. He with one or two of his men performs the task; this takes all night. In most cases, he completes the task in the early hours of following day.

The Paraiyars in the Parish Annual Festival

Before we come to a description of the festival, it will be helpful to consider briefly the background of Christianity in Pappanallur. The parish church belongs to the Roman Catholic Archdiocese of Madras-Mylapore. The Pappanallur parish was created in 1978. This was originally under the Cheyur parish, the oldest parish in the then Chengalpattu district, from 1716 until 1969. It later became one of the substations of the Madurantagam parish. Then for some time it was attached to the Valayaputhur parish in the

1980s, since parish priests found the Pappanallur village extremely remote and there was no road and transport from the village to other places. At the time when Father K.V. Nilappanar became the parish priest, the Pappanallur parish flourished in many ways and the present church was built at this time; he arranged to have a road laid that would link Pappanallur with the Vedanthangal high way tar road.

The Paraiyars were originally Hindus. They converted to Christianity in 1941. The main reason for their conversion was to get away from the Hindus of the village who persecuted them in many ways. In fact, it was a conflict over a piece of land between the *Ūr* higher castes – at that time, the Brahmins, the Reddiyars and the Vanniyars – and the Paraiyars in 1939, which we shall discuss in detail later in Chapter 4. Reverend Father S. Paul the parish priest of Cheyur from 1934 until 1942, was instrumental in helping the Paraiyars out in the conflict, filing a case in the court against the *Ūr* higher castes, and later won the case for the Paraiyars. This gave them an impetus to convert to Christianity. With this background, we shall describe the festival, that I hope will illustrate the way in which they have practiced Christianity while continuing to perform their traditional roles in Hindu festivals and rituals.

Like every Catholic festival in Tamil Nadu, in Pappanallur the festival of St Theresa of the Child Jesus is celebrated every year from 22nd September until 1st October. Unlike the other parishes in the diocese or elsewhere in the state, which are mostly multi-caste parishes (Mosse 2000), here the participants of the festival are all Paraiyars, and there is no regard for structuring the festival according to different groups. The Paraiyars in the village celebrate the festival with the guidance of the parish priest. The nine-day festival, called a *novena*, begins with a meeting two weeks before when the parish council works out a plan of the festival. In the beginning, before 1985, each day was honoured by the *Vagaiyarā*, but after the parish was taken over by the Jesuits, each day is celebrated by different sections of the parish: the women's association, the men's association, youth, children, but the beginning, and of the final day celebrations are common. It is also called *manṭakapadi*, 'the donor holds the day's festival'. This does not mean that each group bears the expenses for that day of the festival, but the day is dedicated to the group in which a theme is selected, and according to the theme, that day's mass and other celebrations are designed. For instance, in the 2001 festival, the central theme was 'Fullness of Life' but each day was dedicated to sub themes such as 'life in sharing', 'life of human rights', 'equality of life', 'life of sacrifice', 'life in justice'.

The ninth day of the festival is the final celebration, the real festival day, which is celebrated in a special way. It is different from the other days, not only for the huge crowds swelled by the presence of the relatives from other villages, but also because of certain factors that significantly contrast with the festivals in the *Ūr*. This is also relevant in the context of the present thesis.

The morning begins with the killing of two or three cows or bulls, which are bought with the common money. This is done openly in a way that the killing of the cows becomes offensive to the Hindus of the village. Particularly, from 1997, the year when the Paraiyars stopped their traditional services to the *Ūr* higher castes, the killing of the cows is deliberately done in such a way. After killing the cows outsidc the village, the dead cows are carried through the *Ūr* streets. This infuriates the Vanniyars, since they could easily be carried through the Colony side of the village. Devasahayam, one of the three persons who usually organise the killing, told me that this was the way we insult the Vanniyars who ill-treated us because of our beef-eating. Then the beef is generously shared among the families and in each house there is great festivity. Also this is a time of the year during which the Paraiyars, men and women, freely consume alcohol, country liquor (*sārāyam*).

In the evening the festival centres on the church. By six o'clock the whole Colony mills around the church in great numbers; hawkers put up small stalls to sell objects like balloons, sweets, stickers and bangles. In contrast to their performance in the *Ūr*, the drummers, who are dressed up in military band shirts and trousers with decorated turbans, start drumming. The drums consist of five circular shaped, one-sided and vertically held *parai*, a large two-sided drum, *satti* parai, and a clarinet type of pipe instrument. The rhythms are different from the ones they have for the Hindu festivals: the clarinet plays songs, mostly familiar to the Paraiyars, and keeping with the beat of the songs the drummers play on, and a group of three or four people dance in front of the drummers, which is watched keenly by a crowd. While this goes on, a group decorates the festival car (*ṭēr*), that will be taken in a procession after the festival mass. About seven o'clock, the church bell goes for mass. Immediately the drumming stops and the crowd enters the church for the mass. Then for an hour or so the whole place is quiet except for the ringing of bells, and a short drumming at the time when the priest lifts the consecrated host and wine. For the drummers this is something important. Their drumming is considered as holy as the eucharist. which they did not felt when they drummed for the *Ūr*.

Once the mass is over, the crowd returns to festive mood. The main celebrant assisted by the parish priest takes the statue of St Theresa of the Child Jesus and mounts it on the decorated car amidst a crescendo of drum music and fireworks. Then the car is pulled through the streets of the Colony, as in the flag procession, to the sound of drum music except when drumming is suspended to tighten the drums' hide over burning hay.

The message that runs throughout the nine-day festival is that Christianity is meant to liberate people like the Dalits from caste oppression. To bring the message home, the sermons, prayers, songs and plays portray Jesus Christ as a Paraiyar, and that is why he was insulted and persecuted and finally crucified naked. One of the women said, 'if Jesus is not a Paraiyar, we have no reason to worship him; I believe he should have been like a Paraiyar in his place at that time, the cross tells us that'. Michael, one of the drummers, said that he had a greater interest in playing the drum in the Christian festival than in the Hindu festivals; not because they were very well respected and paid enough that we could not imagine in the Hindu festivals in the *Ūr*, but because we feel closer to the god we worship who is half naked as we are and suffered like us, the drummers, due to his resistance to the higher castes of his place'. Most of the Paraiyars in the village, even schoolboys and girls, hold a similar opinion. Later, I was told that many from the parish regularly attend seminars on theology in which such themes are handled and these have a great influence on their life. Later, I will argue that this is one of the major reasons that contribute to the project of identity construction. Apart from their training through seminars, the parish festival is used to spread this ideology. A strong proof of this is that the priests invited for each day of the *novena* are mostly Dalits by birth. In their sermons, they tell the congregation that the church in Tamil Nadu is a Dalit church, and so the administration of the dioceses should be handed over to Dalit bishops. The parish, priest, who normally holds the central role in such festivals elsewhere in Tamil Nadu to the level of a king, plays a secondary role in the case of Pappanallur.

The present parish priest, Father Jeyaraj Elankeswaran, a Jesuit, said that he did not want to hold a central and dominant role among the Paraiyars who were gradually coming out of subordination by the higher castes, if he did, he would be just a replacement of the Vanniyar leaders, which he hated to do. He further observed that although the Paraiyars gave up Hinduism in the 1940s, they had taken a long time (1941-1997) to come out of their traditional life-patterns in relation to the Vanniyars, fully demonstrated the fact of how emancipation of the Dalits was a difficult process. Now in 2003, the Paraiyars in Pappanallur are completely cut off from the *Ūr*, and they no longer perform their traditional services to the higher castes. Instead, they make every attempt to imagine their life independent of the *Ūr* and reconstruct their new identity.

This is not to suggest that the Dalits in Tamil Nadu who converted to Christianity liberated themselves from untouchability. Many studies (Raj 1992a, 1992b, 1995; Jayakumar 1999; Stanislaus 1999; Sivasubramanian 2001) have discussed the situations in which Christian Dalits are discriminated against in church rituals and practices. Amongst the Christians of Tamil Nadu sixty-five per cent are Dalits (Paraiyars, Pallars, Arunthathiyars and Valluvans, and under these four divisions there are seventy-eight sub-Dalits), and the rest are high caste, Vellalars, Gounders, Udaiyars, Mudaliars, to name but a few, (Grafe 1990: 138).[22] But the high caste Christians dominate and control the church resources, and the Dalit Christians suffer discriminations in terms of being segregated in the church activities. Even among the Catholic clergy in Tamil Nadu there is a sharp divide between high caste Christians and Dalit Christians (Raj 1995; Fernandes 1993; Amaladoss 1994). Movements like Dalit Christian Liberation Movement (DCLM) have been agitating for equal treatment of the Dalit Christians in the church, and for allotment of seats and jobs for them in the educational institutions run by the Catholic Church. There is fresh evidence in the Kanchipuram district and in the Madras-Mylapore Archdiocese that tell us that the high caste Christians refuse to treat Christian Paraiyars as equals. To give but one example, in four village parishes – K.K. Pudur, Manambathi Kandigai, R.N. Kandigai, Thatchur – the churches have remained closed for the last five years (1998-2003) on account of conflicts between Christian Paraiyars and high caste Christians, such as Telugu Naidus and Reddiyars. The Christian Paraiyars demanded equal treatment in church activities in their parishes which were in control of the Reddiyar and Naidu Christians, and the Arch-diocese was unable to do anything, since, apparently the Reddiyars and Naidus had the support of the priests who belonged to these two caste groups (Philomen 1999). I made five visits to the four parishes to talk to both the groups that I thought would help me compare and contrast the Paraiyars in Pappanallur and the Paraiyars in those parishes. Unlike the four parishes, Pappanallur has only one group, that is, the Paraiyars, and they need to fight with the Hindu Vanniyars. For this, the Pappanallur Paraiyars received support from the parish priests since the 1940s. Michael, leader of the parish council in Pappanallur, told me that if they have had high caste Christians in Pappanallur as those for parishes, they would have to fight with too many enemies, which he reasoned could not have given them the progress they have made in Pappanallur by fighting against the Vanniyars. Many Paraiyars are happy that they had only one enemy to focus on and thankful to the successive parish priests who were a great support and a source of inspiration in their struggle to get rid themselves of untouchability.

Notes

1. The concept of the mini-bus was conceived by the DMK (Dravida Munnetra Kazhagam) government in order to provide people in remote villages with access to city centres and the towns, which was very difficult in earlier times.
2. The Vanniyars are called 'Gounders', a term used to denote another high caste group in the places like Coimbatore in the west of Tamil Nadu.
3. In Part, II-B (ii) of the 1991 Primary Census Abstract (Tamil Nadu Series – 23) for Scheduled Castes lists 76 Dalit groups.
4. Earlier this group was called Sakkiliars but most of the Dalit leaders felt the name had negative connotations. Now the name 'Arunthathiyars' is regarded as culturally correct.
5. See for the studies on the origin of Paraiyars: Hanumanthan (1979); J. Massey (1996: 1-52); L. Stanislaus (1999: 6-9); Moffatt (1979: 32-58); Kumar (1965); Sathianathan (1998: 64-75).
6. This is one of the nine months of the Tamil Calendar.
7. The term *paṭiyāl* is employed for the Paraiyars who get a fixed daily allowance of food for their work. (*paṭi* (fixed allowance + *āl* (a labourer). '*Paṇaiyāl*' (pannai-farm) referred to a permanent agricultural labourer with a long-standing relation to a single member of a dominant caste.
8. *ethu asingamo athu engalukku palam tharum*. The word 'shame' is often used in the village to mean 'pollution'. Similarly, they use '*karaipadithal'* – to mean that their person has been stained.
9. Ninety percent of this figure is the Paraiyars.
10. For a discussion of the Dravidian terminology, see Moffatt (1979: 174-6).

11. See Good (1991: 54-74), for a discussion on eZDy marriage, particularly his critique of Dumont's Dravidian terminology.
12. The *Ūr* higher castes refer mainly to the Vanniyars. The Reddiyars and one Idaiyar come under the sixth category (5 acres). The source of this data is from the village record kept in the Panchayat office.
13. *paraipayalgalukku pontātti sugam kēkkutho*
14. In other places in Tamil Nadu rent-free landholding given to the Dalits as *mānyam* for the services they provided to the *Ūr*. See Mosse (1994).
15. I will elaborately discuss each role in the section on the drum in Chapter 5. Here I restrict my focus to the religious significance of the roles.
16. At the time of the fieldwork done (2001-2002) for the present study, the Paraiyars did not participate in the festivals, since they had stopped all their services to the *Ūr* in 1997, including the drumming and ritual assistance in the festival. So, I draw upon the Vanniyars' information, particularly, the interview I had with Elumalai Gounder, who is in his nineties and who had been the village leader from 1950 until 1989.
17. For a detailed study of the two festivals see Manuel Moreno and McKim Marriott (1990: 158-68); Whitehead (1921: 32); Beck (1972: 118); Dumont (1986: 425-27); Clarke (1998: 80-90); Fuller (1992: 44-56).
18. For a detailed description of Mariamman festival see Moffatt (1979: 250-270).
19. Elsewhere in Tamil Nadu, this is called *salli kaṭṭu* meaning the bulls that carry silver coins and bells on their forehead to be snatched in the race by the bull fighters in a game, see Dumont (1986: 422-423).
20. Mines (1990) explains in detail, in her well-researched paper using rich variety of material collected from all over India, how death is viewed by Indians and the impact of this on the social life of the people.
21. In other places in Tamil Nadu, this is done by Pallars, another dominant Dalit group. In the cases that Dumont (1986: 272ff) and Good (1991: 133ff) describe, Pallars, Ambattan and Vannan Dalits deal with the corpse. It could be speculated that since there are no Pallars in Pappanallur the role has fallen to the Paraiyars.
22. There are sixteen Catholic dioceses and seven dioceses of the Church of South India (CSI). The ratio between Protestants is 2:1. In the total population of Tamil Nadu (5,58,58,946, according to Census of India 1991) Christians comprise 5.69 per cent.

3

Ethnicising Paraiyar Identity: A Theoretical Argument

This chapter offers the theoretical framework of the present study. I intend to provide the reader with the basic idea of the processes through which the Paraiyars of Pappanallur in Tamil Nadu attempt to form their identity. This is a skeleton of the present study, which the other chapters will flesh out by empirical substantiation. The project draws its inspiration from Bourdieu (1977, 1990) who insists that theorising should emerge out of and be interwoven with empirical reality.

There are three reasons for giving the theoretical framework here in this chapter, which comes between the descriptive foregoing chapters and the following chapters, which are mostly analytical. The first reason is to demonstrate explicitly the universal validity of this study of the Paraiyar ways of constructing their identity. This facilitates the possibility of reinscribing this same theory in any context beyond the original context of Pappanallur village. For a theory that grows out of reality must be able to provide tools and guidelines of a more general nature. It can be of help to people who are even far away from the reality from which the theory came. For abstraction facilitates 'cross-cultural comparability' (Schröder and Schmidt 2001: 4) and justifies the relevance of reading this study by people who are not directly concerned with the Paraiyars of Tamil Nadu, because the basic idea of this study is applicable beyond its original context. The second reason is methodological in the sense that the basic idea of the present study is placed before Chapter 5, the core chapter of the investigation, in order to make it easier for the reader to follow the general drift of the discussion and have greater clarity in understanding it. This is to present the argument as a whole first and then, later, break it up into parts in order to help the reader in the end to see the whole picture and come to a better understanding of the Paraiyar way of forming identity. The third reason is that this chapter provides space to introduce the works that lie behind this theory and its emphasis and confirms the universal application of the present study.

The gist of the Paraiyar ways of forming identity can be explained in the following way. Conflict, symbol and identity are a triad of moments or phases of identity construction in the life of the Paraiyars of Pappanallur village. First, conflict with the Vanniyars breaks open the Paraiyars' selves and makes them become conscious of their personhood, both at the level of individuals as Paraiyars and as a community. In the process of becoming conscious of themselves, they realise that they had been so far not only identified with and defined by symbols such as the drum, beef-eating, and land that gave them a low identity as a polluted and segregated community, but also that the life they had led until then had been inhuman, they were only objects to be used by the higher castes of the village. As we will see in Chapter 4, that in and through conflict the Paraiyars realise that they should have lived as *subjects* of their history, culture and society not as *objects* for the *Ūr*. They feel that they should recover their human ability to act and assert themselves as persons and as a community. More than anything else, the Paraiyars came to realise that the symbols had been powerful instruments in defining them as untouchables and Dalits.

Secondly, such self-realisation persuades them to form a new identity of their own different from the one given to them by the *Ūr* higher castes. To do this, they need either to abandon the symbols that defined them as low or to re-claim these symbols and reinterpret them in such ways, as would give them a new positive identity. They decided to do the latter, because they came to realise that the very symbols they were once identified with have the potency to give them a new identity if only they can change their meaning. However, they realised that it is impossible to do this by remaining within the fold of the *Ūr*. So they decided to detach themselves from the *Ūr* by converting to Christianity, by stopping eating carrion (dead cow meat), coming out of the village council and forming their own *Vagaiyarā* council, and finally discontinuing all the services they had been doing for the village. After every conflict there has been an act of coming out of every village institution in which they were treated as polluted, and therefore excluded from the *Ūr*. Earlier, by their performing their services to the *Ūr* they were excluded, but now the Paraiyars do a similar thing by dissociating themselves from those institutions. The former was passive and the latter active in the sense it helped them recognise their own ability to act independently. By distancing themselves from polluting services and institutions, they made an effort to reinterpret and to reverse the meaning of the symbols themselves, from subordination to the assertion of power in the hope of finally forming an identity of their own creation. This change of meaning of the symbols was done by evolving counter – myths to the myths conventionally attached to the symbols, and which, in fact, gave new meaning to the symbols and determined the use and the consequences of the use of the symbols. This came from their conviction that the higher castes were successful in defining them as Dalits, mostly and effectively, by the formation and popularisation of myths. Every symbol that defined them as low, they argued, contained, or was accompanied by, a myth or myths. This in fact made the symbols powerful in the definition of their community in the way the higher castes intended. More than the symbolic objects themselves, they reckoned, the myths that had defined them as polluted persons, gave them a caste hierarchy. Now, therefore, in order to form a different identity and create different social arrangements, in which their new identity will be recognised, they considered that they should form counter – myths that would be able to give a new meaning and understanding of the symbols. By doing so, the symbols, that until then had been used by the higher castes to define them negatively as Dalits, are now used by the Paraiyars to define themselves positively, because they have become the symbols of their unique culture, history, and social life.

Finally, for the Paraiyars change of identity means disowning, not the symbols themselves, but the meaning given to these symbols by the higher castes in order to define them as low and polluted. It means giving new meanings to the symbols by creating counter-myths and re-possessing the reinterpreted symbols to define themselves as people with land, a culture, a history, and a community. To put more sharply, the Paraiyars want both the symbols of the past and the symbols of the present to highlight the fact of how they once were and what they want to become. As they become increasingly conscious of just how much their identity was once an imposed identity, they think, this provides energy and direction to take over their own formation.

Conflict and symbol are the two major building blocks of the Paraiyar identity construction in which conflict leads to symbol, and both conflict and symbol together give rise to the evolution of an identity. Speaking simply, conflict and symbol are the two wheels in the processional journey towards identity construction. There is continuity and consistency between the three phases. For instance, the process does not end at the level of conflict; instead it continues through looking at the symbols and goes on to form a new identity. The process goes on and on and they feel that it should go on until they have achieved the complete transformation of their identity. The process from conflict to symbolic reversal to identity formation is to continue and repeated in order to sustain the Paraiyars' urge to form their new identity.

I should note here that they did not sit down one day, planned the whole process, and used some magic wand to be freed from all domination. Nor did they have this idea of the process from conflict to symbolic reversal to identity formation. It was a gradual building up for a long time. As things developed in the course of more than fifty years, they used all kinds of sources available and ideas that occurred to them to challenge the higher castes. In this constant support of successive parish priests, Dalit movements and political parties helped give them confidence to challenge the higher castes and form their new identity.

What lies at the core of the processes, in which the Paraiyars change their life in the village and causes the transformation of its social institutions, is the meaning that was given to the symbols before, and the meaning that is being given to them now. It is not that the symbols such as the drum, beef-eating, and land have a meaning of their own intrinsically from the beginning; they come to have the meaning given to them by a group of people to favour a particular result. The higher castes gave meanings to the symbols in a way that helped them succeed in defining themselves as a higher and purer community, and the Dalits as lower and impure. Moreover, this became an accepted social norm in Indian society, forcing every community to follow the norm faithfully to maintain the social order. After centuries of the functioning of this norm, it came to be considered that the given meaning of the symbols was natural and divinely determined. The symbols had this meaning for human beings who reacted toward them and brought about the particular social behaviour that was intended by the group that gave the meaning to the symbols in the first place.

The fundamental concern of the study of symbolic anthropology is not symbolic forms *per se*, but how people formulate their reality, their actions towards symbolic forms, or praxis – the uses of symbols (Dolgin 1977: 34). In other words, in symbolic analysis what is important is the focus on the symbolic processes in which people give meaning to their reality and form dynamics of their life. The questions, how the Paraiyars were defined before, and how and why they now attempt to define themselves differently, must be located in symbolic action and the processes in which meaning plays the central role.

The approach is pursued well in symbolic interactionism. Blumer (1986) explains that meaning does not 'emanate' from the symbols, nor is it the expression of the human psyche, in the sense that meaning is brought to the symbols by the human beings for whom alone the symbols have meaning. Instead, what we find in the efforts of identity formation by the Paraiyars is that the meaning of the symbols for a group is born out of the ways in which the one group acts toward another group with regard to the symbols.[1] Meaning is the production in the process of interaction between the two groups. Moreover, that is why symbolic interactionism sees meaning "as social products, as creations formed in and through the defining activities of people as they interact" (1986: 5).[2] In social interactions, one group provides meaning for, or attaches meaning to symbols in such a way that the meaning attached will demand a type of social behaviour, which finally will lead to the formation of a culture and a social structure. In this sense, culture is not an imposed social fact, but is something formed or created in and through social interaction which gives rise to social structure (Geertz 1993; Cohn 1985). The symbols of the drum, beef-eating, and land were given a particular meaning by the higher castes that made the Paraiyars polluted beings and therefore to be segregated outside the *Ūr*. Now, the Paraiyars reinterpret the symbols giving new meaning to the same symbols in the hope that this will dictate a different social behaviour, and in the end, form a new social order and culture. In addition to Cohn's assertion (1985: 17) that social interaction is the transaction of meaning in the process of interpretation of symbols between two groups, I want to argue, that it also helps a social group to form identity. It is this interconnection or interrelation between meaning and symbol, which is fundamental to identity formation in the sense that from the perspective of the Paraiyars reversing the meaning of the symbols, from negative to positive, produces an identity with which they want to identify themselves. In this meaning functions as an ideology that helps deconstruct the village social organisation and forms a new social order. Structurally, the use or change of meaning of the symbols in the process, from conflict to symbol and then to identity, causes a significant change in the Pappanallur village system and beyond it, perhaps it has implications for the caste system in India as a whole. Now I want to discuss briefly each of the three phases – conflict, symbolic reversal, and identity construction – and show the interconnection between them and bring in the works that inform the three phases of the identity formation.

Conflict as the Foundation of Identity Formation

Many older studies (Nader 1968; Coser 1956; Rex 1981; Simmel 1955; Weber 1964; Gluckman 1956; Evans-Pritchard 1940) discussed conflict positively in terms of maintaining social order and a cultural product in the sense of a clash in the social relationship between peoples. But very rarely have they seen conflict as way of restructuring or breaking away from social structures, which would be helpful for the present study.

Therefore, I prefer to draw mainly on five studies, Jayaram and Saberwal (1996), Lewis Coser (1956, 1968), Schmidt and Schröder (2001), Varshney (2002) and Touraine (1985, 1987), which privilege conflict in studying society and social change, particularly in the way how social groups use conflicts as a source of identity formation. Space precludes a detailed review and analysis of each of these works. Therefore, what I plan to do is just use the helpful points that these works can offer in my study of the Paraiyars' conflicts with the Vanniyars.

The first two works directly use the term *conflict* but the third work generally views conflict from the point of view of violence; the fourth one, by Varshney, while it focuses on religious or communal conflict, its main aim is conflict-resolution. The fifth study, although it considers conflict as the prism of understanding and study of social change, gives social movements a privileged focus to the extent of slipping more into advocacy than providing a clear and rigorous analysis.

Nevertheless, what I consider helpful in these studies for my own investigation is that all five works understand conflict largely as a positive form of community-building and identity-construction.

The first three works base their discussion on Coser's definition of *conflict* as a "struggle over values and claims to scarce status, power and resources in which the aims of the opponents are to neutralise, injure or eliminate their rivals" (Coser 1956: 8). Such conflict is "mediated by a society's cultural perception that gives specific meaning to the situation, evaluating it on the basis of past conflicts, and storing it as objectified knowledge in the group's social memory" (Schröder and Schmidt 2001: 4). As Jayaram and Saberwal (1996: 5) think, the definition 'encompasses a variety of phenomena' of conflict and leaves the nature, situation, objectives and methods of conflict open to further exploration rather than rigid and closed definition, which some times may not be applicable to different contexts. Touraine is more helpful here. He proposes eight types of conflict: the competitive pursuit of collective interest, the reconstruction of a social, cultural or political identity, political force, the defence of status and privilege, the social control of the main cultural pattern, the creation of a social order, national conflicts, and the conflict of neo-communitarianism (1985: 50-60).[3] But he settles down to one integrated concept of conflict that he calls 'the unity of conflicts' by which he defines 'conflict' as a source of definition of the actors and the opponents, and of the totality of the cultural field for which the conflict is created (1985: 760). The atmosphere of conflict gives the actors in the conflict the facility and power to define the concepts of 'we' and 'they' and 'ours' and 'theirs'.

This definition is explicated more sharply by Schröder and Schmidt (2001: 18, 19) who view conflict not as a "sudden outburst of aggressiveness devoid of historicity, meaning and reflexivity" but as something "performed as well as imagined by reflexive, socially positioned human beings under specific historical conditions for concrete reasons". In this, there is a process that starts from small competitions to minor confrontations and to major conflict. It is in the final stage of the process, according to Schröder and Schmidt, that violence is used as a cultural resource. This definition and process of conflict I find helpful in understanding the conflicts the Paraiyars encountered. However, I think that it is a restricted understanding of conflict that does not allow the actors any kind of spontaneity, and it is impossible to regulate the time and situation in which violence should be used. Secondly, although the emphasis on the purposeful character of conflict is important, it is impossible to dictate to the actors to be purposeful at all times. In addition, Schröder and Schmidt fail to include unintended effects of conflict and the constraints in achieving the purpose of conflict. Keeping these remarks in mind I will discuss the nature and characteristics of conflicts in Pappanallur.

In Pappanallur village, the word they use to refer to conflict is '*pirachinai*', which could be literally translated as 'issue' or 'problem'. To refer to violent clashes between two groups costing human lives, they use the word '*thaharāru*'. But sometimes, for all kinds of clashes they use the word '*pirachinai*'. Nevertheless, the two terms can mean both violent clashes and non-violent feuds. Conflict in Pappanallur is understood in three ways: (1) physical violence; (2) verbal feud; and (3) symbolic. It is, therefore, only by getting into a deeper dialogue with the people in Pappanallur that we can discover whether the clash between the two groups was serious, in the sense of the loss of lives, or was only a verbal brawl. Generally, what we mean here by conflict is this: the Paraiyars are not in agreement with the higher castes, in general with the *Ūr*, but especially with the Vanniyars, with regard to the village social organisation, and they refuse to perform the traditional services to the *Ūr* that once constituted order in the village. To put it more pointedly, conflict in Pappanallur for the Paraiyars is the violation of the norms and values of the social organisation, as arranged by the higher castes of the *Ūr*, the deconstruction of the conventional boundaries and definitions, and the reconstruction of new boundaries and definitions for the communities in the village.

More sharply still, the Paraiyars of Pappanallur village view conflict both as a symbolic source, and a form of political strategy. It is symbolic in the sense that when they create conflict over the playing the drum at festivals and funerals, beef-eating and the use of land, what they are really aiming at is the recovery of their identity as positive and non-polluted equals to the other higher castes in the village. Secondly, conflict is used as a political strategy. After every conflict, they realised that they acquired a power to oppose, to confront the higher castes, and refused to obey their orders, something they could not have imagined doing in a non-conflict atmosphere. This ability to refuse to obey the orders of the higher castes is further enhanced by their cutting off all social links with the *Ūr*, by changing their religion, founding their own school, and stopping their services to the *Ūr*. The severing of these links helped them build trenches from which they could fight against the higher castes. In addition, it gave them autonomy and the ability to imagine their world in a way far different from what they had been given so far to know or had imposed on them by the *Ūr*. What Schröder and Schmidt (2001: 10) call the 'polarised structure of "we: they" 'gives clarity to the definition of boundaries between the two groups and reorganises the socio-cultural space for both groups in the village. Finally, it leads to a focus on the symbols of identification that serve finally as the locus of identity formation.

In another sense, the conflicts become avenues of performance, what I call performance conflicts.[4] The conflict is a theatre in which acts are performed in order to create an impact on the audience – both the *Ūr* and the Colony – and to demonstrate their vision of reinterpretation of the symbols towards a new identity formation. The idea of theatre becomes more emphatic when we realise that it has only been on the occasion of the Pongal festival that all the major conflicts have occurred, and all their opposition to the *Ūr* has been shown. During the Pongal festival, the whole village gathers in one place, even people from nearby villages take a part, and in front of such a large audience the conflict is performed. For the rest of the year the whole village is quiet and normal, although there are times, when individual fights break out between an Dalit and a member of a high caste, but these are not as theatrical as those that take place during the festival time. Even when the need arises for a conflict the performative part of it waits until the next year's Pongal festival.

With this understanding of the term 'conflict', I will now go more deeply into some important dimensions of conflict as it occurs in Pappanallur, for conflict is the starting point, and the source of the Paraiyars' identity formation. My understanding of the conflict between the Paraiyars and the Vanniyars of Pappanallur rests on three fundamental premises, which can demonstrate specifically how the Paraiyars of Pappanallur view conflict, and use it in their efforts to assert their identity. The first premise is that conflict is a form of positive and creative activity for the community. The second premise is that conflict opens up their self-consciousness, making the people aware of the nature of their social roles, and that the structure and dynamics of the symbols which once gave them an imposed identity can now give them a different identity of their choice. The third premise is that the state of self-consciousness brought about by conflict opens the way to the reconstruction of their identity by changing the mcaning of the symbols. These three premises explain how conflict is one of the effective sources for identity formation, and in this sense they will help us come to the conclusion that conflict is a necessary phase in identity formation. I shall discuss briefly each of these premises.

Conflict as a Creative and Positive Act

Let us take the first premise: *conflict as a creative and positive act*. Conflict is neither an isolated act nor a senseless or meaningless act, arising from the spontaneous outburst of emotions, though at times it may seem like that. Instead, it is closely associated with 'instrumental rationality' that it provides power for a group to bargain with power and re-form its place in society (Schröder and Schmidt 2001: 3, 8). It is a 'meaningful action in pursuit of goals' (Rex 1981: 104) and 'it entails the formation of collectivities and has implications for interconnected institutions' (Jayaram and Saberwal 1996: 5); in addition, it is a "source in world making, to assert one group's claim to truth and history against rival claims, with all the social and economic consequences this entails" (Schmidt and Schröder 2001: 9). The first consequence of conflict is that it serves as a cleansing force that frees a group from the shackles of subjugation and servitude, and makes them 'fearless and restores self-respect' (Coser 1968: 214). More than these studies, Bowman (2001) directly provides a striking similarity to the emphasis of the present study. Conflict and violence is a force that helps create or construct identity, which violates and destroys already existing identities. Therefore, conflict is planned, deliberate and cultural as well as a political act towards the formation of identity.

This we can see in the ways in which the Paraiyars of Pappanallur and the Dalits in Tamil Nadu, and elsewhere in India, have come to view conflict and the violence in conflict as having a redemptive value. They have no hesitation in creating conflict and indulging in violence because they are convinced that new life can spring only from the blood that the Paraiyars shed in conflict'.[5] The Paraiyars create or engineer conflict after conflict in order to assert their power and form their identity, although the first conflict in 1947 was not a deliberately intended act of the Paraiyars, but born out of the situation at that time. They need conflict in their project of identity formation. However, there is a difference between intending a conflict to be creative before that conflict happens and considering the conflict as having redemptive value after it has happened. Employing the former approach, the Paraiyars of Pappanallur use conflict as a "rational strategy of bargaining for power", "a form of symbolic action that conveys cultural meanings, most importantly ideas of legitimacy" and "a resource in world making, to assert one group's claim to truth and history against rival claims" (Schröder and Schmidt 2001: 8, 9). The creative dimension of conflict and, more clearly, the efforts of the Paraiyars and the other Dalits in Tamil Nadu, force us to contest the assertions of structural holism primarily proposed by Dumont (1980) and furthered by Moffatt (1975, 1979a, 1979b) through his theory of replication and consensus.[6]

For Dumont, what is important in the analysis of caste are not the individual castes, what is considered the 'substantialist fallacy', instead, the caste 'system' as a 'whole' should be fundamental in the analysis. It is the relations between castes, between the elements and the whole system, that should be the parameters for understanding the reality of the caste system, in this sense, structure means a *system of relations, not a system of elements* (Dumont: 1980: 40), and therefore what is important here is not the nature of a caste group, but the nature of the relations between caste groups. Individuals or particular castes do not have any substance, they may exist in empirical reality, but 'they have no reality in thought, no Being' (Ibid: 272).

This is directed against an empiricism that would normally place emphasis on the elements, the castes as discrete categories, not the whole system, or the caste system. Therefore, the reality for Dumont, following strictly the principles of structuralism, is the creation of mental categories. Consequently, the caste system is viewed as an ideology, a fundamental ideology of Indian society, consisting of a set of ideas of values shared by all the members of a society. Indian society, perceived as a traditional society, is based on an ideology of hierarchy as against the Western principles of liberty and equality. In the hierarchical Indian society the stress is placed on the collectivity, the overall social order, not on the individuals, and consequently hierarchy takes the form of 'holism'. Thus, when you create a hierarchy what you are really doing is that you are creating an order. Dumont constructs the caste system, as a whole, in terms of values of hierarchical opposition and separation based on an ideology of purity and pollution. The Brahman, who is at the apex of the hierarchy, is most pure, ranked on top, and the Dalits, who are the most impure, ranked at the bottom of the hierarchical structure. As Appadurai has beautifully argued, contesting Dumont's view, structural holism "is above all a matter of the subordination of parts, that is, the castes, to the "whole," that is, the system of castes" (1986: 758).[7] More sharply, Cohen (1998) argues that Dumont is one of those scholars whose neglect of the parts in favour of the whole in a society, based on the conviction that the individual is not an Indian concern, but a peculiar Western phenomenon, firstly denied any space for the voice and values of individuals in a society, and secondly, created an 'axiomatic dichotomisation between individualistic and holistic sociologies and ideologies' that, for Dumont, is the nature of the societies (Cohen 1998: 15). Furthering this argument, Cohen says that structural holism not only stressed the importance of society's imposing itself on individuals and on their consciousness but also led to the reduction of symbols and myths as binary structures; this went so far as to say that individuals are incidental to society.

And many have argued with ethnographic evidence against the structural holism for assertion of the Dalits all over India (Berreman 1963, 1971, 1979; Cohn 1955; Gough 1969; Khare 1984; Charsley 1998; Parish 1996; Omvedt 1995; Zelliot 1998; Yadav 2000; Shah 2001 and several others). The overemphasis on the ideology of structural holism that amplifies only the totality, and obscures the individuality in the totality, ignores the actual reality of people inside the holism who feel that they are denied in terms of "their aspirations and discontents, much of their suffering, the texture of their lives and flow of their experience", and "it precludes a discussion of culture's discontents, of agency and resistance within culture, of the tensions and quandaries of cultural life" (Parish 1996: 6, 7). The fact that the Dalits, especially in our case the Paraiyars, create conflict with the higher castes shows that they reject the idea of cultural consensus and structural holism. Moreover, they view the resistance to caste hierarchy as a positive and creative part of their existence. To that extent, the present study focuses on what the people within the caste system think about themselves and others, how they conceptualise the social organisation and the ideology that segregates them from others and gives them an identity.

Conflict as a Source for Self-Consciousness

This brings us to the second premise: conflict opens the way to self-consciousness. I hasten to point out that by 'self' here I mean the social, or to be more accurate, the community as well as the individual self. This is an awareness of who we are and who I am, and how this is manifested while interacting with others in a society. Moreover, what the Paraiyars do by way of constructing their identity is that they form their selves as well as their community, forming self and community at the same time; it is a politics of self as well as of community. For individuality is formed, reformed, and contested constantly in the context of sociality, and to understand society and its relations, the study of individuality is a necessary condition (Cohen 1998: 192).[8]

By consciousness, I mean an ability to perceive who I am and who the others are: perception of self and of society. Damasio (2000) says that consciousness is an interior state of the human person that is formed by public acts during a period, and is strengthened by repeated public manifestations. The core element that is vital in the formation of consciousness, according to Damasio, is feeling, experience and thought of oneself. Such experience is stored as a social memory that is repeatedly recalled in order to produce a particular type of human behaviour. There are three kinds of self: the *autobiographical self*, the *core self* and the *proto-self*. The autobiographical self is 'an organised record of past experiences', the core self is 'a transient but conscious representation of the multiple dimensions' of a person, and the proto-self is 'a non-conscious collection of the representations of multiple representations' (Damasio 2000: 199). More clearly, Bruner (1986) makes a critical distinction between reality, experience, and expression, which together form consciousness, and life should be viewed "as life lived (reality), life as experienced (experience), and life as told (expression)" (Bruner 1986: 6).[9] In this way, persons in a community not only form their selves but, more importantly, they also form their social organisations, their culture and their political institutions. It is a form of power that gives identity as subjects to people and recognised also by others.

Archer explains the source of such power and its realisation. This emerges from what we learn to do in nature (embodied knowledge/natural order), the skills we acquire in our practical actions (practical knowledge/practical order) and how we verbalise, formulate discourses about our actions and their meanings (discursive knowledge/discursive or socio-cultural order), which are the foundations of the perception of the self-identity and the social identity of a person (Archer 2000: 177-88). The three orders, as Archer argues, are the locus in which both personal identity and social identity are assembled and finalised: our physical concerns in the natural order, our performative abilities in the practical order, and the realisation of self-worth in the social order shape both 'I' and 'We' (2000: 312-14). In human beings there are four modes of being: self, person, agent, and actor, meaning thereby that every human person knows his/her person, acts in ways by which he/she is the agent in respect of what he/she is and becomes. The self is realised early in life through simple practices with nature, in other words, we have a sense of self by the fact of our being in the world; person or personal identity is born out of the considered response to the outside reality (natural, practical and socio-cultural); one becomes an agent in three phases: (i) what impact society has on the human self, what Archer calls the 'primary agency', (ii) the ways in which the socially influenced self transforms itself, and society, (which is called 'corporate agency') which explains that this agency is both active as well as passive, and (iii) the social transforming agent reproduces the role and behaviour of the agents, giving the identity of a social actor. All these together renders wholeness of identity. In all this, being aware of the human ability to act is crucial to human identity in the sense of maintaining it and of actualising it both personally and socially.

The Paraiyars realise today that until they had their conflicts with the Vanniyars, they were not aware of themselves in the sense that they did not know exactly what they did in terms of their activities for the village, and what impact these activities had on their persons. They simply accepted the status of being servants to the *Ūr*, and performing polluting services that gave them a marginalised and powerless existence. Prior to the conflict, they never had any realisation that what they were doing as services – clearing dead cows and cremating dead bodies and playing the drum – was something that made the higher castes pure, and therefore of a superior social status, and portrayed themselves as impure and as belonging to a lower social status. They did not realise their powerlessness in working on the land of the higher castes as bonded labourers, which further confirmed their status as impure and of low identity. More importantly, to lead such an existence of impurity, they thought, was to follow the way defined by God. The Paraiyars behaved as if they were machines that performed without being conscious of the subjective impact that their traditional services had on their persons.

As sharply noted in *The First Report of the Commissioner* in 1951, "by force of habit the Harijan has lost his self-respect to such an extent that he regards his work to which his caste is condemned not as a curse from which he should extricate himself, but as a privilege or preserve, which he must protect. He has not much courage to seek another job in a field or a factory. He has thus become lazy in mind and body and callous to his own condition; and he will not educate his children" (quoted in Massey 1997: 25). One may find this opinion, offensive today but the Dalit intellectuals who theorise on untouchability do speak of their life as Dalits in similar terms (Illaiah 1996, 2001; Guru 2001). The case of the Paraiyars of Pappanallur also confirms this. They told me that they were not aware of their selves as human beings, capable of possessing human dignity in terms of knowing themselves and the world, and asserting their humanness by expressing that knowledge. Instead, they were conscious only of how the higher castes perceived them as impure people, and that perception defined their identity, negating totally their self-identity. Passively, they received what they were told to be and to do, and they were refused the possibility of being active agents of their life and existence: they were only *objects* in the higher castes' life when they should have been subjects in their own life. Therefore, their identity could be defined only in relation to the higher castes, and separated from them they had no identity of their own. To that end, they had constantly to perform polluting activities that made the higher castes pure and themselves impure. The identity of the Paraiyars, as almost every Dalit group in India, was located, conditioned, and governed by what Dumont (1980) called *the hierarchical opposition of purity and pollution*. Until they came into conflict with the higher castes, the Paraiyars were not conscious of what their subservient life under the higher castes had done to them.

In other words, the repeated services carried out for the high caste developed in the Paraiyars a generative scheme of mental and physical dispositions, similar to the ways in which one learns in childhood. This could also be compared with the *habitus* of Bourdieu (1977: 78-86; 1990: 52-65) that the Paraiyars developed, and which had the disposition to generate attitudes and practices leading to the formation of the Dalit identity of pollution and marginality. Such identity they treated as natural and intrinsic to their way of life.

The conflicts helped the Paraiyars to break open that non-self-consciousness and made them realise what they were and who they intended to become; the conflicts helped them to see their inner selves and their community[10]. They re-formed their habitus in ways, which would generate positive practices and attitudes, quite the opposite of the former habitus that was not only negative but more importantly, denied their human dignity. It is a breaking of what Coser (1968: 219) called 'pseudomorphosis', which is a state of being in which an alien identity overwhelms the indigenous or original identity, and stifles its self-expression. Conflicts serve as a force that breaks the seal of the 'crushing objecthood' (Fanon 1967), constructed by the symbolic forms given by the higher castes, and brings to the fore the 'personhood', and the 'socialhood' of the Paraiyars and creates a metamorphosis in group identification.

As Dirks (2000: 173) argues, colonialist anthropology or ethnography considered that the "colonised subject was first and foremost a body, to be known and controlled through the measurement and interpretation of physical subjects organised in caste and gender categories. In all this attention to the body, there was little interest in the subjectivity, will or agency of colonial subjects". Conflict gives them the power to realise the importance of subjectivity in a way to be defined 'from the outside in', what gave them an inferior status and socially constructed identity, comes to be challenged and redefined "from the inside out', and the give themselves an identity that is meaningful to them (Parish 1996: 7,8).

An important dimension in this ability to define is that they realised their human agency, or human capacity to act and change their ways of life,[11] which they were not conscious of before the conflicts. Earlier they were only actors, who just followed willingly, or unwillingly, the rules offered by society, whereas now they have become persons, who have realised that they possess the ability to act in a way in which they can change or imagine their world in a new way (Karp 1986: 137; Ahearn 2001: 113). As Giddens noted, the notion of being able to act means that people are capable of transforming things and of forming their future (1993: 78-82). And power, for Giddens, is intrinsic to the ability to act realising that individuals have the capacity to intervene in a series of events causally, and power is not an obstacle to freedom but it is a medium by which freedom is achieved, and it is by power the subordinated influences the dominant power (Giddens 1984: 14-16; 1993: 118).

The Paraiyars have largely realised their human agency in and through conflicts with the higher castes, who they think had refused this to them but which the higher castes themselves enjoyed in instituting the caste hierarchy. This human agency in fact enabled the Paraiyars to reflect upon their life in the village caste hierarchy, and act reflexively on it in the sense of becoming capable of imagining their world as individuals and as a community. This made them the subjects and active shapers of their own life, rather than objects and passive recipients of what was given to them by the village. The Paraiyars becoming effective in asserting their human agency is one of the important dimensions of self-consciousness. Theoretically, this gives due place to the properties and powers of those human beings who form a part of society but who, for a long time in social theory, had been denied this; instead it was society that mattered and occupied every realm of social analysis (Archer 2000: 306).

This realisation of the human ability to take action leads to the creation of a boundary between the *Ūr* higher castes and the Colony Paraiyars, cutting them off from the *Ūr* on which their life had been dependent and their identity defined. Every conflict the Paraiyars had with the Vanniyars separated them from the *Ūr* and the higher castes of the *Ūr*. Conflicts enabled them to come out of the folds of Hindu religion, the village council, the school, the village festival, and finally, they gave up their traditional services to the *Ūr*. This was to build one's own trenches from which one could fight the enemy. Tearing themselves away from the bonds that made them dependent on the *Ūr* has given them a sense of autonomy and independence to look at themselves and the higher castes and imagine a new world for themselves. For boundary marking is the first vital step towards identity-construction, a boundary is a locus where interaction between groups takes place and identity is formed (Barth 1969, 2000; Cohen 1985, 1998, 2000).

Symbolic Reversals

Power of Myths in Symbols

Realising the power of symbolic performance, the Paraiyars, after every conflict, focused on the symbols that defined their low identity and reinterpreted these symbols of social exclusion as symbols of identity. The Paraiyars of Pappanallur reversed the symbols of social exclusion and pollution – the drum, the beef-eating, and the land – into symbols of their own culture and identity. The reversal arises out of a realisation that there is nothing intrinsic in the objects such as the drums, or the use of it, that makes them polluted. This was due, rather, to the myths these symbols carried along with them, and the discursive practices about the symbols, and about the Paraiyars themselves who handled the symbols that were largely responsible for defining them as low and polluted people. The myths of their origin told and retold by the *Ūr* higher castes and repeated by the Paraiyars themselves gave them their identity, and justified their polluting services to the *Ūr*. This they became increasingly aware of in the process of conflicts with the higher castes. Through the help of the parish priests, their participation in Dalit social and political movements, they came to realise that they should be treated essentially, as human persons, equal to the other people in the village. And they refused to accept their low, negative, and impure identity given to them. What was central to their identification with impurity and marginalisation was the power of symbolic discourse, and that had led them even to think about themselves in this way.

Therefore, to form an identity of their own making they needed to form reverse discourses, that is, to evolve counter myths, and use the same method and categories by which they had previously been negatively defined. About the drumming, beef-eating and ownership of land the Paraiyars are evolving new myths, in opposition to the conventional myths, which give positive meaning to the symbols, and help assert their culture, history, and community. What they once held to be negative symbols of identification have now become a positive means of identification, and they have taken these over as their own, not something imposed on them but something formed by and for themselves.

To show what informs the way the Paraiyars form their identity we need to clarify the concept of symbol and myth. First, I will discuss the basic premises of symbolic interactionism.

Secondly, I will explain the power of symbol and mythologising in the formation of identity.

To understand best the Paraiyars' way of identity formation by the use of symbols we need to bring in the theory of symbolic interactionism.[12] Symbolic interactionist theory and its methodological position is, according to Blumer (1986), based on three basic premises: (1) human beings act towards different things, places, persons and events, on the basis of the meanings they have for them; (2) such meanings are born out of the social interaction one has with others; (3) these meanings are then modified by the interpretative process one uses in the interactions (1986: 2).

Linked closely to these three premises is Blumer's idea of 'joint action' referring to "a societal organisation of conduct of different acts of diverse participants" and "made up of diverse component acts that enter into its formation, is different from any one of them and from their mere aggregation" (Blumer 1986: 17). By a collective action a group or groups are bound together in terms of sharing symbols and symbolic actions that provide meaning in their life and organisations, for example, this is what people do in marriage, in festivals and so on. As Baert (1998: 73) reckons, what Blumer explains in terms of 'joint action' is not in the sense of a social fact as discussed by Durkheim (1982) for whom the concept of social facts is external and pre-existed in forms of social life independent of any interpretative process, but on the contrary for Blumer, social facts are born out of component acts and are mainly dependent on the interpretative process and the attribution of meaning.

For Blumer, society means symbolic interaction and it is the space where individuals or groups interact with each other through symbols. He draws our attention to the fact that individuals in society during their interactions are capable of symbolising themselves and interpreting what they had symbolised. More deeply, he views meanings as "social products, as creations that are formed in and through the defining activities of people as they interact" (Blumer: 1986: 5). The social actors interpret and reinterpret the meaning of objects and events, as and when they feel, the need for this. Both Mead, and later Blumer, assert that the social self emerges from the necessary condition of society in which human beings share symbols with one another in their social interactions.

Symbolic interactionism does not refer to social structure that constrains people's conduct. Perhaps, Blumer has closely followed Mead, who although recognises the existence of the generalised other but does not see it as constraining the agency of interacting human beings. Secondly, symbolic interactionism does not account for unintended effects of human interactions. It is hard to accept the argument that every action will bring the intended consequences.[13] Having said that, this does not prevent me from saying that the identity given to the Paraiyars by the higher castes and the identity the Paraiyars aim to construct now are formed out of component facts and joint action, and more specially, is born out of an interpretive process, which is the core aspect of symbolic interactionism. The reversal of the meaning of the symbols of the drum, beef-eating and land, attributed by the higher castes, from negative to positive, that brings forth a new identity is, I argue, helpfully informed by the symbolic interactionist theory.

Paul Ricoeur defines symbol as "any structure of signification in which a direct, primary, literal meaning designates in addition another meaning which is indirect, secondary and figurative and which can be apprehended only through the first" (1986: 12). The definition demonstrates that a symbol has a plurivocal or polysemous character: (i) it has a direct or primary meaning; (ii) an indirect or secondary meaning; (iii) the primary/ direct meaning designates the secondary/indirect meaning; (iv) and the indirect meaning can be apprehended only through the direct meaning.

The most important aspect of double intentionality is the revelatory and the evocative functions of symbols (Kuruvilla 2000: 16). It reveals what is absent through what is present and evokes a sense of affectivity in us with the symbolised reality beyond. The revelation is indeed done through a discursive elaboration, through stories, or mythical narratives. In fact, symbols come alive by the stories attached to them, in the sense that every symbol has a story to tell that explains not only the lives of people but also the organisations by which their lives are directed and governed. For myth is an elaborated and extended form of symbol, in that sense that "myth is a kind of symbol, a symbol elaborated in the form of a story and articulated in space and time" (Ricoeur 1969: 18) and the language of the stories is symbolic, more clearly it is a symbolic discourse (Fawcett 1970: 101).

Mythical narratives are crucial in giving the content and the structure to symbols, and they help people harmonise human experiences and justify a particular social order, shaping the identity of societies. This is why myths are not descriptions of things but expressions of determination to act (Coser 1968: 213).[14] Myths are used to explain the meaning of the social order set by one group for the others who have to follow it. Myths are necessary for the dominant group, not only for explaining the meaning of the system, but to 'secure its own conceptual edifice' that fails to justify the system (ž ižek 2002: 10). In this sense, myth must be understood in a political dimension.

Although the Paraiyar myths of origin (Moffatt 1979: 120-5; Mosse 1985: 242-4; Deliege 1999: 71-88), are generally classed under sacred myths, the ways in which the Paraiyars today look at the myths demonstrate that they should be viewed in political terms that they helped to form the identity of the Paraiyars as polluted and 'stupid' and the higher castes as pure and 'wise'. Even if we agree with the reflection of Moffatt (1979: 121) that the Paraiyars feel it is the curse of god in the myths that has made them impure and stupid, it will be difficult to disagree with the fact that even such a reflection results in the formation of the identity of the Paraiyars. More sharply, the god who remains as the arbitrator, finally decides the fate of different individual actors in the myths, and this serves to hide the original intention of the myth-makers and the intenders, the higher castes. In this way, myth is not only a form of information and explanation about the relationship between cosmic reality and human beings (Levi-Strauss 1978: 17; Eliade 1958: 367-87; 1989: 12-21), a vital ingredient of human civilisation (Malinowski 1974: 101) and models of and for the social reality (Lincoln 1989, 1999), but more importantly, myth helps to form community, sanctifies social segmentations and the political hierarchy (Cohen 1998; Burland 1970; Frankfort 1949; Graves 1968), and it is used for the "maintenance or imposition of hierarchical domination by one group over others; it can sustain a balance between groups of equal rank within a hierarchy; it can be coupled with active or passive resistance to hegemony" (Flood 2002: 41).

The field reality in Pappanallur village persuades us to recognise above all the political dimension of the Paraiyar myths of origin. The self-consciousness, gained after their conflicts, made them realise that there was nothing intrinsic in the objects like the drum, beef, or land that define them as polluted and segregated, but the kind of symbolic discourses, or the mythical discourses about them, constructed by the higher castes, provided meaning and justification for defining them in that way. More deeply, the mythical/symbolic discourses were based on the intentions of the higher castes that led to the construction of an account of the past that defined social life and organisations. These intentions I consider as ideologies that take the form of mythical/symbolic discourses (stories), which function as an evocative force to give form to a society and its members. Every ideology, as Feuer (1975: 1) explains, has an invariant mythological structure, which remains as the base ingredient on which two other ingredients of ideology such as "an alternating set of philosophical tenets, and a historically determined chosen group" are formed. The way the story is structured and the meaning it gives decide the ideology, which in turn guides the people in the intended direction, and the narrative, with its form and content, serves to define a community and its life in a society.

Nations have been formed, defined, and sustained by myths. This is clearly seen in India and elsewhere. The mythification of the past has largely been a helpful strategy for Hindu fundamentalists in India in their attempt to form a Hindu India (Bhatt 2001; Jaffrelot 1993; Vanaik 1997). More directly, the work of Kearney (2002) is instructive for the present study of the Paraiyars' identity formation. He skilfully enlightens us by his treatment of story as something that not only entertains us but also defines the identities of nations and people. Because he points out that it is story, that becomes history and history is narrated as story in the sense that there is a very thin line between history and fiction.

Story-telling is one of the basic ingredients of any meaningful society. It can be in many different genres – myth, epic, legend, sacred history, folktale, allegory, satire and novel and so on, but the underpinning character is that there is someone communicating about something to somebody; the communicative act creates *catharsis* (a purge of emotions), which helps imagine a new way of being in the world. For Levi-Strauss (1968), stories also functioned as therapeutic and transformative, as in his example of the woman who had difficulties in giving birth due to a blocked womb. When the woman was told of the story/myth of the warriors liberating people from monsters, she gave birth to her child. In addition, stories also serve to get over a loss of somebody close to us, or a separation and they "fill the gaping hole within us, to assuage our fear and dread, to give answers to the great unanswerable questions of existence" (Kearney 2002: 6-7). More than the narratives we tell about what happened in past, the narratives we tell about what we want to happen are important in the life of nations.

This is why Kearney argues that nations are narratives, in other words, nations are 'constituted', invented and sustained by stories. The Roman foundation myths of Aeneas and Romulus, the narratives of the British people about the Irish and counter stories of the Irish about the British, and the stories of the 'Other' and 'aliens' by the Americans of the United States were constructed in order to define national boundaries and create cohesion among themselves and vice versa. Although it is difficult to accept Kearney's argument that it is merely the story-telling that defined and shaped identity of nations, his insights such as that story-telling is one of the powerful ways of recalling the ways in which individuals were shaped their selves and how re-enacting such memories helps heal the wounds of the past are helpful to understand the Paraiyars' use of myths and symbols.

The symbols, which we have chosen for the present study, are based on the myths of Paraiyar origin, explaining why the Paraiyars are treated as polluted, excluded from the *Ūr* and remain landless labourers. Each myth had a plot (*mythos*) to give sense to the way the Paraiyars lived their lives, how they were subjected to the marginalised life by god. Such myths about the Paraiyars were repeatedly 'talked about' 'recreated' (*mimesis)* and narrated as true history. Every time the Paraiyars heard the story, they experienced emotions (*catharsis*) of sadness, frustration, and dejection so that they failed to hold on to the superior position and felt resigned to a marginalised existence. The purging of emotions was such that it had 'authority' (Lincoln 1989: 24) and 'example' (Eliade 1958: 430) to formulate definitions of untouchability that gave the identity of the Paraiyars in particular, and of the Dalits in general. For the Paraiyars, the myths were not taken as fiction but as a true historical accounts that had legitimising power on their present polluted existence. Over a period of time, the marginality and pollutedness became innate to the Paraiyars and it was accepted as natural to be subservient to the higher castes. In addition, the ideology of the purity of the higher castes that divided society into pure and impure was constantly reinforced in the minds of the Paraiyars and the higher castes as well through the myths. Finally, the ethos of the myths was that the Paraiyars were *objects* of history and eventually refused their right to be the subjects and agents of their life. In brief, the identity of the Paraiyars as defined by the higher castes is the product of symbolic discursive formulations.

Therefore, to redefine their identity in addition to all other efforts – economic self-dependence, political awareness – they focused on the de-definition or deconstruction of the traditional myths by creating counter-myths that would accord the symbols of the drum, beef-eating and land a new meaning and thus an identity of their own making. This is based on the conviction that there is nothing intrinsic in the objects like the drum or beef that makes them polluted, their life as segregated from the *Ūr*, but it was the discursive formulations in the myths that gave the meaning to these objects and actions. Moreover, what they are now as individuals and as a community is the product of mythical discursive practices about them by the higher castes. Discursive formulations are central to the formation of identity and we need to discuss them briefly and the power they have in identity formation.

Discursive Power and Identity Making

Discourse is defined as a relational or differential ensemble of signifying sequences in which meaning is constantly negotiated and renegotiated, with a tacit assumption that every discursive formulation has an implicit power to structure or de-structure a society, or to construct or deconstruct an identity (Torfing 1999: 85-93). According to Laclau (1993), the concept of discourse has its roots in classical transcendentalism from which theory of discourse is derived. He says that "the very possibility of perception, thought and action depends on the structuration of a certain meaningful field which pre-exists any factual immediacy" (Laclau 1993: 431-7).[15] The discourse, understood as the relational totality of signifying sequences that determine identity, leads either to the construction or the de-construction of meaning. It is often understood as an identity of an object or a person or a community.

Foucault (1985) in his analysis of the archaeology of knowledge, for the first time demonstrated that formulation of discourse and 'episteme' carries within it the implicit thoughts and rules about a social reality.[16] To uncover the thoughts and rules that help to construct the identity of the present, Foucault suggests, we must go back to the past to find the discontinuities between past and present and to uncover the conditions of discursive formulations (as mentioned in Baert 1998: 122-28). For Foucault, discourse is a political commodity and the articulation of discourse adds power, that is, a phenomenon of exclusion, limitation, and prohibition (Gordon 1980: 245). Particularly, power, for Foucault, is not simply an entity that can be 'held, taken' or 'alienated' but also a problematic of circulation within various channels and networks governed by discursive formulations and relations of power that constitute a social body and "can not themselves be established, consolidated or implemented without production, accumulation, circulation and functioning of discourse" (Yon 1999: 30; Gordon 1980: 93).

Advancing this argument a little further, in a post-modern theoretical background, Laclau (1985) and Mouffe (1985) focus their discourse theory on the construction of identity. By studying different discursive formulations, they argue, we can disclose the discursive construction of meaning and the ideological configurations that lay beneath the discourses. From this we will get a lead to understand the effects that the employment of such discourses has upon the workings of society (Torfing 1999: 290; David Howarth 1998: 268-93). In brief, every discursive formulation, by lending fixity to meaning, exercises power through a set of symbols and words "that delimits a field and legitimises perspectives and norms for the elaboration of concepts that govern and keep intact certain social ordering" (Franco 1996: 81-108). It must be noted here that the development of Laclau and Mouffe's theory of discourse is predicated on the idea of Althusser's (1971) critique of ideology, and furthers the line of Foucault's argument of discourse and power that intersect with systems of domination. In a sense, Laclau and Mouffe's theory emerges as a development from the intellectual trajectories of Althusser and Foucault. For Laclau and Mouffe, "all objects are discursively constituted by articulatory practices such that the determinants and limits of discursive formations are not an extra-discursive 'reality' but 'other discourses" (Torfing 1999: 279) and the practice of articulation fixes meaning to a social relation or to an object and thereby provides an identity. Drawing on Foucault, Butler (2002:

46-47) focuses on what is excluded and how by formation of discourses, the powerful (sexists, racists, and imperialists) make 'normalising' discourses by which they create the 'abnormal other'. In this sense, the discourses help create subordinate identities that are to be excluded from the society. Since the dominant groups give such identities they are made to look natural; people talk about them as if they were facts of nature and internalise them through repeated practices for a long time, without realising that they were constructions. Once people realise this 'episteme', strengthened by the conscientisation of the Non-Governmental Organisations (NGOs), parish priests (the Catholic Church), and the Dalit political parties, they begin to see possibilities of change.

Central to discursive or articulatory practice is its nature of openness allowing it to be deconstructed and thereby replaced by another discursive practice or formulation. The social ontology of Laclau and Mouffe is based on the open texture of discourse allowing possibilities for re-constructing a social identity, and gives primacy to politics, and formulates an idea that "systems of social relations-or-discourse – are always political constructions, and, as such, involve the exercise of power in their formation" (Howarth 1998: 275). Accordingly, the social system is viewed as having a fundamentally political character, in which conflict, what they call 'antagonism', occurs when a group tries to assert its identity against a group that prevents it. One group sees the impossibility of a possibility of an identity from its social position in the system, and the opposing group asserts the possibility of the construction of its identity. Each group insists on its agency and power to construct and protect its identity. Finally, the discursive analysis is placed within the hermeneutical tradition of social enquiry rather than the naturalistic methods of enquiry, that is discursive formulations have socially generated meanings that have to be interpreted and understood.

This serves my purpose in looking at the symbolic discursive formulations by the Paraiyars. The realisation of the importance of discourse and power in the construction of identity that we gain from the foregoing discussion confirms and informs the Paraiyars' ways in which mythico-symbolic discourses help change the meanings of symbols, leading to the formation of a new identity. The symbols of pollution and social exclusion that were used by the higher castes to give a negative identity to the Paraiyars are reversed into symbols of Paraiyar culture and identity. In this process, the formulation of counter-mythical discourses to the conventional mythical discourses is central in formation of new meaning of the symbols, leading to construction of a new identity for the Paraiyars.

Identity and Identification

The core of the Paraiyars' way of forming identity now and of the ways in which the higher castes had given an identity to the Paraiyars is the identification with symbols. For identity is a question of identification, identifying *with* and *against*. In effect, identity is a process of identification. In logical terms, the process consists of "a going out from oneself, a journey through difference, and a return to oneself, including all difference in oneself, crowning oneself as emphatic identity" (Susin 2000: 79). It is a circle of identity and identification: going out of oneself, journeying through differences and finally returning to oneself. In this process, understanding and meaning are the basis of the identification, in which an individual or a group understands activities and objects, and gives meaning to them, constantly existing as a reflecting, conceptualising, categorising and acting subject. The circle includes sameness, and excludes, even demonises, difference to strengthen sameness.

The identification reveals two kinds of relations with people and things: one is a relation of similarity and the other is a relation of difference (Jenkins 1996: 4). *The Oxford English Dictionary* explains these two aspects of *identity*. The word identity comes from a Latin root 'idem', meaning 'the same', which suggests both absolute sameness and distinctiveness. Further still, in the notion of identity, another important dimension of identity is that it has to be identified, there is something active about it. As

Jenkins (1996: 4) rightly observes, "identity is not 'just there', it must be always established", we need to actively identify with and against equally. And it is a process in which continual identification produces a state in which we come to realise who we are and who others are, and also, others' understanding of who we are and our understanding of who they are. Largely, in the sense of the political, the psychoanalytical category of identification is the key element in identity-construction; one has to identify with something to enjoy a social space and position, which is often apparently absent when a group does not explicitly assert its identity (Laclau 1994: 3). Identity is made, not given or innately endowed, Laclau calls it the 'making' of political identity. At the same time, the act of identification can be either born out of the coercive force of social structures or it may arise from one's own initiative. Nevertheless, repetitive social practices of identification enable a person or a group to assert an identity in the process. All identity and social reality is a constructed, not a given universal reality; both self-identity and social identity are socially constructed.

In the process of identification, according to Jenkins (1999: 20, 21), there is a dialectic of internal and external identification. Internally an individual has to define him/herself, and equally the definition should be recognised by others. If not, one should at least strive to be recognised. This also applies to groups. Closely following Goffman's interactionist method, Jenkins considers that in the construction of social identity, both self-image and public image are important constitutive elements. A group identifies and defines itself – group identification, and the group is identified and defined by others – social categorisation. In this, social categorisation is crucial in the sense that depending on it a group gets its social position in a society that bestows identity for people. The social identification or categorisation is negotiated and produced, as Barth (1969, 1981) and Cohen (1985) say, at the boundaries between two opposing groups, where the internal and the external interact, for which conflict between groups is a necessary condition to maintain heightened self-consciousness and the consciousness of the other, that is, the division between 'us' and 'them'. What a group identifies with and defines itself by is tested and negotiated across the boundary, and social identification is formalised. Such a process, more importantly, has a great influence on social institutions both for their structuration and maintenance. At the boundary, when a group negotiates its identity, it does so by the effective use of power and agency for the construction of social as well as individual identity. Further still, in this process, as Giddens notes, there is a communication of meanings and an application of power that functions between social interaction and social structure, giving rise to the transformation of the structure (1984: 29, 33), and in this the people are 'knowledgeable agents' and they have the practical consciousness to imagine their world and their future. In this sense, social structures are not merely a constraint but a *stimulus* for social change; if there is no social and group identification and practices related to them, social structures cease to exist. Giddens is helpful at this point. In his attempt to overcome the Durkheimian dualism between structures and action, he argues that structures are internal to human actions and they are the memory traces that are instantiated in social practices (Giddens 1984: 25). For instancc, a language is what it is because people speak it; if people stop speaking a language, it will ceases to exist.

In brief, to reiterate the central notion, identity is not a given, static reality, but is constantly negotiated in social interaction and constructed by people. In Jenkins' words, 'social identity is a practical accomplishment, a process' (1999: 25). Moreover, it is essentially a question of identification that results from the process of internal-external dialectic in which communication of meaning, and uses of power and agency remain very important elements.

Such an approach to identity answers the postmodern critique of the essentialist view of identity.[17] Essentialism views identity in the sense that "individuals or groups have an immutable and discoverable "essence" – a basic, invariable, and presocial nature" and it has the tendency to form a single category such as gender, race, sex, etc. to determine social and cultural identity (Moya 2000: 7).[18] Essentialists understand that meaning, which is vital in identity formation, is generated by experience and it is self-evident, and the identities we have, for instance, gender and sex, are seen as natural. Though it was mostly helpful to minority groups for emancipatory purposes through social movements, this approach does not explain so many other problems in social identity.

The earlier identity the Paraiyars had was thought to be essential for their human existence and therefore was unchangeable. Later, through conflicts, created with the support of parish priests and Dalit political parties and movements, they realised that the identity was constructed by the higher castes to serve their own interests, which could be easily changed, if they stood firm in their conviction for change. What they would form as a new identity, they envisioned, would be their real identity with which they could positively identify. So for them, identity means identifying actively with the symbols of identity, such as the drum, beef-eating and land, which have their meanings changed, first through conflicts, and later by symbolic reversal. Earlier, the identity given to them by the caste system was passively received as the natural and divinely-willed order, but the identity they now construct is actively what they make, an activity of their own. The identity that was imposed on them so far by the higher castes was born out of the symbols of identification, which gave them a polluted and socially excluded identity. Constantly, the Paraiyars were forced to identify with the symbols of pollution and social exclusion. Now after the conflicts and their consciousness awakened from these, they do not reject the symbols as such or look for other symbols for identification. Instead, they take those very symbols of the drum, beef-eating and land, but before identifying with them, they change their meaning by, as we have just seen in the previous section of the present chapter, creating counter-myths. The identity given to them earlier is in the words of Castells (1998: 8-10) a 'legitimising identity' that was produced and given by the higher castes to rationalise their domination. The identity the Paraiyars form now for themselves is, according to Castells, both a 'resistance identity' and a 'project identity'. The former means the identity generated by the resistance of the marginalised people who have had stigmatised positions and conditions by domination; the latter identity is that of the social actors who build a new identity by using available cultural resources that will henceforth redefine their position in society. Resistance to the given identity and the reconstruction of their own identity are the twin faces of the Paraiyar identity formation.

What is vital in this is the change of meaning and the practice resulting from it. The change of meaning in a way leads to a change of practice in the sense that what the Paraiyars had been doing before with the symbols of pollution and social exclusion has to be changed. So they decide not to play the drum at the funerals of the higher castes rather they would like to play it on auspicious occasions like marriages and festivals. Along with that, they narrate myths about the drum being once upon a time an art and used for the proclamation of war. Earlier beef-eating was pollution, but now to make it their social and cultural custom they have communal meals with a celebration of beef-eating publicly to do away with the stigma of pollution. Alongside this, they also create stories of people being cured of serious illness and of people becoming healthy and brave by eating beef. Similarly, the land was used earlier by the higher castes to socially exclude the Paraiyars and to make them powerless and marginalised, politically and socially. Now by creating myths according to which they were the original inhabitants of the village and that all the land belonged to them, they forcefully occupy common lands, and even buy the land of higher castes, which, they feel, makes them landed and powerful people, equal to the higher castes.

In this process, we see a logic of identification: on the one hand there is a rejection of the meanings of symbols given by the higher castes, and on the other there is the formation of meaning by myths relating to the symbols. They identify *with* the latter and identify *against* the former. The symbols remain the same but only their meaning is changed. More sharply, to identify with the symbols in the sense that they will give them the identity they need to 'de-mean' the symbols and to 're-mean' them.

In this sense, I agree with the definition of identity given by Castells (1998: 6) as "the process of construction of meaning on the basis of a cultural attribute, or related set of cultural attributes, that is/are given priority over the sources of meaning". Meaning, for Castells, is seen as 'the symbolic identification by a social actor of the purpose of her/his action' (1998: 7). Therefore, more than the symbol it is the meaning of the symbol that is central in the formation of identity, which, as we have seen earlier in this chapter and much more we will come to realise later, is evolved in and through the construction of discourses, in our case, symbolic/mythic discourses. It is instructive to learn from the present study that in the formation of identity the symbol (signifier) is not changed, only the meaning. In that way, identification is more with the meanings that symbols have for people rather than with the symbols themselves. The change of meaning gives them an opportunity to alter their perception of themselves and it helps them gain self-respect (*suyamariyāthai*) and self-dignity (*thanmānam*). Self-respect and self-dignity form the core of the new consciousness of the Paraiyars and of their identity, and serves as the basis for their renewed understanding of their personhood. Vincentnathan (1993: 55) notes this clearly in his study of a group of Paraiyars in a village in northern Tamil Nadu. The Paraiyars in that village told him that their major concern is 'getting *mariyaatai* (respect) from others and having self-respect'. Further along this line, he sees that to rid themselves of the low status and identity given by Hindu society and the caste system, they need to 'cognitively' evolve different concepts of person and society that will uplift their self-esteem. This is true also in the case of the Pappanallur Paraiyars in their efforts to reverse the meaning of the symbols of the drum, beef-eating, and land. Now pursuing the line of Paraiyar identity, we understand that the identity unique to the Paraiyars is indeed an act of identifying with the symbols that are redeemed from the given meaning of pollution and exclusion to become symbols of Paraiyar culture and identity. In the redeemed identity the Paraiyars feel that they are equal as human persons to the high caste men and women – 'sameness' – and they are unique by way of their life as musicians (drummers) and who eat beef as their social custom just as Brahmins eat vegetarian food – 'difference'. The sameness or commonalities and uniqueness or type provide them with an identity of their own, from which they derive their self-esteem and self-dignity. This is the way that identity is understood in anthropology (Byron 2002). Put simply, they have pride in calling themselves Paraiyars: "Say you are Paraiyar; lift up your head and stand tall".[19] To stand tall, by coming out of their submissiveness and passivity to the ways in which the higher castes categorised and identified them, they reverse the meanings of the symbols of pollution and social exclusion into symbols of identity and their culture.

Therefore, what the present study tries to do is to look at the process, which began in the 1930s from a conflict over the public land, went through many directions and used many strategies and resources, and discerns the general pattern of the process of the conflict-symbolic reversal-identity formation, which can possibly explain and help us to understand the social change in Pappanallur village.

Notes

1. There are two traditions of understanding the origin of meaning. One is that meaning is intrinsic to the thing or symbol, which contains it, as if it is natural to the thing. The second tradition is that, in philosophical realism, meaning is a psychical expression of the person for whom a thing is meaningful, or has meaning, what Blumer (1986) calls 'psychical accretion'.
2. Many have remained critical of the theory of symbolic interactionism. Among the many criticisms, two major ones are that in the Durkheimian approach it does not look at social structure that constrains people's behaviour, and in the Weberian view of social theory, symbolic

interactionism does not focus on unintended consequences of any purposive act. In Blumer's thesis I find that he purposely ignores any reference to structure. What the construction of meaning through social interaction results in other ways is not discussed. In my study of the Paraiyars I cannot ignore the consequences of the construction of new meaning into the symbols on the social arrangement of the village and on the caste system beyond the village. For a critique of symbolic interactionism see Baert (1998: 67-74).

3. See R. Singh (2001) for a detailed discussion of Touraine's conflict typology, especially pp. 116-131.
4. I adapt the term 'performance conflict' from the use of the term 'performance violence' by Juergensmeyer (2000: 122ff) who in his discussion on terrorism sees it as a theatre in which terrorists demonstrate their vision. In our case, although the conflicts are not violent in the sense that terrorism is, the idea of theatre helps us to understand the ways in which the Paraiyars view their conflicts with the *Ūr*.
5. *ratham sinthinālthān vāḷvu pirakkum* (only when you are ready to shed blood, can you achieve life and progress).
6. Allen defines structure as "a totality made up of several elements, at least two…a totality which is systematic and coherent in the sense that the component elements stand in definite relationships to each other, such that neither the totality nor the elements can be properly described independently of these relationships" (1990: 279).
7. There are many others who have successfully refuted Dumont's structural holism; I am not going into the details, as I am not in the present study concerned about it. See Quigley (1988) Berreman (1971), Inden (1990), Dirks (1987), Selvam (1999), Deliege, (1998), (1999); Vicziany, (1998), R.S. Khare, (1984); S.M. Michael, (1999)
8. Cohen (1998) differentiates between individualism, individuality and selfhood: Individualism is for him "a dogmatic posture which privileges the individual over the society"; individuality, the term he prefers, is "the perception of individual's distinctiveness', which is 'a property of selfhood" (p.168), see pp. 168-192, for further details on this theme. See also pp. 13-14 for his discussion of the comparison between Durkheim's understanding of the relationship between the individual and society and the Marxian approach to this.
9. Appadurai (1996) says that 'Life as told' should mean also 'life as imagined'. This is better explained in his term 'ethnoscape' that speaks of the landscape people who move from one place to another create and live in (p. 33-34).

10. Scott (1990: 72) calls such state of mind 'false consciousness', which he divides into 'thick' and 'thin' versions. The former means that a dominant group is able to persuade a subordinated group to believe actively in the values that justify their subordination by the use of rhetoric or discourses and the latter means that a dominant group is able to gain compliance of a subordinated group by convincing them that the social order they live in is natural and inevitable.
11. I follow Ahearn's definition of agency: "agency refers to the socioculturally mediated capacity to act" (2001: 112). I view agency more as social than as individual. But at the same time, I must not fail to recognise the fact that multiple types of agency are exercised in a social situation, particularly in the case of the Paraiyars. For different types of agency, see Jackson (1990); Goddard (2000); Davies (1991); Davidson (1980); Comaroff and Comaroff (1997); Archer (1988).
12. I do not intend to discuss the theory of Mead in the limited scope of the present study. Instead my reference to Mead's theory of social behaviourism, which gave rise to the theory of Symbolic Interactionism, is just to indicate where Blumer gets his inspiration from. The term was coined by Herbert Blumer and introduced in an article in *Man and Society* in 1937 (Baert 1998: 211).
13. see Baert (1998: 72-74) for a detailed critique of symbolic interactionism.
14. 'Myth' is defined and understood in many ways: in a generic sense it means something that is not true; the writers on religious history use the word myth to refer to a representation of the sacred in words; while anthropologists use it to refer to narratives about the formation of social order or institution or behaviour. See Lindow 2001: 1-33. Malinowski (1948) views myth as a useful strategy to justify the *status quo* whereas Lévi-Strauss (1969, 1978, 1981) argues that myths do not refer to any empirical reality but are the reflections of the cognitive world. From the point of view of my present study I agree with Malinowski rather than Lévi-Strauss.
15. Torfing refers to Western Philosophy, in which Immanuel Kant who inquired into the *a priori* categories of cause, substance, etc., which, together with intuitions for Kant, were the necessary conditions for the constitution of phenomena and later the line of thought was furthered by Husserl who placed emphasis on intuition which is basic to all acts of experience, which are anchored in a transcendental ego giving historical possibility very little space, what is called ahistorical, *cf.* Torfing (1999: 84).

16. See Skinner (1997: 65-81); also see Baert (1998: 114-131).
17. See Varshney (2002: 27-38) for a detailed discussion on the four traditions of enquiry on conflict and identity: essentialism, instrumentalism, constructivism (postmodernism), and institutionalism.
18. For further reading on essentialism see Fuss 1989 and Kripke (1980), for a critique of essentialism see Lyotard (1988).
19. *paraiyar endru solladā, thalai nimirnthu nilladā* (say with pride that you are a Paraiyar and hold your head high): this is a slogan that is used by the Paraiyars in their public meetings and by the Paraiyar children in their schools.

II

From Symbols of Pollution to Symbols of Culture and Identity

4

A History of Conflicts between the Paraiyars and the Vanniyars

In this chapter, I propose to present a history of the conflicts between the Paraiyars and the Vanniyars in Pappanallur village and the impact this has had mainly on the life of the Paraiyars and others in the village and beyond. In doing so, I hope to trace the process of identity formation of the Paraiyars which had the conflicts as a constitutive element. To anticipate, I will explain that conflict has been the process through which the Paraiyars have so far negated their low identity as Dalits and imagined their new and positive identity.

Conflict remains as a starting point in the Paraiyars' assertion of their identity and, more importantly, it has been the powerful sustaining impetus in their efforts to form a new identity. These conflicts opened up a whole world of possibilities for the Paraiyars and presented them with some important ways in which they could transform their life. More specifically, it was in and through conflicts that the Paraiyars became conscious of their state of life and came to notice how they were defined by the symbols of social exclusion. Such self-consciousness led them to imagine their world. Had there not been conflicts with the Vanniyars, it would not have been possible for the Paraiyars to reach the state they are in today. More sharply, conflicts were for them a theatre in which they were able to perform their acts of identity formation. Most of the conflicts occurred only at the time of festivals, particularly at the time of the Pongal festival. At other times of the year, the whole village is largely quiet and both groups relate to each other with an ease that disguises the animosity between them. In that sense, conflict remains as a base structure on which the whole project of identity formation is built. Therefore, conflicts need to be discussed in-depth in order to understand the other two phases of the process of identity-formation–symbolic reversal and identity consolidation.

I begin by giving a broad picture of the conflict situation between the Dalits and higher castes by considering cases at the national and the state levels. Secondly, I go on to discuss the factors that have influenced them to openly create and face conflicts with the higher castes in Pappanallur. Thirdly, I will give a historical account of conflicts that took place in Pappanallur from 1930 until 1997, taking only the major ones from more than thirty cases that I had gathered during my fieldwork. Finally, I will discuss some important characteristics of the Pappanallur conflicts that will lead to Chapter 5.

Caste Conflicts: An Overview

Conflicts between the Dalits and the higher castes in India are not a recent phenomenon. From the time of the colonial rule until now, thanks to the political democracy that the British left behind in India, many forms of struggles by the Dalits against socio-economic exploitation and discrimination have been taking place in India (Shah 2001: 28-38; Gupta 1985; Suresh 2000; Kananaikal 1982; Ilaiah 2001; HRW 1999; NCDHR 2000; Krishnan 2002). The conflict situation in Tamil Nadu, though it shares in many respects the national situation, has a different nature and dynamic. The origin of the caste conflicts in Tamil Nadu between the Paraiyars and the Vanniyars can be traced to the non-Brahmin movement in the 1920s (Geetha and Rajadurai 1998; Kshirsagar 1994; Jacob 2000), which helps us understand the social change that the Dalits in general were attempting to bring about and more importantly, it serves as a useful background against which we can better understand the Paraiyars' identity-construction in Pappanallur. In addition, the non-Brahmin movement had been in many ways a catalyst for the rise of the Dalits in the state.

In his seminal study of Tamil society in the 1930s, Irschick (1986) says that the non-Brahmin movement did everything to alter the structure of Tamil society and politics in the sense of mobilisation of non-Brahmin castes, both the low castes (the Backward Castes (BCs) Shudras in the Varna model) and the Dalits against Brahmins who dominated the state public institutions. To this movement the contribution of the Dalit leaders was very significant. Although the main architect of the non-Brahmin movement was E.V. Ramasamy Naicker, alias Periyar, the Dalit leaders such as M.C. Rajah, Iyothi Das and Irattaimalai Srinivasan were prominent figures in terms of their contribution to the formation of the Dravidian ideology. For instance, Iyothi Das said that in the past India was a nation of Dravidas, which was invaded by Aryans, and more importantly, he claimed that the original inhabitants of India were the low castes and the Dalits (Aloysius 1999; Cited in Geetha and Rajadurai 1998: 43-108).[1] As many non-Brahmin associations adopted the name 'Dravida', the Dalit associations changed their names into Adi-Dravida. For instance, the Pariah Mahajana Sabha, founded in 1890, was changed into Adi-Dravida Mahajana Sabha. M.C. Rajah who became secretary of the Sabha moved a resolution that the Dalits should be called the Adi-Dravida (Jafferlot 2003: 169).

The low castes in many a way showed the path on which the Dalits could also organise themselves to receive better treatment by the state. The South Indian Liberal Federation, later popularly called the Justice Party, in 1916 in Chennai, and the Self-respect movement by Ramaswamy Naicker (Periyar), P Sundaram Pillai and C.N. Annadurai, fought relentlessly against the evils of untouchability and popularised rationalism and atheism. The low castes with the support of the Dalit leaders like Iyodhi Dass and M.C. Raja founded the Dravida Kazhagam (DK) that attacked primarily the Brahminical caste hierarchy and persuasively argued for the importance of the Tamil language and opposed vehemently the imposition of Sanskrit and Hindi on the Tamils. The core belief and ideology of the non-Brahmin movement was that the sons of the soil are the backward castes and the Dalits who were invaded by the Aryans, in this case the Brahmins, and the main object of all non-Brahmins was to regain their original status by attacking the values of the caste system and the Brahminical values of purity and pollution.

Many backward castes such as Nadars, Kontaikkatti Vellalars began to organise themselves as caste associations to negotiate with the state for aid, reservations and support for their castes (Jaffrelot 2003: 148ff). More importantly, these caste associations distanced themselves from the Sanskritisation process by making themselves separate ethnic-like groups. The case of the Nadars in South India illustrates this point well (Hardgrave 1969). They were one of the lowest caste groups among the BCs (backward castes) who were mainly involved in the toddy-tapping business. In 1891 they started claiming *Kshatriya* status, first, by Sanskritising themselves by wearing the sacred thread characteristic of the twice born Brahmins, but later, by shunning this method they claimed a separate identity. To that end, they started *Nadar Mahajana Sangam* (The Nadar People's Association) through which they founded schools and organisations to 'encourage industriousness of the community' (Jafferolt 2003: 167). Under the leadership of W.P.A. Soundrapandian, the Nadars discarded the sacred thread and boycotted marriages officiated by Brahmin priests; instead they united all the sub-groups of the Nadar caste as one ethnic group (ibid.). This process of ethnicisation set a model to be emulated by other low castes as well as the Dalits.

Later, the low castes (mainly *Vellalas*, *Mudaliars*, *Chettis*, *Mukkulathor*) in the non-Brahmin movement worked for reservations in jobs in different administrations and in the legislature and left the Dalits out and formed their own associations. But we cannot ignore the contribution of the movement in terms of providing a precedent for the Dalits to assert themselves. In fact, it inspired many Dalit movements that at the grass root level in villages and towns fought against Brahmin domination. The Dalits began to organise themselves both against the Brahmins and the low castes. This became a source of conflict between the Dalits and the low castes. The Dalits realised that in actual reality the groups who dominated and oppressed them were the low castes, like Thevars in the south and Vanniyars in the north, who, for the Dalits, were the higher castes. In this sense, for the Dalits the low castes are in fact higher castes, more particularly, for the Paraiyars, the Vanniyars are higher castes.

Hutton (1973: 205-6) reports a conflict that took place in 1931 between the Paraiyars and the Thevars in Ramnadu district and it gives us the first instance when the Dalits of Tamil Nadu challenged the higher castes, although one can find similar conflicts in other parts of the state (Ludden 1989; Hardgrave 1969; Alm 1996; Mosse 1994). The first major incident that left an indelible mark on the psyche of the Dalits in Tamil Nadu was the murder of Immanuel, one of the staunch leaders of the Dalits (mainly Pallars) in Mudukulathur village in the Ramnad district in 1948. After this incident, Immanuel's statue or his portrait became the symbol of caste oppression and the fight against it. Every Dalit house was adorned with a photograph of the leader who had provoked militant reactions among the Dalits, particularly among the Dalit youth. Later in the 1960s, although most of the conflicts between the Dalits and the higher castes were over the issue of wages, the implicit motive was to oppose caste discrimination. One such case comes from Keelavenmani village in the Thanjavur district in which forty-two Dalit agricultural labourers were burned alive because they demanded an increase in the wages they received for their work on the land of the higher castes (Jacob 2000: 24). But in the late 1980s the conflicts between the Dalits and the higher castes – in the south the Pallars versus the Thevars, and in the north the Vanniyars versus the Paraiyars – became increasingly centred on the question of the identity of the Dalits, which also heightened the consciousness of identity of the higher castes; more and more the Dalits challenged untouchability and made efforts to redefine themselves by freeing themselves from the status of the polluted people.

Among one hundred and ninety nine cases of conflicts in Tamil Nadu, published in newspapers and magazines from 1990-1997, most centre around the issue of the Dalits' challenge over the symbols by which they were defined as polluted and socially excluded people (Thangaraj 1998).[2] In addition to the newspaper reports, I have used two major compilations of cases of conflicts: 1) the National Public Hearing report on Dalit Human Rights Violence, atrocities against Dalits in India; 2) the report by Human Rights Watch on caste violence against India's untouchables. In all these reports we can perceive unambiguously that land, drumming, cremating the dead and participation in festivals had been the issues over which the conflicts were primarily based. These had been the services (*tholil*) for the higher castes all over Tamil Nadu that defined the status of the Dalits. More sharply, a close reading of the cases of conflicts all over Tamil Nadu stated in the reports reveals not only that the Dalits would no longer live a life of social exclusion but also that they had decided to challenge the practices that defined them as polluted and to redefine their identity. In many villages, after the conflicts the Dalits discontinued their traditional services to the higher castes. In addition, they have taken an active role in state politics, hoping that this would give them the means to challenge the system democratically. In southern Tamil Nadu, the political party called *Puthiya Thamiḷagam* (PT, literally 'New Tamil Nadu') led by Krishnasamy mainly for the Pallars was formed, and in the north, the DPI (*Viduthalai Siruthaigal*) led by Thirumavalavan for the Paraiyars.[3] Similarly, in the south, the conflict had been between the Thevars (a dominant high caste group) and the Pallars (a dominant Dalit group) and in the north mainly the conflict was between the Vanniyars and the Paraiyars.

In northern Tamil Nadu, the conflict between the Vanniyars and the Paraiyars started on a large scale during the latter part of the 1980s. Although the Vanniyars started organising themselves to demand reservations for them in the state and central services, it was only after the founding of the Vanniyar Sangam (Vanniyar Association) later as a political party called, *Patali Makkal Kacci* (Toilers Peoples Party, PMK) by Dr Ramadoss, the conflict between the Paraiyars and the Vanniyars came into a sharp focus and the state witnessed many violent incidents between them in the northern districts. What started as an anti-state struggle for job reservations became an anti-Paraiyar movement, because, as Murugesan, the Vanniyar leader in Uthiramerur, told me, they needed an enemy to fight with; otherwise, it would be difficult to organise their caste group. Specifically, the Vanniyars considered the Paraiyars as potential competitors in the reservations for state and central government jobs and seats in educational institutions. The growth of the Paraiyars in terms of literacy and economic advancement, the Vanniyars openly acknowledged, would decentre them from power and domination in the villages of the northern districts (Jacob 2000: 40). Gradually, it escalated into violent confrontations between them and the Paraiyars, who rallied behind Thirumavalavan, the leader of DPI. In a major conflict in 1987-88 eleven Paraiyars were killed, to which the Paraiyars' reaction was slow and ineffective, since they could not stand against the strong organisational network of the Vanniyar party, PMK. It was only in the 1990s that the DPI became stronger and able to react to the Vanniyars. For instance, on 7 November 1997, in reaction to the Vanniyars' attack on the Paraiyars of Nantheesvaramangalam village, the Paraiyars, mainly organised by the DPI, burnt six state-owned buses and destroyed the shops owned by the Vanniyars (Thangaraj 1998: 256). All over Cuddalore, Perambalur and Villupuram districts the Paraiyars put roadblocks and demanded the arrest of the Vanniyars who, they claimed to be behind the attack on the Paraiyars. The pamphlets and posters on walls said, 'the storm of Cheri [Colony] will soon one day cross the limits of patience and history will be rewritten.'[4] Many Paraiyars consider that this was one of the significant events in Paraiyars' history that demonstrated their opposition against the Vanniyars much more effectively. The DPI volunteers held public meetings in most of the towns in northern Tamil Nadu to rally the Paraiyars against the Vanniyars, in which thousands of Paraiyars from many villages took part. This provided the much-awaited confidence for the Paraiyars in other villages to resist the domination of the Vanniyars. From Pappanallur more than forty men and women took part in the meetings and in the agitations organised by DPI. It is in this context that the conflicts in Pappanallur should be viewed, that what was happening all over the state gave an impetus for the Paraiyars to challenge caste discrimination in the village.

Socio-Political and Religious Role of Institutions

There were many factors from which the Paraiyars derived inspiration and the confidence to challenge the *Ūr* higher castes, and to generate conflicts consistently over the symbols by which they had been rendered untouchable and given a low identity. I would say that these sources of support and inspiration were institutions and organisations such as the parish council (the Roman Catholic Church), their membership in the Village Panchayat, the Women's Association (*Māthar Saṇgam*), the help they received from non-governmental organisations (NGOs), the Paraiyar children's education and the Dalit Panthers of India (*Viduthalai Siruthaigal*). These institutions and its individual members had been instrumental in making the Paraiyars realise the need for getting themselves rid of polluted identity, and that to do so they should challenge the Vanniyars. It explains where the motivation to challenge the higher castes came from. It is hard to see whether without the support of these institutions the Paraiyars could at all have made the progress they did so far in their attempt to form their new identity. However, every Paraiyar I talked to was keen to convince me that the starting point of their opposition to the higher castes was their own conviction to get rid of their identity as Dalits, and the institutions only helped them to make their conviction become a reality. I realise that although it is difficult to find out the origin of conflicts and the attempts to form a new identity later, it was a collective effort of both the Paraiyars who were seeking a way out of their low identity, and the institutions that not only perceived the desire but also helped the Paraiyars translate it into concrete actions.

The Parish Council

The Pappanallur Roman Catholic parish belongs to the Archdiocese of Madras-Mylapore. Its only members are the Paraiyars of Pappanallur, Koliyalam, Vaippanai and Valayaputhur villages as no other high caste family in the area is Christian and other Dalits (i.e., Vannan, Irulars) are Hindus. The parish is organised by a parish priest, a Jesuit, with his parish council. The council consists of a leader, secretary, treasurer and four members representing four *Vagaiyarās*. The other three substations of the parish do send members to the council, but the Pappanallur Colony has the power to decide for the whole parish, which is accepted by the Paraiyars of the substations. On the day of annual parish feast the council is elected through formal voting. Each *Vagaiyarā* is represented by two members from the sub-stations of the parish. Once the council is formed, it deals with any issue that concerns the Paraiyars. Nobody in the Colony is allowed to ignore the council in terms of the Paraiyars' life and activities. If anybody does, he or she with their whole family would be in the first instance fined. In the event of repeated deviant acts the family would be ostracised from the parish and they would no longer enjoy any financial assistance and other benefits from the parish and the Archdiocese.

The parish council is the only major decision-making body now, although there are other smaller associations. Every Sunday it holds a meeting. Even though the council is a church-centred institution, it functions as a political organ for the Paraiyars in many ways. All the conflicts with the Vanniyars were organised by and discussed in the council before and after the conflicts. Particularly, in the 1996-97 conflict with the Vanniyars, the Paraiyars told me that it had functioned as a powerful organising force in terms of designing the strategies of what and how they should counter the Vanniyars. Often, the council meeting is the time when the Paraiyars discuss the ways in which they should make efforts to improve themselves and how they should confront the higher castes. Once a month a workshop is conducted on different themes: Paraiyar identity, the Paraiyar history of untouchability, the caste system, social analysis and so on. In this way, the parish council remains a resource for the Paraiyars from which they receive guidance and support. Once a decision has been made in the council the whole Colony stands by it united until they achieve their objective, and when it fails the council supports the Paraiyars who are affected. The Women's Association considers the council to be something that gives them enormous support to face the challenges from the *Ūr*. They recall the time when they were refused work in the Vanniyars' fields; the council took the decision to provide financial assistance by the collection of a tax (*vari*) from each family (*kuṭi*) in the Colony. On another occasion, when the police arrested three Paraiyars following a conflict with the Vanniyars, it was the council that arranged to bail them out.

The contribution of the parish priest is vital in the council in terms of guiding the Paraiyars in their opposition to the higher castes in Pappanallur. Although there had never been a conflict in which the parish priests from the 1940s were involved directly against the *Ūr*, but they had been a great support and without this many Paraiyars think they would not have done what they have done so far. Particularly, the Paraiyars remember the support given by Father Paul Puthannangady and Father Raja who were the parish priests in the 1940s and in the 1970s respectively. However, not all the parish priests had the same ideology with regard to the Paraiyars' efforts to improve their position in the village. Some parish priests such as Father Nilapanar have taken a neutral role and helped both the Vanniyars and the Paraiyars. Even the Vanniyars agree that he was the one who financed the deepening of the village pond and arranged to lay the main road in the *Ūr*. By and large, all the parish priests directly appointed by the Archdiocese have been supportive of both groups since they viewed their job as merely religious, they were not meant to get involved in the village politics, although they did not put any obstacle in the way of the Paraiyars when they challenged the higher castes. The Vanniyars too have a great appreciation for these priests and even now they remember their good relationship with them. It was only the Jesuit parish priests of Pappanallur, who became involved in village politics by actively supporting the Paraiyars against the Vanniyars, and are not liked by them.

The Jesuits as parish priests of the village have worked and still were working, at the time of my fieldwork, with the Paraiyars, making them aware of their state of untouchability, and the ways in which they should reform themselves. The Jesuit parish priests considered their role as not merely religious. They view it as both religious and political, or rather, an integrated ministry that helps the Paraiyars improve their life politically, socially and culturally as much as they do in matters of religion. That was why while they helped the Paraiyars to increase their political consciousness, they also built houses for them and provided scholarships for their children. More importantly, they arranged to get jobs for the Paraiyars in other cities and towns. This kind of support from the parish priests gave them great confidence in their opposition to the Vanniyars. Arulappan, a Paraiyar, said that had there not been those parish priests, the Vanniyars would have made it hard for them to live in the village.

Village Panchayat Board

The Village Panchayat consists of seven members including the president. From the Paraiyars' ward – ward II – there are three members; one of whom is chosen to be the vice president. Nevertheless, the Vanniyars usually get the post of treasurer, since the president is from their caste. In addition, they have four members compared to three members from ward II. The dominance of the Vanniyars is seen in implementing welfare programmes for the development of the village. In the last three decades where Vanniyars have been presidents of the panchayat, whatever welfare schemes the state government allotted to the village were mainly made use of by and for the Vanniyars and other *Ūr* castes. For example, in 1996, the government allotted a fund for building three houses for the Dalits in the village. The Paraiyars told me that with the support of other Vanniyar members in the Panchayat, the president, Mrs Anchalai Devi, diverted that fund to build a nursery school (*bālvādi*) where no Paraiyar children went as they had their own school in the Colony. When this was brought up in a meeting of the panchayat, the president said that although the government allotted the money for building houses for the Dalits, it was left to the discretion of the Panchayat to decide keeping in mind local needs. She further added, "you have your church fathers who build houses for you and according to the government rule Christians are not Dalits". Similarly, drinking water for the Colony has not been provided for the last two years. Most of the pipes that bring water to the Colony are under repair. Whereas the Vanniyars have had a constant water supply in their residential area. In October 2001, the Paraiyars first went and complained about it to the president. She did not want to do anything. Then, in the board meeting, the Paraiyar members brought it up. Although it was promised that the board would look into the problem, nothing was done to repair the pipes that carry drinkable water. So, the Paraiyar members went to the Panchayat Union office in Maduranthagam and complained to the Union president who visited Pappanallur village and asked the Panchayat to arrange to lay on drinkable water pipes to the Colony. The Paraiyars told me that the work was completed in two days. Similarly, the Paraiyars use the panchayat as one of the resource points to assert their rights in the village.

The Paraiyars feel that being a part of the panchayat committee brings substantial benefits for them. Not only in material terms, but also it serves the platform for asserting their political power in the village. The Paraiyars are confident that without listening to them the Vanniyars could do nothing in the village, and no government programmes could be implemented in the village without the support of the Colony. This confidence in fact has created some kind of fear among the Vanniyars who realise that without the help of the Paraiyar members in the Village Panchayat they will not be able to bring any state sponsored programme into the village. This is for the Paraiyars a resource towards the formation of their new identity. The Paraiyar women say that the panchayat is one of the places in which they feel equal to the Vanniyars;

The Māthar Saṇgam (Women's Association)

The Paraiyar Women's Association has been another resource through which the Paraiyars have been successful in all their conflicts. In fact, the ways in which the women of the Association had participated in the conflicts of with the Vanniyars made it all the more effective and productive. In addition, it has remained the most powerful organ for the Paraiyars in organising themselves against the Vanniyars. The women from the Association have taken front line roles in all the conflicts. They have no fear of police arrests and intimidation; instead, the Paraiyars told me that the police were afraid of them. A police constable from Uthiramerur station said that "the Pappanallur Paraiyar women are not women, they are more than men; they are men in women's dress (*sēḷaikatina āmbaḷaigal*)."

At the time of my fieldwork in 2001-02, there were 32 members in the Association, most of whom had joined voluntarily, without any outside pressure. It was formally registered in 1992, though it had been functioning since 1986. The Association was divided into two sub-groups named after Dr Ambedkar and Mother Teresa. The division was to satisfy the state government's demand that each women's group should not have more than fourteen members to be eligible to receive loans in the village reconstruction scheme called '*makalir thiṭṭam*' (the plan for women). But for all other purposes the Association functions as a single group.

Every week they assemble to discuss matters concerning the *Ūr* issues and the thrift scheme. The thrift scheme is one of the ways by which the Paraiyar women help the Colony become self-sufficient and independent of the higher castes. In the scheme, every member pays monthly subscription of fifty rupees. Once it grows into a sizeable amount, a member is allowed to apply for a loan. In 2002, the scheme had seventy thousand rupees. Mostly, women take the loan for the purposes of marriage and medical expenses. Issues of the Colony are often kept to a minimum in the meetings as the parish council takes care of them, but problems regarding the thrift scheme consume a major part of the time during the weekly meetings. In the discussion of the financial status of the Association many other issues of the village figure for which every member has an opinion and a suggestion for a strategy. For example, in the February 2001 meeting, they discussed why some members did not pay back the loan they had received from the Association. The women who failed to pay said that they could not do so because their husbands were irresponsible and failed to save the money they had earned. Seven out of ten women said that it was due to their husbands' excessive drinking of *arrack*. One woman, while narrating how her husband behaved when he was drunk, cried profusely and said she thought she would better hang herself and die rather than go through such suffering. Immediately, some women suggested that a few representatives should meet her husband and reprimand him on this. The president and secretary volunteered to do this. They were successful in persuading the man to give up drinking. Like this, the Paraiyar Women's Association has been effective in solving internal and domestic problems in the Colony. More than that, the Association is involved in public issues that concern the Paraiyars.

In 1994, when the sale of *arrack* was allowed within the village, the same Women's Association, I was told, had decided in one of their monthly meetings to destroy all such shops and barrels of *arrack*. More than thirty Paraiyar women went from place to place in the village and destroyed as many as fifteen barrels. The Vanniyars confronted the women and told them that they had no right to destroy the *arrack* barrels kept for sale to the *Ūr* people. They told them: "control your drunkard husbands from drinking, we have every right to sell and drink *arrack* here in the *Ūr*; all your power (*athikāram*) should be kept within the Colony, it should not be displayed to us. If you do so, you will have to face dire consequences". The Paraiyar women told me that they scolded the Vanniyar men in vulgar language in front of the crowd that had gathered to see the fight. In addition, to counter this more effectively, the Paraiyar women went to the police station in Madurantagam and filed a case against the owners of the *arrack* shops and informed the police that the Vanniyars were brewing *arrack* illegally and selling it in many villages and the people who consumed it would surely die.

The police were initially hesitant to arrest the Vanniyars who brewed the illegal *arrack*, fearing the pressure from the PMK party leaders. But the women were adamant that the Vanniyars should be arrested, and staged a *dharna* (protest) before the police station. Then the police were forced to arrest some of the *arrack* shop owners to de-fuse the situation, as it was the day of the District Collector's routine visit to Madurantagam town. From that time onwards, the sale of *arrack* was forbidden within the village. But during my fieldwork, I saw that many Paraiyar men went to nearby towns to buy packs of *arrack* in large quantities and hide it in their houses from their wives. This goes on even although the Association has a strategy to eradicate it.

Whenever an issue arises in the Colony, it is the *Māthar Sangam* that takes the front line to settle it. For instance, when there was no power supply in the Colony for three months the Association went to meet the *Ūr* leaders and threatened them that they would set electricity transformer on fire that was in the *Ūr* area. Within a few days, the power supply was restored. Similarly, when the Vanniyars refused to lay pipes for the drinkable water supply, women from the Association went and complained to the District Collector. Later, the Collector's office had to send a notice to the Vanniyars to lay the pipes in the Colony area as soon as possible.

More importantly, the Association's participation in the series of conflicts with the Vanniyars described above has been commendable and in fact, their role in the 1997 conflict with the

Vanniyars was instrumental in initiating the decision finally to stop the *Ūr* services. In any conflict, the Paraiyars say that they would always send their women first to confront the higher castes, which would be humiliating to them. In addition, the Vanniyars would hesitate to confront or physically attack women easily since it would lead to serious charges against them. Using this to their advantage the Paraiyar women challenge the *Ūr* people freely. Pushpa, a member of the Association, said, "every Vanniyar man is terribly afraid of us, we have beaten them in public, I have stripped a Vanniyar in public in Uthiramerur town". Another Paraiyar woman, Sasikala, said that if any Vanniyar man spoke to her disrespectfully [calling her *Paracci nayē* ('Paraiyar bitch')], she would slap on his face. She further said, "I have no hesitation to sleep with a Vanniyar, because that is a way of making him polluted and the next time if he does anything against us I will expose his relationship with me".

Such militancy is feared by the Vanniyars, who told me that they could easily handle the Paraiyar men, but not the women. One of the Vanniyars said that the Paraiyar women would be ready to take their clothes off in public to insult them and that was why they kept away from them. The aggressive approach of the Paraiyar women has remained a powerful force by which the Paraiyars have asserted their rights successfully.

The Paraiyar women, I found, are more politically active and more articulate than the men. And they a are very important resource for the Paraiyars' challenge to the Vanniyars. More than their activities, they teach their children why and how they should fight the *Ūr* people and come out of their state of marginalisation. Not only are the Paraiyar women assertive inside the village, they have also demonstrated their power outside the village at the state level organisation of rallies and protests by the Dalits. To give one example, they went in great numbers to participate in the rally in Chengalpattu on October 10, 1994, for the Panchami Land struggle[5], in which one of the Pappanallur Paraiyar men, John Thomas was shot dead by the police. More than thirty-five

Paraiyar women along with their men were arrested by the police and sent to prison in Velur Jail.[6]

Many non-governmental organisations (NGOs) have also contributed to the political awakening of the Paraiyar women in particular, and the Paraiyars in general, which I will discuss briefly in order to understand where they get the confidence to challenge from the higher castes in Pappanallur.

Non-Governmental Organisations (NGOs)

One of the main sources from which the Paraiyars of Pappanallur receive training to become politically conscious of themselves is the NGOs. In Pappanallur, the Association of Sarva Seva Farms (ASSEFA)[7] and the Chengalpattu Rural Development Society (CRDS) have played a pivotal role in the political awakening of the Paraiyars by making them economically independent from the landlords and the higher castes under whom for centuries the Paraiyars were bonded and semi-bonded labourers.

The ASSEFA was founded in 1969 and celebrated its silver jubilee in 1994. Its origin dates back to the concept of Gram Swaraj (self-governance of villages in India) of Mahatma Gandhi, and more directly to the concept of *sarvodya*[8] by Vinoba Bhave, who was a poet and philosopher who lived partly as a recluse in central India. As the spiritual heir of Gandhi, Vinoba Bhave went on walking tours (*padayātra*) across India in 1951 to propagate his project of the *Bhoodhan Movement*. This meant the gift of land (*bhūmi*)[9] by a person to landless people all over India.[10]

The movement swept through Tamil Nadu in 1968 but actually took root in the state in 1981 under the name of Serva Seva Farms. The first farm was started in Sevalur near Madurai city, about three hundred miles from Chennai. From 1980 onwards, the Paraiyars used the ASSEFA lands that were given to the landless Paraiyars for cultivation. Initially, the organisation provided loans to spend on cultivation and irrigation. Later, it urged the Paraiyars to become self-sufficient. Some Paraiyars because of their hard work, the ASSEFA officers told me, obtained a few acres of land from ASSEFA for their permanent use, gradually to come to own them. Apart from the land distribution, the organisation also provided them with goats and milch animals to make them further economically self-sufficient. In addition to 26 per cent of the ASSEFA agricultural programmes, 28 per cent had a focus on educational, social and political amelioration of the Paraiyars. This was intended to make them get out of their dependence on the *Ūr* castes. The ASSEFA programmes were helpful particularly when the Paraiyars were in conflict with the Vanniyars. It helped them to have their own income, though it was meagre, yet of assistance in gradually becoming independent. For the first time, only through the ASSEFA, the Paraiyars say that they had the experience of owning a piece of land. Michael, the first Paraiyar who was given two acres of land by the ASSEFA, said, "I cannot describe how I felt on the day when the officers from Manithottam [from the ASSEFA] handed me the land *paṭṭa* [the title]; it was on that day that I became hopeful for our future and one day we will employ the Vanniyars on our land. I did this last year when I hired two Vanniyars to plough my land for three days."

The ASSEFA also gave the Paraiyars goats to rear and later sell back to the organisation. Through this they earned a quite sum of money. The organisation also provided the Paraiyars with scholarships to educate their children. Later, the role of the ASSEFA became marginal in the lives of the Paraiyars of Pappanallur, as there were other Christian organisations like the CRDS, which, at the time of my fieldwork, was active in organising the Paraiyars in general, and the Paraiyar women in particular. At one point, the leaders of the ASSEFA who functioned in Manithottam, the officers I met told me, felt that they needed to concentrate on the Hindu Paraiyars of the area. In Pappanallur village the presence of ASSEFA was almost extinct by the time of my fieldwork, except for three families who had the land of the ASSEFA for paddy cultivation.

The CRDS, unlike the ASSEFA, is much more explicitly political in its thought and action in terms of Dalit empowerment. The role of the Society in the political awakening of the Paraiyars has been to a large extent vital for their becoming conscious of themselves and escape from living a dependent life at the mercy of the higher castes in the village, particularly, the Vanniyars. This is an organisation run by the Roman Catholic Archdiocese of Madras-Mylapore. It was started in July 1990 as a registered society with the District Registrar of Kanchipuram district. In its aims and objectives, the Society was intended to "to promote integrated human development…without distinction of caste, creed or colour"[11] but later it became a political organ for the Dalits by the Dalits. At the time of the fieldwork, the director the Society was a Catholic priest, Father Jeyaseelan, who comes from a Paraiyar background.

Despite its name, the Society's core principle is to help the Dalits assert their identity. In the Society's annual report it is mentioned that it was "founded on the principles of justice and truth" with the concrete aim of helping the downtrodden to 'live with self-esteem, self-confidence and self-governance', and to help create political consciousness among the Dalits to form and assert their identity (CRDS Annual Report 1996-97: 2, 4). It conducts a series of training programmes in the Kanchipuram district on social analysis, thrift and credit associations, and politics (socio-political analysis and awareness programmes). In Pappanallur, the Society conducts an evening study centre (*mālaipaḷḷi)* and a crèche aiming to help the Paraiyar children not only to get educated but also to realise the evils of caste system. Although the Society appears to be concentrating more on economic programmes, such as providing loans for raising milch animals, and goats, sewing machines for the Paraiyar girls who have dropped out of school, credit unions for saving money, it is also involved largely in the political issues that concern the Paraiyars. More specifically, it conducts programmes to train Paraiyar women to fight against the higher castes when they are discriminated in work and in other walks of life. Every year on Women's Day, i.e., 8 March, the *Madharsangams* organise rallies in the district to protest against atrocities against Dalit women in the state. On 23 March, 2001, the Society organised a massive women's rally in Chengalpattu in which most of the slogans were against caste discrimination. One of the placards read: "O, Paraiyar women, you have conceived the fire of our times; if you point your finger at the oppressors they will be burnt into ashes; by your brave leadership the liberation of the Dalits will be achieved."[12]

In the training programmes in which the Pappanallur Paraiyars participate, they are urged to abandon the polluting services to higher castes and to become aware of human equality. Concretely, the Society provides financial assistance to the Paraiyars who come forward to abandon the traditional services to the higher castes and are in search of alternative jobs. The Director of CRDS openly criticises the church for discriminating the Paraiyars in its programmes in favour of the people in the diocese. In my conversation with him, he told me that the Archdiocese was dominated by Telugu Naidus and Reddiyars who prevent the church officials from allotting sufficient funds to the Society that was meant for the Paraiyars. Because of his critical stance against the Archdiocese, he thinks that the Archbishop is ostracising him from the diocese. In the conference of the Dalit Christian Movement (DCLM) in which more than twenty thousand Christian Paraiyars had assembled in Chennai at Valluvar Kottam, Father Jeyaseelan spoke in the presence of the Archbishop against the atrocities committed against the Paraiyars by high caste priests in the diocese. The gathering mainly organised by the CRDS shouted slogans against the church. Even at other times, he often asserts that he is first a Dalit, and second only a Catholic priest, and if the church continues to discriminate against the Dalits, he wishes not to die as a Catholic. His conviction seems apparently to have influence in the programmes of the CRDS, and unlike in earlier years, the Society has almost become a Paraiyar organisation, when it is supposed to be one for the poor in general.

At the time of my fieldwork, I noticed that the ASSEFA, and the CRDS had made important contributions to the Paraiyars in realising the power of becoming self-sufficient, and thereby self-assertive, particularly when they needed this badly. Although the two NGOs are still active in Pappanallur in terms of conducting their programmes, the Jesuits who run the parish are the most dominant group working for the Paraiyars.

Formal Education

In 1942, Father S. Paul Puthanangady, who was the parish priest of Cheyur, thirty-eight kilometres from Pappanallur, started the first school of the archdiocese of Madras-Mylapore in the Colony area (see Map 4).[13] In 1944 the school received government approval. Initially, I was told, children from all castes studied in the school, except the Brahmins who sent their children to Chengalpattu and Kanchipuram. However, the Vanniyars could not accept the fact that Paraiyars' children sat equally with their own, and so it was difficult psychologically for them to send their children to a Paraiyar school. Everyday, there were problems in the school between the children from the *Ūr* and the Colony children.

As we have seen earlier in this chapter, this was, the Paraiyars felt, an advantage that they could educate their children to become aware of their life of exclusion and exploitation by the *Ūr* castes. In 1994, the Colony school, called R.C. Middle School, was moved outside the village (see Map 4) in the hope of training the Paraiyar children and keeping them away from the distractions of the Colony. At that time there were one hundred and thirty two pupils in the R.C. Middle School, where the children study upto the fifth form.[14] The Catholic sisters of a Foreign Missionary congregation are in the management of the school. Since 31 May, 1989 these sisters have been working for the Paraiyars, and their special role in the education of the Paraiyar children has been significant. Before they came to the village only four girls had been to school and many children had dropped out for various reasons. One main reason was that most of the Paraiyar children were either sent by their parents to graze the cattle of the Vanniyars or to take part in the *padiyāl* work in the

Vanniyar houses. It was difficult for the Paraiyars to stop their children doing the *padiyāl* work because they were afraid of sanctions from the Vanniyars. Realising this the nuns visited the Paraiyar houses regularly to convince them to send their children to school. In 2001, all the Paraiyar children were going to the R.C. Primary School and once they passed out of fifth standard they were sent to Loyola High School in Kuppayanallur, twelve kilometres from Pappanallur, run exclusively for the Dalit children by the Jesuit priests of the Madurai province of the Society of Jesus.[15]

Loyola High School was started in June 1995 with 455 students on the roll among them 440 were Dalits.[16] In the year 2001, the total number of students rose to 740, from thirteen Dalit colonies in and around Kuppayanallur. From Pappanallur village there were 52 students (16 boys and 36 girls) in the school. All the teachers of the school are instructed to teach at least one hour, particularly making use of the moral instruction period to speak on the history of Dalit oppression and in what ways they can be liberated from it. The students are taught about the lives of the Dalit leaders like Ayotidhās Pandithar, Irattaimalai Srinivasan, and M.C. Raja. Among these Irattaimalai Srinivasan hailed from Koliyalam, which is seven kilometres from Pappanallur village and comes under the Pappanallur Catholic parish,[17] and his achievement, as a Paraiyar, remains a model for the school children, and one whom the Paraiyar leaders persuade their children to emulate.

Table 8

Literacy in Pappanallur Village[18]

Divisions	*Total Population*	*Educated*		*In education*		*Total*
		Men	*Women*	*Boys*	*Girls*	
Paraiyars	433	33	19	45	67	160
Vanniyars	702	21	11	26	30	88

Srinivasan was born in 1860 in the village and completed his university studies in Coimbatore, one of the northwestern cities of Tamil Nadu. Later, when he worked for European companies in the Nilgri hills as an accountant, he experienced caste discrimination. In 1890, he travelled across Tamil Nadu, mainly Chidambaram, Kumbakonam, Tanjore, where the Dalits were forbidden to enter temples. He spoke against this and published handbills about the temples in those cities that stood as symbols of high caste power. He argued boldly that the temple in Thiruvarur was built on *Sāmbān*, a Dalit place, but the Brahmins had changed the name into *Jambukesvarar* to make it sound Brahminical. At a time when the very use of the word 'paraiyan' was considered polluting, he published a monthly under the title *'Paraiyan'*. In it he wrote: "we Paraiyans should be bold enough to accept our status as Paraiyans; to accept our oppressed status is to take the first step towards final freedom" (Revathi 1997: 45-6). In 1894 he led a struggle to demand land for the Paraiyars of Chengalpattu. Later as a member of the State Legislative Assembly he fought for the rights of the Dalits. The then British government awarded him the title of 'Rao Sahib' (later this was changed to '*Rao Bagadur*') for his services to his community and to the nation. He was the first to organise a conference for the untouchables in 1892. More spectacularly, when he participated in the Round Table Conference in September 7, 1931, in London, he wore a badge that read '*Srinivasan-Paraiyan*' to demonstrate to the participants of the conference that members of his community were treated as untouchables in India. He spoke for the Dalits, insisting that they were not Hindus[19], and hence should be treated as a separate community, with political security and representation in the state and central assemblies,

He is popularised as a model to all the Dalit children in the school. Small leaflets are distributed on his life and achievements. Ninety per cent of the 72 boys and girls in Loyola School whom I personally interviewed to find out how they felt about being Dalits and how they would like to form themselves for the future, told me that their role model was Irattaimalai Srinivasan.[20] On every festival a meal of beef is provided for the students with the intention that they should accept this as their food and thereby a part of their culture and that there is nothing to be ashamed about in doing this.

Similar training is also imported through study centres, called *Senthalir Mālaipalli* [red shoots ('*Senthalir*') evening schools] in twenty-six villages, enabling the school children to develop the habit of studying at night. The Dalit dropout children are also encouraged to join the study centres including those from Pappanallur. Apart from coaching the usual class lessons, the teachers teach the Dalit children about Paraiyar life and society, especially through stories and songs; they show them how their ancestors were excluded socially and how important it is for them to become educated in order to be able to rise up to the higher castes, occasionally referring specifically to the Vanniyars' treatment of the Paraiyars. Evening study begins with an oath-taking ceremony by a boy or girl and repeated by the whole group:

> "I feel proud to have been born as a Dalit [Paraiyar]. Because the word *Paraiyar* and the land where I was born, denote a sense of heroism and superiority. By birth I am not an untouchable, it was by the unjust arrangement of the Hindu society I was made untouchable. By an inhuman and unjust philosophy, I was refused education and I was indoctrinated to live in servitude. To rewrite this unjust history, I resolve to become educated in the footsteps of Ambedkar and Irattaimalai Seenivasan. I am sure that only by education will I be able to regain my lost human dignity. Learning is my duty; learning is my right; learning is my gift. I promise I will improve and I will surely succeed."[21]

In the education of the Paraiyar children another important strategy followed is that the school is residential, so that the children can be isolated from the villages where their families experience untouchability and social exclusion, and it teaches them how to come out of the low status of Paraiyar life. There are two hostels, one for boys and another for girls within the campus.

In the hostel for boys, in 2001, there were one hundred and forty five boys from seventeen villages in the Kanchipuram district and fifteen boys from other northern districts like Cuddalore, Thiruvannamalai and Dharmapuri. In the hostel for girls, there were one hundred and fifty girls from thirteen villages. Unlike the boys, the girls are mostly from the nearby villages except for seven girls who come from villages of Cuddalore and Thiruvannamalai districts.

In addition to the two hostels there is another hostel called the Good Samaritan Project in Ongur village, three kilometres from the school. This was started in June 1995 with the help of an American Agency known as the Christian Foundation for Children and the Aging (CFCA). When it was started there were ninety Paraiyar children, both boys and girls, but in 2001 there were two hundred and twenty eight children. Eighty-two of the children go to the primary school in Ongur village, run by the Roman Catholic Archdiocese of Madras-Mylapore, and the rest go to Loyola High School. The unique character of the Good Samaritan Project is that ninety five per cent of the children are orphans and destitute.

In the other two hostels about 91 per cent of the boys and girls have parents who are day agricultural labourers and are uneducated. These are the first generation to have entered school education. Quite a number of the boys and girls are from single parent families; either the father or the mother is dead. Keeping the Paraiyar children away from the villages facilitates a situation in which, apart from projecting the three Dalit leaders – Irattaimalai Srinivasan, Ayothidasar, M.C. Raja – as models of Paraiyar liberation, they are taught the importance of education by which the Paraiyars can liberate themselves from untouchability. More importantly, this helps them understand the positive elements of drumming and beef-eating, which in their native places, are looked upon as polluting and demeaning activities. Although I will say more about the question of symbolic reversals, I shall briefly explain how the Paraiyar children are educated in the ways in which they can form their new identity.

The boys and girls are taught to appreciate the artistic elements of drumming, and in the school, among many programmes organised for the children, drumming is the main programme. The students are persuaded to reject what they have been told at home about drumming as a polluting activity; instead they are asked to appreciate it as their own traditional and unique artistic talent. They are also taught the advantages of eating, beef learning that it is not only healthy but also medicinal for coughs, tuberculosis, and their eyesight. Of the two hundred boys and girls I talked to, one hundred and twenty four said that beef was good for their health, though they had earlier considered it to be shameful (*asiṇgam*). To make it more convincing, many stories are told about people who had been cured by taking beef from different diseases. On every Sunday, lunch is provided with beef, and on important days of feast a cow or a calf is bought and killed in front of the hostels, and the cooked beef meal is eaten in a festive atmosphere. The communal meal begins with a prayer which runs like this: "Eating beef is not a pollution, not a shameful act, but it is our traditional food; it signifies our unique culture; we shall eat beef and we shall live healthily, and with dignity."[22] Such sharpened political and cultural consciousness is further enhanced by the Dalit Panthers of India (DPI), a Paraiyar political party in the state.

Dalit Panthers of India (DPI)[23]

In northern Tamil Nadu, the dynamics of regional politics centres on how the PMK party of the Vanniyars and the DPI party of the Paraiyars conduct themselves. Although there are political parties led by Paraiyar leaders (see Table 9), the DPI party led by Thirumavalavan is popular among the Paraiyars of northern Tamil Nadu. Opposition is always between PMK and DPI as the social conflict always persists between the Vanniyars and the Paraiyars. Depending upon this dynamics all other major parties (DMK, AIADMK, BJP, Congress) make alliances with them, during elections and at other times to set up their power networks. In the last two assembly elections, both the DPI and the PMK never aligned themselves with any one party on a permanent basis; when the DPI made alliance with the DMK, the PMK party joined the AIADMK, later when the PMK party joined the DMK, the DPI left the DMK to join the AIADMK. Gauging the political moves between the PMK and the DPI parties, all major political parties in Tamil Nadu change their alliances and shape and reshape their policies. Mainly, this is due to the numerical strength of the Vanniyars and the Paraiyars in northern districts. In addition, both the parties aggressively represent the interests of their community and claim themselves as the protectors of their respective communities. Among the caste riots in the last five years in the northern districts almost all of them had taken place between the Vanniyars and the Paraiyars, in which both the PMK and the DPI were involved (Thangaraj 1998; HRW 1999). One can say that the two parties set the trends of the regional politics and patterns of power relations. Keeping this in mind we should look at the role of the DPI political party in the lives of the Paraiyars in Pappanallur.

Table 9

Dalit Political Parties in Tamil Nadu[25]

Dalit Group	*Leader*	*Party Name*
Paraiyars	R.Thirumavalavan	Viduthalai Siruthaigal
Pallars	K. Krishnasamy	Puthiya Thamilagam
Paraiyars	Ilayaperumal	Manitha Urimai Katchi
Paraiyars	Vai.Balasundaram	AmbedkarMakkal Iyyakam
Paraiyars	Poovai Murthi	Puratchi Bharatham
Paraiyars	Krishnaparaiyanar	Ambedkar puratchi puligal
Arunthathiyars	Ira. Athyaman	Athithamilar Peravai

Source: The 2001 Assembly Elections Supplement to *Dinamani* Tamil daily newspaper.

Although there are some Paraiyars who hold membership of the Dravida Munnetra Kazhagam (DMK) and All India Anna Dravida Munnetra Kazhagam (AIADMK), the main political parties in the state, it is the DPI which is the most powerful party among the Paraiyars of the northern districts of Tamil Nadu, where the Paraiyar population is more concentrated than in the southern districts of the state. This is an offshoot of the parent party started in the state of Maharashtra in July 1972 after Dr Ambedkar's death.[24]

The DPI in Maharashtra insists on radical and violent means to avenge the atrocities done to the Dalits by the higher castes of Maharashtra. This appeals to the urban Dalit youth to such an extent that in 1974 there were 25,000 members in the party. But later, due to internal party squabbles, the party was dissolved and its regional branches started functioning independently. In this way, Maviran Malaichamy headed the DPI of Tamil Nadu in 1982 in Madurai. After his death Thirumavalavan became the organiser of the party. Until 2000 it was kept alive as a merely social movement dissociating itself from the electoral system of Indian Politics.

But in the Legislative Assembly elections of 2001 it fielded candidates to contest election to the state assembly; Thirumavalavan was elected as a Member of the Legislative Assembly (MLA) from the Mangalore assembly constituency. From the beginning, continuing the parent party's radical ideology, Thirumavalavan has been a strong advocate of violent means to resist any caste discrimination. Additionally, the party disseminated a new kind of history of the Dalits: the Dalits are the people who challenged the *Varnashrama dharma*; because of this, they were labelled as *panchamar* (fifth caste) and *sandālā*, and ostracised as untouchables; even the epics like the *Mahabharatam* and the *Ramayanam* are, for them, the result of the conflict between the Dalits and the higher castes of early Indian society. Though it is hard to prove the validity of these ideas, the Paraiyars of Pappanallur strongly believe in these views and treat what the DPI party says as true Dalit history. Booklets and audio cassettes explaining such ideas are found in every house of the Paraiyars in Pappanallur and elsewhere. Even the Paraiyar boys and girls at the elementary school have memorised the slogans of the Party: 'Refuse to obey, break laws; force yourself out and retaliate'; 'We are not sheep, but ferocious panthers'; 'When your head is held high the *cheri* [Dalit Colony] will rise up and the nation will be turned upside down'; 'Burn like fire and spread in all directions'; 'The *cheri* storm will one day go beyond its limits and history will be rewritten and you will hear lamentations in the high caste villages'.[26]

One of the basic approaches that the DPI takes is that it tries to oppose Pattali Makkal Kacci (PMK), the Vanniyar political party, and the Vanniyars as a whole, as the enemy of the Paraiyars. The DPI deliberately constructs and invites the Paraiyars to erect enemies to maintain 'unity and internal cohesion'; even though a threat is not always present there, the DPI party imagines threats from the Vanniyars in order that the Paraiyars will always keep the threat alive. All the time the DPI puts the Vanniyars forward as the archenemy of the Paraiyars. This is evocative for the Paraiyars and builds up cohesion in the Paraiyar community. After the 1999 elections, the Paraiyars of Chidambaram apparently indulged in violence, which resulted in the burning of Vanniyar houses in Alapakkam, near Cuddalore.[27] Practically in all his speeches Thirumavalavan pictures the Vanniyar community for the Paraiyars as their only enemy. Their enemies are not the Brahmins but the Vanniyars (*paraiyanukku ethiri papan alla, namakku irukira ore ethiri vanniyan*). This appeals to the Paraiyars of Tamil Nadu and encourages them to oppose the Vanniyars in their own villages. For Thirumavalavan, constructing an enemy is a very important and he organises the diverse Paraiyar groups and get them to assert their identity. On occasions, the Paraiyars take to violent means in their resistance to the Vanniyars. The only way for the Paraiyars to be secure and assert their identity is, Thirumavalavan argues, that they should retaliate against the Vanniyars; if one Colony hut is burnt by the Vanniyars, ten Vanniyars' houses should be burnt. In my interview with him, he said that violent resistance to the Vanniyars is the only weapon, at least for the present time by which the Paraiyars can improve their status in Tamil society. Such ideology and praxis of the DPI has an enormous influence on the thought and behaviour of the Paraiyars of Pappanallur.

Arulappan is the local DPI leader and he takes up many issues of the Paraiyars; in the recent conflicts with the Vanniyars the DPI have had an important role in countering the Vanniyars' PMK party. When necessary he informs the head office of the DPI in Chennai about the happenings in the village in relation to the *Ūr* castes. There are thirty-two registered members of the party including fifteen women in Pappanallur, though all the Paraiyars are members of the party unofficially. Every month they hold meetings to review their activities and share information received from the head office. Some times, they call for emergency meetings to organise people for a rally or demonstration at other places in the state and to select representatives for state level meetings and consultations.

On the part of the Paraiyars, to show constantly to the *Ūr* higher castes their link with the DPI party is to realise themselves as more powerful to face up to any challenges from the Vanniyars. To reinforce this gesture regularly, once a week, the local DPI broadcasts the speeches of the DPI leader, Thirumavalavan, which are considered provocative by the Vanniyars. To that extent, the DPI party adds to the political power acquired through the different resources discussed above. One of the DPI members said, 'if we did not have our own political party like the DPI we would have been destroyed by the Vanniyars a long time ago. The party gives us the courage (*thairiyam*) to challenge the Vanniyars".

For the Paraiyars, power means that they have the courage to speak out against caste discrimination, and they know it well that if anything happens, the party is there to protect them. They realise that this is the difference from earlier times when they were unable to utter anything unpleasant to the Vanniyars from their subordinated situation. As Arockiasamy has said, they were not allowed even to wear their sandals in the presence of Vanniyars or have the towel on their shoulders, but now they can do all this boldly. The power from the political networks have helped them assert themselves as respectable individuals and as a community like any other high caste communities.

Role of the Roman Catholic Priests

Among the institutions that built up the Paraiyars' confidence gradually, and sharpened their conviction to get rid of their low identity, the Roman Catholic Church remains a significant institution in all respects. Through its parish priests of Pappanallur and CRDS, the Archdiocese of Madras-Mylapore has provided the Paraiyars with a seminal boldness in conflicts and in their efforts to form a new identity. From the 1940s until the time of my fieldwork, the eight parish priests have stood by the Paraiyars consistently, and have provided them with financial assistance and legal help during the time of conflicts with the higher castes. Not that all of them followed the same method or approach to the whole issue from the beginning, but all of them have shared the central idea and concern that the Paraiyars have to change their social status of a low identity and that it was their duty to help the Paraiyars in the process. Father Paul Puthanangady for the first time in the 1940s helped the Paraiyars who were arrested after the first major conflict to get released on bail. Later he invited them to convert to Christianity and helped them build a school and put up decent houses for them. His main focus was, the Paraiyars told me, on the Paraiyars' spiritual advancement although he helped them financially. In the 1950s, Father Neelapanar concentrated mainly on development works. He financed the laying of the five-mile long road from Vedanthangal to Pappanallur and deepened the village tank (*ēri*). During his time there was no major conflict between the *Ūr* and the Colony, since he was good to all the caste groups in the village, and although he was a parish priest only for the Paraiyars, he was helpful to all the higher castes in many ways. Understandably, he is the only priest for whom the Vanniyars have high respect. From the latter part of the 1960s until 2003, the emphasis of the priests had been on the political identity of the Paraiyars. The Jesuit priests especially took a preferential option for the Paraiyars and have organised them politically against the Vanniyars. It was during the time of Jesuit parish priests that the Paraiyars stopped their traditional services to the *Ūr,* and began the process of identity formation focusing on symbols of identity. To do this, the Jesuits trained them through seminars and agitations in which they were made to realise the importance of changing their low status and forming a new one.

In my conversation with the Paraiyars, they singled out Father Yesumarian, a Jesuit lawyer, who helped them fight their court cases, and Father Sahayaselvan, a Jesuit sociologist, and parish priest of Pappanallur from 1995-99, who stood by them when one of them was shot dead by the police in a land reclamation agitation, which I will discuss later in this chapter. Although the Paraiyars of Pappanallur narrate many incidents that demonstrate the important role played by the priests, they refuse to accept the view that it is the priests who gave them the idea of fighting against the Vanniyars, and, later ways of reconstructing their identity. They assert that their self-consciousness came from themselves and they are the architects of their new identity. I argue that the origin of the Paraiyars' opposition to the *Ūr* could have originated from them, but this was made a reality only by the help of the priests. This will become clear in the following sections.

History of the Conflicts in Pappanallur Village

The history of the Paraiyar community is textured by conflicts and the chronology of their past is defined by their conflicts with the higher castes of the village It is only by these that they recall their past. In my interactions not a single Paraiyar could tell me about anything without referring to a conflict or two. Even after I came away from my fieldwork, the one word that lingered in my mind powerfully was 'conflict'. I realised that what they are as persons and as a community is shaped and being shaped by the dynamics and nature of the conflicts they had and are having with the higher castes; to ignore this would make it hard to understand the inner core of the Paraiyars' life.

During my field study in 2000-02 I collected thirty stories of conflicts that the Paraiyars have had with the higher castes – both the Reddiyars and the Vanniyars from the 1950s until 2002.[28]

From these I have chosen only seven major conflicts to examine, for they are directly related to the symbolic reconstruction of identity, which is my central concern. This is not to suggest that other conflicts do not have any significance in the identity formation. Rather, every conflict, be it minor or major, has contributed to the making of major and spectacular results.

In addition, the conflicts that I describe below have had a direct influence on the Paraiyars in their efforts to remove their negative identity. For the Paraiyars in Pappanallur, their history means what they have experienced in the major conflicts. It is by these that they remember their lives in the past and guide their present and future life.

Conflict and Conversion, 1941

In the early 1930s, the Paraiyars in Pappanallur told me, that they had been landless labourers. They worked on the land of the higher castes – the Brahmins, the Reddiyars and the Vanniyars – as permanent farm servants (*paṇṇaiyāl*) and hired farm servants (*paṭiyāl*). They received no income in cash, but many families of the Paraiyars were only fed in the houses of the higher castes.[29] Around the year 1939, the whole district of Chengalpattu experienced drought and famine. In Pappanallur, the people who had wells for irrigation were able to survive, since they could grow pulses and lentils; others survived on government rations. It was extremely difficult for the Paraiyars to survive with the limited supply of rations from the state government. Barnabas, the eldest Paraiyar in the village, recalls that three of his children died of starvation in that year.

The experience of the drought made the Paraiyars realise that if they had had a piece of land like the *dargos*[30] land they would have survived the drought. For a long time, many in the Colony have had plans to ask for land from their landlords. One of the Paraiyars pleaded with Elumalai Gounder, leader of the village (*nāṭṭāmai*), to give them a piece of land or at least allow the Paraiyars to use the dargos land kept common for the village cattle grazing. Since the Paraiyar was his bonded labourer,

Elumalai Gounder was generous enough to allow the Paraiyars to make use of the *dargos* land.

Thus, the Paraiyars cleared all the thorn bushes and removed stones from the land to make it arable for cultivating pulses. In the next two years, they produced more than seven bags of *payitham paruppu* (a pulse). Consequently, it forced some Paraiyars to concentrate on that land to the extent of withdrawing themselves from working on the land of the higher castes, who became increasingly displeased about it. Yet they could not openly do anything, since it involved the village leader. The dissatisfaction remained a private matter within the circle of a few Vanniyar families, who were waiting for an opportune moment to bring it up in the *Ūr* council.

In 1939, the Paraiyars distinctly remember, on the day of the Pongal festival, some Vanniyar youth chased cattle into the *dargos* land where the Paraiyars had been cultivating pulses and destroyed the pulse plants. As soon as the Paraiyars heard about this, about fifteen Paraiyars went to chase the cattle away from their fields. In doing so, they had so beaten some milch cows to the extent that two cows were killed on the spot. This infuriated the Vanniyars who went into the Colony in large numbers, burnt some of the huts of the Paraiyars, and beat up Paraiyar men and women. This led to a riot between the *Ūr* and the Colony. Although there was no death, more than twenty Paraiyars and five Vanniyar men sustained serious injuries. The Paraiyars recalled to me that the Vanniyars lodged a complaint against the Paraiyars with the police that they were creating communal riots in the village. The police from Achirapakkam arrested about hundred men and women from the Colony and ten men from the *Ūr*. The Vanniyars with their influence bailed their men out, but the Paraiyars were helpless. For the Paraiyars this was the first time they had been to a police station so they did not have a clue about what they should do.

Some Paraiyars who had known about Father Paul Puthanangady, the parish priest of the Cheyur Catholic parish, ten miles from Pappanallur village, proposed that they should go to

Cheyur to meet the parish priest, who would probably help bail them out.

A few Paraiyars went to Cheyur and narrated the whole incident to Father Paul who promised to do what was necessary. The Paraiyars remember that since the parish priest had good rapport with the police, he persuaded them to release the Paraiyars. The elder Paraiyars have a vivid memory even to this day about the way in which the priest brought them from the police station and gave each family ten kilos of rice. One of them said, "if Father Paul had not been there to help us we would not have survived the attack of the Vanniyars that day".

After the incident, Father Paul began to visit the Colony regularly. He talked to them about how they should become economically self-sufficient, and the importance of educating their children for them to be able to get out of the domination of the higher castes. This made a great impression on the Paraiyars, and later they expressed their wish to become Christians. The Baptismal register kept in Cheyur parish records that on 19th June 1941 forty-nine Paraiyars, and later on 8th August in the same year, twenty-eight Paraiyars went through baptism. Other Paraiyars gradually converted to Christianity, and by the year 1949, the whole Colony of the Paraiyars had become Christian.

This conflict has remained foundational in serving as the starting point of all other processes that had taken place, and even now not in only in terms of the Paraiyars' efforts to redefine themselves but equally so in terms of the events leading to the reordering of the village institutions. It is interesting to note that the Paraiyars do not remember anything or any event before 1939/41.* The conflict set a pattern or a template that provided them with a guide map to every other conflict with the Vanniyars. More sharply, it served as a frame of reference for their new life and approach, and in particular, it was helpful at a time when there had been some slackening in their resistance to the

---

* From the conversations I had, I understand that the conflict should have happened in 1939 and later in 1941 the impact of the conflict was realised tangibly. This is a reason why there is no clarity on the exact year of the first conflict.

discrimination by the higher castes. Whenever the Paraiyar leaders decided to reinvigorate their vision of identity formation they recalled this conflict.

I followed the conflict from Pappanallur to Cheyur parish where the present parish priest told me that Father Paul had converted more than three thousand people in Madurantagam area and showed me the diary of Father Paul in which he had written about his daily visits to villages. Older members of Cheyur parish recounted to me stories of how Father Paul used to visit Pappanallur regularly and of the Paraiyars of Pappanallur who went to meet the parish priest when the police arrested them in 1939. More importantly, the example that Pappanallur Paraiyars showed in challenging the Vanniyars inspired the Paraiyars in other villages in their fight against the higher castes, the Vanniyars, the Naidus and the Reddiyars.

Formation of the Paraiyar Vagaiyarā Council, 1960

Like the first primal conflict, this one also took place on a Pongal festival day of 1965. Even before the festival began in the Colony the Paraiyars talked about how in the previous conflict their cultivation was destroyed and how they were arrested. Barnabas, who had taken part in the previous conflict, said that the Paraiyar boys who were grazing the cattle of some Vanniyars drove the cattle into the paddy fields of two Vanniyar leaders in revenge for the Vanniyars' act earlier. He further added that some of them had even planned to kill at least one bull of the Vanniyars who had masterminded the previous conflict. Some Paraiyars promptly communicated these to the *Ūr*. This infuriated the Vanniyars and made them ready to face any challenge. All this led to a build-up for a fight between the two communities.

After the usual ceremony (*sāmikumbiduthal*) at the village temple where all the cattle were taken for blessing, the cattle procession went from the temple towards the village lake for the game of the bulls' race. While the procession was in progress two Paraiyar youth snatched the balloons from the horns of one of the Vanniyars' bullocks. Immediately the Vanniyars accompanying the bullocks started to beat the Paraiyar youth, using bamboo sticks used for chasing the bulls. One of the youth, Thomas who sustained injury on his forehead dropped down unconscious. Rumour spread all over that the Vanniyars had murdered the young Paraiyar. The procession was immediately halted and the Paraiyars started beating the Vanniyars who were caught by surprise and rushed to their houses, but the Paraiyars continued to run after the Vanniyars all over the village. The Paraiyars claim that more than twenty Vanniyars were beaten and there seemed to have been no resistance. The Vanniyars to whom I spoke to about the incident accepted that they were beaten up by the Paraiyars but refused to accept that they were chased all over the *Ūr* streets. The conflict lasted for more than four days, and since the Vanniyars would not allow the Paraiyars to walk the *Ūr* streets, the Paraiyars retaliated by picking a quarrel with whoever from the *Ūr* came along the main road leading to Vedanthangal.

In the *Ūr* council, the Vanniyar leaders decided that what the Paraiyars had done during the festival was wrong and also that it was they who had been the main cause for the continuing antagonism. The best way to contain the situation, the leaders decided, was to fine both parties who had been involved in the main incident that day and later in the village. Moreover, the seven Paraiyars would not be allowed to work on the land, not only of the Vanniyars but on any land in the village. Although the Paraiyars agreed to pay the fine, the elder Paraiyars recall, they did not agree on the additional sanction, which they thought was unfair. So the Paraiyar leaders requested the *Ūr* council leaders to drop the additional sanction. The *Ūr* council refused to accede to the request, and ordered that if the Paraiyars did not abide by the decisions of the council the whole Colony would have to face serious consequences.

Although they considered this judgement as partial and unjust, the Paraiyars had no other option except to give in. The seven Paraiyars from that time had to struggle to get work in the nearby villages. Realising that they had become involved in the whole conflict for the sake of the Colony, the Paraiyars did not sufficiently argue their case in the council. The seven Paraiyars complained first to Father Nilappanar, the then parish priest who had his presbytery in Vedanthangal. But he could not do much in this regard. Since the Paraiyars who had rapport with the Paraiyars in Kattukollai village went to them for help. The Paraiyars of Kattukollai village, had some rapport with many non-governmental organisations (NGOs) and they took the Pappanallur Paraiyars to meet organisers of SAM movement. The NGO people suggested to the Paraiyars of Pappanallur that they should build their system of governance up and become powerful so that they could influence the decision making process in the village. And the NGO promised to help them if there was any problem, which gave the Paraiyars confidence to stand up to the Vanniyars.

Apart from this outside pressure, after the incident the Paraiyars themselves started gradually to realise that they were unable to argue their case at the *Ūr* council because they had no representation from the Colony. Since all the members of the *Ūr* council were from the higher castes, the Paraiyars thought that they were partial to their own people in their decisions. After a long debate the Paraiyars decided in a meeting of the Colony to form their own council in which all the *Vagaiyarās* of the Colony would be represented: the *Vagaiyarā* council. Whenever there was a conflict with the *Ūr* castes, they decided, the *Vagaiyarā* council would meet to discuss the issue and form an opinion, which would be conveyed to the *Ūr* council where they would demand a proper hearing of the case. They demanded that this representation by the *Vagaiyarā* council in the *Ūr* council should be respected. Although there was some initial resistance to this from the higher castes, later gradually they came to recognise the Paraiyar *Vagaiyarā council.*[31]

After the formation of the *Vagaiyarā* council all conflicts that involved only the Paraiyars were settled in the *Vagaiyarā* council, and in the conflicts involving both the Vanniyars and the Paraiyars the *Vagaiyarā* council began to have a strong representation in the *Ūr* council. At the time of my fieldwork there were three political institutions in the village: the *Ūr* council, the Paraiyar *Vagaiyarā* council, and the Village Panchayat. Whatever issues involved the two communities – the Paraiyars and the

Vanniyars – are taken care of by the *Ūr* council. If something relates only to the Paraiyars it is handled in the *Vagaiyarā* council, and in the same way the Vanniyars sort out their community's problems in the *Ūr* council. The formation of the *Vagaiyarā* council gave the Paraiyars the power to assert themselves as a community and to represent their cases in the village strongly.

Abandoning Cattle Scavenging, 1965

Like the previous conflict, one of the best-remembered conflicts is the one they had over cattle scavenging. They often recall this on the days they come together for communal beef-eating. One day in 1967, Kannappa Gounder, leader of the village, sent for the Thotti Paraiyar. When he went to the house of Kannappa Gounder he was asked to remove a dead cow from the cowshed. Realising that the dead cow was exuding a strong and foul smell because it must have been days since it died, the Paraiyar suggested that he needed help to carry the carcass away, and said he would go back to the Colony to get some more Paraiyars. But Kannappa Gounder insisted that the Paraiyar should do something immediately. But the Paraiyar refused to obey him. This made Kannappa Gounder angry. He took his sandal and beat the Thotti Paraiyar up brutally. Later on the Paraiyar *Vagaiyarā* council decided to report the matter to the police. Hearing this, Kannappa Gounder and his men vowed to teach the Paraiyars a lesson, saying if the Paraiyans who ate the carcasses of cows had such pride (*koḷuppu*), how greater would be the pride of the Vanniyars who were the higher castes. The Paraiyars say that one-day when the wife of the Thotti Paraiyar was working in the paddy fields of a Vanniyar, two men sent by Kannappa Gounder dragged her away to a spot nearby and allegedly raped her. Having come to know the incident some Paraiyar youths battered Kannappa Goundar's brother and his family members and burnt the hut in which more than fifty bags of rice was stored.

The Vanniyars retaliated by damaging the properties of some of the Paraiyars and beat some youths up who sustained minor injuries. The Vanniyars decided in their *Ūr* council that the

Paraiyars were not be hired any more to work in their fields. The Paraiyars in Pampayamputhur, three and a half kilometres from Pappanallur, came to the rescue of the Pappanallur Paraiyars. From my conversation with the Paraiyars in Pampayamputhur I gathered that it was in Pampayamputhur that the Pappanallur Paraiyars regularly met to discuss the conflict and took decisions about how they should act. The experience of the Paraiyars of Pampayamputhur in abandoning the cattle scavenging in their village in the previous year provided the Pappanallur Paraiyars with some clarity with regard to their future course of action.

Later the Paraiyars decided in the Paraiyar *Vagaiyarā* council to discontinue the cattle scavenging service. In addition, the Council ordered that no Paraiyar should thereafter eat the meat of dead cows; instead they could buy a cow, kill it, and share the meat among the Colony people. Many Paraiyars and most of the Vanniyars take a different view of this.

In this issue, Father Raja, the then parish priest, played an important role in persuading the *Vagaiyarā* council to decide to discontinue the service, and he promised to give them money to buy a bull or a cow every Sunday that could be killed and the meat be shared among the Paraiyars. Even today many Paraiyars remember that the priest had often in his sermons at Sunday Masses implored the Paraiyars to give up eating the meat of dead cows, telling them, "you are human beings, you are not animals to eat carcasses". Michael, the Paraiyar leader, remembers the sermons which he heard when he was a small boy and he agreed that they were very powerful so much so that immediately after the Mass many Paraiyars went to the priest and vowed to give up eating carcasses.

Many Paraiyars feel that the conflict discussed above ushered the awareness for the first time that they could oppose the Vanniyars and be successful in it as well. Michael, the leader of the Paraiyar *Vagaiyarā* council, said that it was wonderful to realise that he had been able to beat up the Kannappa Gounder's brother. His description of the change they experienced after the conflict is vivid: "when we were bent down we had no idea of our strength, but when we stood straight up and held our heads high, we realised that we had discovered enormous power within us and that we could even burn down the Vanniyars' house". This made it clear that till so far they had been on the defensive and submissive, whereas the conflict suddenly gave them the courage to rebel against the people who dominated them; they were now on the offensive. The feeling of 'standing up' was so persuasively seductive that they stopped eating meat from carcasses in order to sustain their state of 'standing up'.

All this helped the Paraiyar finally abandon the scavenging service and stop the habit of eating meat from carcass. Instead, with the help of many Dalit movements and with financial assistance from Father Raja, they started the practice of buying a cow every Sunday and sharing the meat among themselves, telling themselves that what they ate was pure meat (*suṭṭamāana curry*) and that this should remain as a unique custom of the Paraiyars. In addition, they began gradually to evolve many myths glorifying the practice of eating beef and treating it as a Paraiyar social custom.

Two Schools in One Village, 1970

The first school in Pappanallur was started in 1943, after the Paraiyars' conversion to Christianity. Father Paul Puthanangady of Cheyur parish helped them financially to construct the building and assigned a teacher from his parish to the school. In 1953 they moved the school from the southern end of the Colony to the centre of the Colony where they built a proper building with two rooms. Even at the time of my fieldwork in the place where the old school building stood there were dilapidated walls. Again the school was shifted still further north of the Colony near the present church building (see Map 4) to build more facilities in the school since the number of students was increasing steadily. Father Martin from a non-governmental organisation called SAM (Social Awareness Movement) and Father K.V. Neelapana, the then parish priest, contributed money to build three rooms, two for the school and one for the use of the priests who visited the Colony once a week to hold Mass for the Paraiyars.

Conflict started when the higher castes, particularly the Vanniyars started sending their children to the Colony school. The Vanniyars demanded that their children should be provided with separate space in the classroom away from the Paraiyar children. The Paraiyars say that the Vanniyars pressurised them so much that the teacher, who belonged to a Naidu caste (equal to the Vanniyar caste, although the Naidus are Telugus who originally came from Andhra Pradesh, one of the four southern states) arranged to provide a raised platform for the children of the higher castes. Separate pots for drinking water were kept for the Colony children and the *Ūr* children.

The Paraiyars say that they opposed this arrangement and complained to Father Neelappana who was then the correspondent of the school. They said that it was their school and that if the Vanniyars wanted to send their children, they should follow the prescribed rules and regulations of the school; it was not fair that the Vanniyars dictated what was to be done. The case was also taken up in the Paraiyar *Vagaiyarā* council where they decided that they would demand that the special arrangements for the high caste children be cancelled and all the children should be treated equally. Some of the elders from both sides persuaded the Paraiyars and the Vanniyars to settle the issue peacefully. Nevertheless, the Paraiyar youth felt that this was an opportunity for them to assert their power, and if they missed it, they thought, they would never get another opportunity. Xavier from the Colony said, "we wanted a fight; we were desperately looking for one; only in such a conflict situation we could get the chance to beat the Vanniyars up, at least we would be able to use swear foul words against them".

No day went off without a verbal duel between the two groups that led to many twists and turns, and every day the hostility between the *Ūr* and the Colony was increasing. Once again that year's Pongal day provided the two communities with the occasion to give vent to their anger against each other.

In 1960, on the second day of Pongal, when the whole village was watching drama (*kūṭṭu*) in the *Ūr* area, some one set on fire to the Colony school building. When the Paraiyars, who were watching the drama heard about the fire they ran to the Colony and put out the fire. There was no major damage to the building but the Paraiyars took it as an issue that would help them settle scores with the Vanniyars. The Vanniyars related to me that they did not set fire to the school but that it was one of the Paraiyars who did it deliberately in order to create a conflict in the village. But the Paraiyars on the contrary insisted that the Vanniyars did it. But the Paraiyars told me during my fieldwork that it was one of them who did it, and it was deliberately planned to generate conflict to assert the Paraiyar power.

Later the Paraiyars decided not to allow the Vanniyar children into the Colony school. In 1965, the Vanniyars opened a school exclusively for the higher castes and petitioned the state government for formal recognition. The reasons given for starting a separate school for the *Ūr* were that they had a sufficient number of students in the *Ūr* and it was difficult to send their children to the Colony during the rainy season as the Colony was flooded being in a low lying area of the village. The actual reason was, both the Vanniyars and the Paraiyars agree, that the Vanniyars did not want to send their children to the school where they would have to sit with the Paraiyar children. To get permission to start another school in the same village, the education department needed signatures of all the castes of the village, and particularly, the approval of the Paraiyars since the existing school was in their territory and was a state-aided school as well. The Paraiyars were more than willing to approve of a new school, which they felt would allow them to have a school exclusively for their children. And making use of their dominance in the Panchayat board the Vanniyars filed a petition to the government demanding a separate school for the *Ūr* people. Since the application came from the Panchayat, the state government officials thought that the Colony people also shared the opinion of the *Ūr* higher castes. The Vanniyars from the nearby villages also used their influence in the state government to recommend the application of the Pappanallur Vanniyars. In course of my visits to the villages – Kattukollai, Katiyambandal, Chitamur – as a part of my methodology of following the conflict, the Vanniyars of those villages told me what had been the issue behind supporting the Vanniyars of Pappanallur. Consequently, a separate school for the higher castes was started fully aided by the state government in 1970 (R.C. No. 484/70, 21 December 1970).

The Paraiyars of Pappanallur invited the Paraiyar children from nearby villages to join their school that increased the roll strength of the students. This incident seems to have inspired the NGOs that worked for Dalits in the area to start nursery schools exclusively for the Paraiyar children.

The new school for the *Ūr* further widened the gap between the *Ūr* and the Colony that was gradually widening first by the conversion and then the formation of the Paraiyar *Vagaiyarā* council. The avenues and institutions through which both groups interacted with each other were being increasingly reduced after every conflict.

Conflict Over the Use of Public Facilities, 1989

For many years, the Paraiyars told me, they had been asking the *Ūr* leaders to provide them with water facilities from the well in the Colony area, which was meant for the whole village (see map 4). All the other areas of the village had a drinkable water pipe connection except the Colony. Every time the Paraiyars asked about why their area had not been given the facility they were told that the Colony was in a low lying area and if connected to the system this would prevent the free flow of water to other areas of the village, particularly to the *Ūr*. The Paraiyars even petitioned the Panchayat union in Maduranthagam but nothing happened. One of the reasons what, Elizabeth, the leader of the Women's Association (*Māthar Saṇgam*) told me, was that the Colony was not united on the issue. Whenever they had planned to raise the issue of water facility in the *Ūr* council, some Paraiyars leaked the information to the *Ūr* Vanniyars, who somehow found a way of making the Paraiyars refrain from insisting on the matter. Pushpa, a member of the Women's Association, told me that the Vanniyars were successful, because the Paraiyar men, or at least some of them, if not all, could easily change their position by receiving a bottle of *arrack* and a meal given by the Vanniyars. More than the men, the Paraiyar women were the ones who were immediately affected by the lack of a water facility, since only the women faced the trouble of collecting water from the water pump, which was in the *Ūr* area. They were allowed to take water only after all the *Ūr* people had taken. Sometimes, the Paraiyar women told me, by the time the Paraiyar women reached the pump to collect the water the tank had already been emptied and the only option for them then was to go on foot for three miles to a nearby well in the paddy field area to collect water for drinking and cooking purposes. Therefore the Paraiyar women were waiting for a way to find a solution to the problem.

On the eve of the Pongal festival in 1989, some Paraiyar women, after having decided in their association meeting, went to the well, washed beef with the water taken from the well, and threw the water into the well. Promptly they spread the news to the *Ūr*. The Vanniyars immediately asked all their people not to collect water from the water pumps. Agitated by this, about fifty Vanniyar men attempted to remove all the pipe connections to the well. The Paraiyar women and some women opposed it. As a consequence, there was a brawl between the two groups, which did not lead to violence because some of the Paraiyar *Vagaiyarā* council members intervened to promise the Vanniyars that they would inquire about who 'polluted' the well.

Everybody in the Colony knew who did it and even the leaders were in fact aware of it but they did not betray their people, since they also, like the Paraiyar women, wanted to find some solution to the water problem. Since they had promised the Vanniyars, they convened the *Vagaiyarā* council where the Paraiyar women refused to accept that they had done it. One of the women who was present in the council meeting told me that as soon as the women, who were thought to have polluted the well, denied that they had done so, the whole council burst into laughter, and that was enough to conclude that the it was the Paraiyar women who had in fact polluted the well. However, the *Vagaiyarā* leaders informed the Vanniyars that they could not trace the persons who polluted well. The Vanniyars did not believe the information. Most of the Vanniyars who spoke to me on this issue said that they knew that it was someone from the Colony who polluted the water, but they were not able to find out who did it.

Therefore, at the *Ūr* council the Vanniyars decided to dig a separate well for the use of the *Ūr*. In addition, the council persuaded the Village Panchayat, in which the Vanniyars were in the majority, to remove all the pipe connections that went from the well in the Colony to the *Ūr*. But members from the Colony in the Village Panchayat were successful in getting the Panchayat to allot funds to lay water pipe connections to the Colony from the existing well, which would then be for the exclusive use of the Colony.

The story of this conflict provided the Paraiyars of nearby villages with the idea of demanding public facilities for their colonies. In this, matter the support of the Paraiyars of Pappanallur was significant. Regularly, the Paraiyar members of the Panchayat boards of nearby villages met to plan out their actions. In Katiyambandal, the Paraiyars told me that the Paraiyars of Pappanallur were a catalyst in bringing about change in their life.

Discontinuing the Traditional Ūr Services, 1996-67

This was the last major conflict that the Paraiyars had with the Vanniyars and through it they finally disassociated themselves completely from the *Ūr*. It is considered to be of great significance, equal to the first conflict by which they converted to Christianity, because it was after this conflict that the Paraiyars discontinued all the services to the *Ūr* that had for a long time been used to define them as having a low and untouchable identity.

On 14 January, 1996, in the evening of the Pongal festival all the decorated cattle and livestock were taken out of the village in a procession called chasing the cattle (*mādukalaithal*). This is what the drummers used to do, as they had always done, going through each street of the *Ūr* accompanying the bulls and other livestock. When the cattle procession was taken out of the village, the Paraiyars told me that the Vanniyars straight away led the procession into the two-acre *dargos* land that was being used by the Paraiyars as a playground for their school children. Their intention was to reclaim the land from the Paraiyars, who had forcefully taken possession of it a few years earlier, with the plan to make it a common land (*purambōkku*). As soon as they realised that the cattle procession was entering their *dargos* land, the drummers refused to proceed further in the procession and stopped drumming. The drummers started arguing with the Vanniyar leaders declaring that it was not fair to chase the cattle on to their land; if they allowed this to happen, the land would be treated as public land, which, in all probability, the Vanniyars would finally claim. While this verbal exchange was going on, one of the Paraiyars shouted that his drum had been broken by the Vanniyar who was standing near him, and pointed at him saying he had used a bamboo stick to break the drum. Immediately, the Paraiyar youths started throwing stones at the Vanniyars and a few other Paraiyars beat up the Vanniyar who was alleged to have broken the drum. Finally, this resulted in a major conflict in which two Vanniyars and seven Paraiyars were injured.

Later, both groups went to the police to register a case against each other. After a series of peace meetings in the presence of the police and RDO the whole issue was put to rest by the decision that neither of them thereafter should use the land for any purpose, and that it should be treated as disputed territory. Both groups promised the officials that they would adhere to the decision.

As the village was getting back to normalcy, some Paraiyar youths divulged to the Colony that the conflict was of their own making. The person who broke the drum was not a Vanniyar, but one of the Paraiyars who did so deliberately and put the blame on the Vanniyar in order to pick a reason for a conflict, thinking they could use this as a ground for stopping to drum for the Vanniyars.

While the Paraiyars were planning as to how they could stop the *Ūr* services they were again faced with another problem. In 1997, without any prior decision in any of the proper forums, the Village Panchayat or in the *Ūr* council, the Vanniyars started digging a well in the land adjacent to the R.C. school and the *dargos* land of the Paraiyars to take water to the *Ūr* overhead tank and to the *Ūr* tank of the nearby village Thiruvenkatapuram. When the Paraiyar leaders approached the *Ūr* leaders to ask why the well was being dug in their land, they answered that they would take over the school from the church and they had every right to use public land. The Paraiyars petitioned the District Collector to allot the land (3.50 acres/S. No 155/3A) adjacent to their *dargos* land for the permanent use of the R.C. School children's playground and prayed for the legal title (*pattā*). In the petition the Paraiyars threatened that if the issue was not settled amicably it would cause a caste riot in the village. Gauging the situation, the Collector's office sent a team of officials with the RDO to Pappanallur village to settle the dispute. The RDO, I was told, had a series of meetings with the two groups. The Vanniyars were adamant in claiming their right to dig a well since the land could be used as public land (*purambōkku*); the Roman Catholic school, they said, should not use the land because the school was mainly for Paraiyar children. But the Paraiyars insisted that the land should be given for the use of the school children, and argued with the RDO that the Vanniyars were planning to take it over gradually. The RDO, both the Paraiyars and the Vanniyars told me, favoured the Paraiyars since the land was useful to the school. But the Vanniyars refused to give in and threatened that they would go to their Vanniyar caste political leader Dr Ramadoss and make it a caste issue. Realising how volatile the situation was, the RDO finally decided that the land should be treated as disputed land until a further decision was taken by the district administration, and that neither the Vanniyars nor the Paraiyars should use the land.

A week later the Paraiyars held a meeting of the *Vagaiyarā* council to discuss the whole issue. Although some elder Paraiyars did not want to create further tension with the Vanniyars, most of the Paraiyars were in favour of stopping the services to the *Ūr* altogether. In one of the council meetings they took the decision to stop all the services – the drumming, the announcing deaths, cremating the dead, and the guarding of the village. Some Paraiyars objected to this, saying that the Vanniyars would not allow them to draw water from the village tank for their cultivation; the drummers feared that if they did not go for drumming the Vanniyars would beat them up. For all this, the local DPI leaders promised that they would protect them from any such eventuality. The parish priest, Father Joe Mike, also assured them that if anything happened he would provide all the support they needed, and promised to provide all the Paraiyars, particularly the drummers, who would stand united with his financial assistance. Then the Jesuit priests in collaboration with DPI members organised a workshop for the whole Colony in which the Paraiyars were given lectures by different Dalit scholars from Chennai city and Pondicherry university on the history of drumming in which the drumming by the Paraiyars was made into a funeral service, and the need to reconstruct drumming as an art form of the Paraiyars. This workshop made an impact on the drummers in the Colony and they decided to drum only for auspicious occasions. More importantly, they decided not to play for funerals, not only in the *Ūr* but also in the Colony. Even for auspicious occasions, the drummers should be booked in advance as is normally done when a musical troupe is invited from Chennai or from any other place. When in future the drummers go to drum, they decided, they should not beg food from the houses of the *Ūr* higher castes, rather should demand that they be fed in hotels (meaning restaurants) in the nearby towns. Some Paraiyar youths came forward to join the drummers and suggested that the military drum, used for a march-past, and the *thavil* drum, a double sided and vertically held drum, used to provide auspicious music in temples, should be taken up so as to transform their drumming from drums of death to proper and respectable percussion instrument.

At the time of my fieldwork, no drumming took place in the village for any occasion. More importantly, the Vanniyars now cremate their dead on their own, a thing that used to be a polluting service provided by the Paraiyars. For instance, when on 23 January, 2002, while I was there, one of the Gounders died, three Vanniyar youths did the work of cremation. Initially, the youths hesitated, but later agreed after the family of Sullippillai promised to pay them each Rs 500; by contrast, previously the Paraiyar, who had been the cremation assistant, used to be given only the coins placed on corpses, mostly amounting to not more than Rs 20. It took a long time to persuade the youths to agree to do the cremation work. Finally they carried the body to the cremation ground around eleven o'clock at night. When the Vanniyar youth went back after burning the body to, their families they were asked by their families to stay away for three days to rid themselves of the pollution. This consisted of a ceremonial walk every morning and in sponsoring puja at the Vinayagar temple; at their homes they slept in the cowshed and their food was served to them in palmyra palms. Kathamuthu, one of the three Gounder youths who cremated the body of Sullipillai, told me that he was afraid that if he continued the cremation work, he and his family would be finally forced to live outside the village like the Paraiyars.

After this final conflict, the boundary between the *Ūr* and the Colony was firmly marked and there was no avenue open except the Paraiyars' membership in the Village Panchayat in which the two groups interacted freely with each other. As Arulappan, a DPI member said, earlier they had been excluded, segregated and marginalised from the *Ūr* by the higher castes even although they formed part of the *Ūr* in terms of their services. Now it is their own initiative to exclude and distance themselves from the *Ūr*, removing all links with the *Ūr*, in order to assert their positive identity.

Conflict as Ritual

In the series of conflicts that the Paraiyars had with the Vanniyars one can see that conflict has been like a ritual in the sense that it has been repeatedly created and it resulted in a pattern by which the whole politics of the Paraiyars with the Vanniyars is conducted. In addition, it developed into a medium that communicated their intentions. All this leads to the construction, deconstruction and reconstruction of identity of the Paraiyars, which Tambiah (1996: 223) calls 'the structuring role of collective agonistic violence'.

We can see this not only from the number of conflicts they have had since the 1930s but also from the way they have handled them. In more than thirty conflicts, minor and major, a similar pattern has been followed. First, although there have been minor conflicts throughout the year, most major conflicts have taken place only during the annual Pongal festivals. Secondly, in every conflict the focus has been on the symbols of their low identity. Thirdly, in all the conflicts the Paraiyars have felt a sense of a breakaway from their identity as Dalits. They experienced a feeling of equality with the Vanniyars in that they have been able to challenge them as equals, and have been treated as equals. Fourthly, after every conflict they experienced a change in their life in terms of rearranging their social activities and their position in the village. This pattern has been followed uniformly in all the conflicts.

All the four points indicate the nature of a ritual that has been constant. The Pongal festival has been the time for the conflict/ritual to be performed and the symbols of identity are the themes of the conflict. All these together have changed their life as Paraiyars in the village. The conflicts have provided a break-away from their identity as Dalits and put them on a status of equality with the Vanniyars, however temporary this has been.

During the conflicts, they hear a voice within to challenge the Vanniyars, beat them up and call them names. Turner (2002: 359, 360) describes this process in two terms: liminality and comunitas. In the liminal phase one experiences a break or 'detachment' or separation from an earlier fixed point in the social structure, from a set of cultural conditions (a 'state'), or from both and in the communitas phase, one has the experience being in a community that is 'unstructured or rudimentarily structured'. In many ways, such an experience has been attractive and so addictive to the Paraiyars that they wanted to repeat it often. Such a ritualising act, in which the Paraiyars deny what they are and accept what they intend to become, almost gives them the identity they want to have, and which they try to form later by reversing the symbols of pollution into symbols of a new identity.

This ritualisation of conflicts helps invent a tradition, in the Hobsbawmian sense, in opposition to the traditions of the village. Hobsbawm (1988: 1) views tradition as an invented and constructed set of practices that inculcate "certain values and norms of behaviour by repetition". Applied to the context of the Paraiyars, they form a tradition in and through ritualising conflicts that can give them a new identity. What is crucial in this process is that conflict at the Pongal festival, which is carried out repeatedly. In the words of Hobsbawm (1988: 3) it becomes gradually a "habit, automatic procedure or even reflex action" and after some time it gradually acquires the status of a social practice. It is not entirely an original act of the Paraiyars, but they have learnt it from, or at least have been inspired by, the ways in which the higher castes invented it at village festivals which, they think, reinforced their low identity in and through their performing of polluting roles.

Festival as Theatre of Conflict

In any conflict, performance is the important element that makes it successful. In the studies of conflicts (Schmidt and Schöder 2001; Varshney 2002; Coser 1956, 1958; Tambiah 1996;

Saberwal 1996) it is noted that without the performative quality, it would be hard to achieve anything. For Schmidt and Schöder (2001: 5, 6), without audience and performance conflict is 'socially meaningless'; it is effective because of its 'staging power and legitimacy'. In addition, in a conflict situation the conflicting parties use narratives and inscriptions (ibid 2001: 10). By narratives they maintain the memory of previous conflicts and in doing so they motivate their communities. Along with the narratives, the parties use images and objects that indicate the intended conflict and provoke the opposite party.

In Pappanallur, the annual Pongal festival remains as a theatre for the ritual of conflict to be performed. It is a space in which the Paraiyars enact their proposed new identity, negating the old low identity as Dalits. As seen earlier, no major conflict has happened outside the festival time. The Pongal festival in the village is the time when the whole village people with their relatives from the nearby villages get together to witness the performances of different people in the village. Unlike time of the year, at the festival each villager realises his or her position and performs accordingly. This helps strengthen and reinforce one's identity and it is internalised constantly. The Paraiyars are especially shown their lowly place by their activities of drumming, cleaning the *Ūr* area, and staying away from the sacred spaces. In other words, at the time of festivals the Paraiyars are asked by the *Ūr* castes to 'perform' their low identity. What were, during the ordinary time of the year, normal functions and occupations become a performance in public. In return, this performance reinforces the idea that the *Ūr* people entertain about the Paraiyars. Dirks (1994: 487)explains this in a similar context of a festival in central Tamil Nadu, where the festival remains a symbolic site in which social relations are reinforced and upheld. It is a time when who dominates whom and who struggles with what are all performed and witnessed openly.

Using the dynamics of the festival, from the 1950s the Paraiyars have used the festive time for creating conflicts with a view to resisting the ways in which they had been portrayed and trying to demonstrate the new ways in which they intend to form themselves. As seen earlier, the narratives the Paraiyars use before the Pongal festival are important for both motivating them and provoking the Vanniyars. Recalling the previous conflicts and what they had achieved from them inspires the Paraiyars to look for a similar productive conflict, whereas for the Vanniyars, it is a provocation to resist them. This actually aggravates and sharpens the conflict benefiting the Paraiyars more than the Vanniyars. In addition, the inscriptive images that the Paraiyars exhibit at the festival every year make the audience recall the previous conflicts, and heighten and intensify the situation. The performative quality of the conflicts opens up new possibilities of existence for them and they need to repeat it constantly in order to counter their low identity that used to be ritualised in the festival.

In addition, the festival is a theatre in the sense that apart from the festival times the groups in Pappanallur village interact with each other amicably. Only on the festival day, do the Paraiyars treat the Vanniyars as an enemy at war. It is like performing a role in a play, and once the play is over the person returns to his normal self. This is what is meant when Michael, one of the drummers, says, "What we are able to do in the festival cannot be done at other times". The DPI party members say "there is no use of fighting with them (the Vanniyars) on other days, because nobody will care about it. When we challenge them on the Pongal day it becomes a big event and the entire village witnesses it. It is a very good opportunity for us to assert ourselves". The festival gives them the licence to fight.

But this does not mean that there is no linkage between how the Paraiyars behave at the festival and the life they lead afterwards. Every conflict brings in changes in the lives of the Paraiyars and in the whole village. The festival can be seen as a drama in which they reconstruct themselves both individually and collectively; it provides a medium through which new values and structures of the new world they want to build are addressed and manipulated. It effects changes in the collective behaviour of the Paraiyars.

Conflict as Paraiyars' Culture

Both in my conversations with the Paraiyars of Pappanallur and with others in some ways related to the village, I realised that for many of them conflict has become synonymous with the Paraiyars. From the very first day of my fieldwork to the time of my writing this book and leafing through the field data, one of the key themes that repeatedly come to the fore is conflict. As seen earlier, in daily discourse the Paraiyars see themselves as a community opposed to the higher castes in the village and their identity can be defined only in opposition to the higher castes and other communities in the caste system. They want us to identify them not as a peace-loving people but as those who always desire conflict with the higher castes of the village: a rebelling community. It seems almost that they do not exist without their sense of enmity with the higher castes. This state of conflict defines their persons and community. To this end, they need to be in conflict ever with the higher castes, by which they contest the ways, others have see them and through which they can now construct ways in which they want to be seen. Raj Gowthman (1993) calls it 'protest-culture' (*kaḷahappanpāṭu*), culture here meaning a way of seeing oneself, because the Dalits need to throw away the identity given to them through their traditional services to the higher castes and create their own identity. This they think can only be possible through conflicts.

Violent action is the way by which they participate in the village effectively. Because the Paraiyars feel that there is no point in negotiating with the higher castes. As one of the Paraiyar women, a member of the Women's Association, said, it would be impossible for the Paraiyars to sit in dialogue with the higher castes to get what they want, "the Vanniyars will never sit equally with us to have a decent dialogue, the only way is to turn our way of being with them upside down". The Paraiyars want to be seen as people who create conflicts and are revolutionaries (*puraccikārarkal*). For them, the conflicts they have had and the violence that they have caused have not been meaningless; instead they have given them the strength to say 'no' to the higher castes for the first time in their lives, to refuse to perform all the services that defined them as untouchable, and to disassociate themselves from the institutions in which they were repeatedly held marginalised. The idea of conflict and its prospect in the mind of the Paraiyars is creative and constructive. As seen earlier, this helps to form a Paraiyar tradition that shows them to others as a people who open conflicts, and the Paraiyars are happy with this portrayal of themselves. As Thirumavalavan, the leader of DPI said, "for centuries we were slaves, but now we want to be seen as revolutionaries, we want to break all the traditions of the caste system, to rewrite the boundaries set by the system". In every public meeting of DPI the Dalits repeat the slogans: 'break all the social limits, refuse to obey, break the chains and retaliate'. The Paraiyars of Pappanallur follow this in the village and especially they wait for the arrival of festivals during which they can show themselves as revolutionaries, not any more as servants. Yesumarian, a lawyer and a Jesuit priest, who is the founder leader of an organisation for the Dalits, says that the Paraiyars need to be rebellious otherwise it will be hard to fight the centuries-old untouchability: "the higher castes and we are not equals to sit together for a dialogue, they are heavily supported by the system and unless we become violent we will not be able to fight them and our voice will not be heard". More sharply, Pushpa, a Paraiyar woman said, "really, violent action has been the way in which the higher castes treated us as untouchables, not the way in which we resist and challenge this treatment; you should view our resistance as a just act". Put simply, conflict is a method and ideology by which the Paraiyars try to alter the social arrangements in the village. More than the physical hurt, the conflicts the Paraiyars have created so far have been symbolic in providing a space for them to define their identity by forming their own institutions and re-forming their own symbols of their community identity.[32]

The higher castes see the situation differently. They see the Paraiyars as a people obsessed with creating disorder in the village, anarchists (*kaḷakakārargal*) against them, who are a peace-loving people in maintaining the status quo. They consider that all the conflicts during the Pongal festival every year have caused disunity in the village and have not been constructive in the development of the village. "The only sign that the village is no longer a village is that we have not been able to celebrate the Pongal festival for the last seven years properly, and all this is because of the Colony people" the Vanniyars say. But they definitely agree that the Paraiyars who were once obedient slaves are now becoming a defiant group in the village, transformed from the state of slaves (*atimai*) into a state of a ruling group (*āndān*); ruling in the sense that they have become assertive.

From the discussion above one would get a triumphalistic picture of the Paraiyars who have overcome the discrimination they have been experiencing for centuries. In fact, it is not the total picture of Pappanallur village. There were voices I did hear during my fieldwork, some of the Paraiyars felt that they should not have severed their links with the *Ūr* and their coming out of the avenues of their interaction with the higher castes had diminished greatly their influence and power among the *Ūr* castes who actually are the leading groups of the village. Kannan, who is the only schoolteacher from Pappanallur, is a main proponent of this approach. According to him, the Paraiyars should fight the higher castes by remaining within the system, not from outside it. Further, he reasons that if a village is to be village there will always be some inequalities. This does not mean that one should abandon one's traditions. Echoing this there are some Paraiyar families, more than ten families, who want to return as bonded labourers (*panaiyāl*) to their former landlords. They think this would be a peaceful life for them. Apart from these people, there are some individual Paraiyars who still interact with the Vanniyars secretly, and serve them as they used to before the conflicts, and do not adhere to the decisions so far made in the Colony, not openly however. These divergent attitudes and the apparent ambivalence among the Paraiyars should not be seen as a failure in their project of identity formation, but it should be viewed as natural in the process by which they attempt to find a way out of caste discrimination. Moreover, as Parish (1996: xvi) said, we always encounter 'polyvocal discourse', in a group some accept a point of view and some others reject it; some want to be part of the social order and some others seek to destroy it. It will be naivety to expect everybody in a group to take a single point of view. In Pappanallur, the divergent approaches among the Paraiyars constitute indeed a minority voice compared to the majority Paraiyars who feel happy that by conflicts they have come out of the situations in which they were treated with contempt and where they were repeatedly made to internalise their untouchable identity. This dominant group is not bothered with those who are against their approach; they are more concerned about how they can assert and sustain the independence they have achieved after the conflicts.

Notes

1. The invention of the term *Dravidian* and popularisation of it was largely the work of the Rev Caldwell (1819-91) which was assimilated by Tamil thinkers, both low caste and Dalit leaders. See Irshick (1969); Jaffrelot (2003).
2. In addition to my research and reading of newspapers and magazines, I used also the compilation of one hundred and nineteen cases by Thangaraj (1998). I have tried to look for cases of conflicts in three ways: (1) I gathered the cases both from villages and towns all over the state; (2) I focused only on the conflicts of the Pallars versus the Thevars in the south and the Paraiyars versus the Vanniyars in the north; (3) still further narrowing down my focus, I concentrated on the cases in which the conflicts centred around symbols such as land, the drum and beef-eating. More importantly, I did not read and use the information in the newspapers and magazines literally, rather I read them interpretively. Mostly the cases reported in newspapers had their headings as 'caste conflicts' lumping all the conflicts, both inter-high caste conflicts and the conflicts between the high caste versus the Dalits,

as caste conflicts. Moreover, the newspapers did not focus on the symbols involved in the conflicts although symbols have been the focus of the conflicts. Apart from this, most of the newspapers had some problems of bias, which I tried as much as possible to identify and remain conscious of it when sifting through information for conclusions. The criteria for my interpretation: (1) if a newspaper or a magazine was generally believed to be biased towards the higher castes or the Dalits, I tried to identify the information that demonstrated the bias and tried to exclude them from my analysis; (2) I tried as much as possible to delve deep into the question of what caused the conflicts, whether it was an economic issue or cultural reasons such as challenging pollution and assertion of identity with an emphasis on symbols. The reports of one newspaper were checked against another newspaper's reports.

3. Although both parties in their public statements say that they work for the entire Dalit communities, they have their clearly marked out territories of involvement. The Pallar party gets seldom involved in the issues of the Paraiyars who are a dominant Dalit group in the north and the Paraiyar party very rarely gets involved in the issues of the Pallars in the south. Many consider this as a case of disunity among the Dalits. But Thirumavalavan, the leader of Liberation Panthers does not see this as disunity, instead he thinks such a demarcation gives a focus for their efforts. Further, he said that for the Dalits who were 19 per cent of the total population they need more leaders and divisions in order to counter the challenge of the high caste power.
4. In Tamil, *Cheripuyal orunāl varampu mīrum, varalāru mārum.*
5. The struggle was to reclaim the lands that were allotted to the Dalits (*Panchamas)* by the British government from the higher castes in the district. In detail we will discuss the land struggle and its symbolic content for identity construction in Chapter 5.
6. I took part in this land struggle in which I had seen the Paraiyar women on the day of the incident who were very vocal against the higher castes who appropriated the Dalits' land.
7. I draw most of my data from my interviews with the directors and field assistants of ASSEFA in the Uthiramerur area with the help of its office in Manithottam village, about eight kilometres from Pappanallur. My thanks are due to the generosity of the officers who allowed me to have access to the documents on their work in and around the area of my present study.
8. *Sarvodaya* meant literally 'prosperity (*udaya*) everywhere' but it actually meant 'welfare for all'. It was believed to be a synthesis and an

extension of Gandhian thought. It had grassroot *mandals* (societies) all over India functioning as foci for construction workers.

9. "Land for Vinoba belonged to none but God, and was given for, and was to be cultivated for, man's enjoyment, and that no one would stop him from putting this into practice" see the ASEFA Silver Jubilee Souvenir magazine, p 13.
10. Almost 4.2 million acres of land were received as Bhoodan land or 1,60,000 villages were declared as Bhoodan villages in 1971 (at this time the Bhoodan transformed to the *Gramdan*). But only about thirty percent of the land was arable land. This was one of the reasons why the movement did not sustain the pace it set in the 1960s. In addition, most of the landless Dalits lacked the capital to invest in land reclamation and irrigation.
11. See Memorandum of CRDS p.1.
12. *kālanēruppai karukkondirukkum peninamē; un viral nuni asaivil kodumaigal norungum; un vīrathalaimayil viduthalia nērungum.*
13. According to the archdiocesan directory of Madras-Mylapore for the year 2000 the diocese runs 12 English medium schools; 4 higher secondary schools; 8 high schools; 17 middle schools; 24 middle schools. In addition, there are 29 vocational training institutes for tailoring, typewriting and computer skills (Cf. Directory 2000, Archdiocese of Madras-Mylapore). Apart from these the state government runs 784 elementary schools, 128 Middle schools, 49 high schools, 56 higher secondary schools, in which 223257 Dalit students are studying. The Adi Dravida Welfare Board manages the schools, for which there is a state minister. Attached to these schools, throughout the state, there are 1075 hostels in which Dalit students are given free board and lodging. The state government in its annual budget allocates Rs. 12 million (120 crores) for these schools, of which very little is spent on the schools, instead the money is alleged to have been swindled by politicians. See *Junior Vikatan*, (27 Feb 2001, pp.24-5).
14. According to the Tamil Nadu education system, until the fifth standard (year 1-5) is elementary school education; until middle school; and if the school goes up to the tenth standard (year 10) it is a high school; beyond that it is plus two or higher secondary, after which the pupils go on to college/university education.
15. The Madurai province Jesuits run educational institutions, social training institutes and mission stations all over Tamil Nadu. There are 56 Jesuit centres starting from Chennai to Tuticorin, at the southern tip of the state (Cf. *Catalogus Provinciae Maduraiensis Societatis Iesu*,

2002). The Jesuits' involvement began in 1981 when they started their mission called 'The Chengai Mission'. The late Jesuit Archbishop of Madras-Mylapore diocese entrusted four Paraiyar dominated parishes to them: Ongur, Malligapuram, and Pappanallur. There are now fifteen Jesuits working in the mission, concentrating mainly on the education of Paraiyar children.

16. A very limited number of non-Dalit children are admitted in the school for two reasons: one is that the non-Dalit children have to be from very poor families; the second is that the non-Dalit children should promise to follow the rules and regulations of a school meant for the Dalits.
17. Since space precludes a detailed discussion of all the three leaders, I restrict the discussion to Irattaimalai Srinivasan who is a native of the area of the present study. However, I will use their ideas later whenever it is helpful. There is a massive two-volume work on Ayothidas Pandithar (G. Aloysius, 1999), which I will use for my analysis later.
18. The literacy rate in the state of Tamil Nadu, according to 1991 Census, was 62.7 per cent (male: 73.7%; female 51.3%) occupying fourth position among states of India, where all-India literacy rate is 52.2 per cent. For details of data on literacy and in other areas in Tamil Nadu see *South India: Human Development Report 2001*, pp. 212-341; *Tamil Nadu Social Development Report 2000*, pp. 41-108 and for data on India see *India: Human Development Report 1999*, pp. 98-131.
19. When Ambedkar decided to convert from Hinduism to Buddhism he sent a telegram saying that the Dalits had never been Hindus and therefore they did not have to convert to Buddhism (Revathi 1997: 57).
20. I intend to use the findings of the interview with the school pupils more fully in my discussion of the symbolic construction of identity in Chapter 5.
21. *Nān uru Paraiyaraga piranthatharkkāha perumaipaduhiren. Enendrāl, Paraiyar endra sollukkum nān pirnatha mannukkum vīram undu. Nān pirappāl thāḻnthavan alla. Anīthiyāna samūhathāl thāḻthapatten. Anīthiyāna sithānthathāl kalvi marukkappaten. Adimaichinthanaiyāl amukkappaten. Intha varalātrai mātri eḻutha Ambedkar, Irattaimalai Seenivasan vaḻiyil kalvi karpen. Kalvi ondre nān iḻantha mānbai mīttedukka mudiyum. Karpathu en kadamai, karpathu en urimai, karpathu en kodai. Uruthi, uruthi, nān uyarvathu uruthi, uruthi, uruthi, nān vetri peruvathu uruthi.*
22. *māttukari thinbathu kēvalam alla, ithu namathu parambarai unavu, namanthu panbāttai kurikkirathu, māttukari thinbōm mānathōdu vāḻvōm*

23. In Tamil Nadu, it is called *Viduthalai Siruthaikal* (liberation panthers) but it is used mostly in Tamil language press, the term DPI is used in English language press.
24. It is called the Dalit Panthers after the American Black Panthers (Shetty, 1987; Murugkar, 1991).
25. There are now 44 Dalit MLAs in the Tamil Nadu State Assembly and 100 MPs in the Parliament elected from the reserved constituencies.
26. In Tamil: *adanga maru, athu mīru; thimiri eḷu, thiruppi adi; nāngal ādugal alla, sīrippāyum Siruthaigal; thalai nimira cheri thiralum, andru thalaikīlai nādu puralum; Thikketum padar, thīyai paravu; Cherippuyal oru nāl varambu mīrum, varalāru mārum, oppāri ōlanagal ūrilum kētkum*
27. The election violence was studied by independent non-governmental organisations to find out the root causes for the violence. The reports stated that both the Vanniyars and the Paraiyars, fully supported by the PMK party and the DPI party, were equally involved in the violence. See Justice V.R. Krishna Iyer, *Independent Initiative Report about Elections, Attacks on Dalits, Denial of Voting Right, Bogus voting.* September 1999; and also Sonamandan (1999).
28. See Appendix II for conflicts other than the ones described in this chapter.
29. Kumar (1965: 42ff, 1994: 87ff) provides sufficient evidence for the cases of slave labourers in South Arcot districts in the latter part of eighteenth century. The *Mirasidars* (land lords) who had propriety rights to buy, sell and pledge the Paraiyars.
30. The term *'dargos'* or '*darkhast*' means petition in Urdu. It is a system established by the British that a person who has used a piece of waste land for more than five years could lay claim to it (Moffatt 1979: xii).
31. The representatives of the *Vagaiyarās* of the *Ūr* also form the *Ūr* council. But all of them were from the Reddiyars and the Vanniyars. Other castes of the *Ūr* are not included in the council. Beyond the two *Vagaiyarā* councils in the village – the *Ūr* council and the Paraiyar *Vagaiyarā* council – there is the village panchayat board, the lowest unit of the state administration, in which the members are elected thorough elections conducted by the state government as we have seen in the second chapter when we discussed politics of Pappanallur village.
32. See Eckert (2003) who discusses the Shiv Sena that uses violence as a method and ideology to construct identity.

5

Changing the Meaning of and Positive Identification with Symbols: Drumming as Art Form

This chapter explains the process by which the Paraiyars of Pappanallur attempt to transform the symbols – drumming, beef-eating, land – that were used to define their low and polluted identity into symbols of their new and positive identity. I will argue that they do this while they have rejected and distanced themselves from most of the avenues of interaction with the *Ūr* and have formed their own institutions after the conflicts. More sharply, this chapter is concerned with the question of what the Paraiyars do in terms of identity formation after their conflicts with the *Ūr*.

Before entering into the discussion proper let me make two observations that I think will orient the discussion. First, I will briefly go over the question about what the Paraiyars think of how they were defined in the past by their traditional services. Secondly, I will explain how the symbol of the '*parai*' remains as the foundational symbol, which contains, signifies, and leads to the other symbols, beef-eating, and land that defined the Paraiyars as low and polluted people and are taken up by them to redefine themselves.

As seen earlier, until 1997, the Paraiyars say, that they were a community both excluded from and dependent on the *Ūr*. This status they acquired apparently by their five distinctive services (*tholil*) – drumming, cattle scavenging, announcing deaths (*vāriyan*), cremating dead bodies (*thōti*), and guarding the village (*kambukūti*) – that they did for the *Ūr* higher castes. These services were associated in many ways, directly or indirectly, strongly or weakly, with the death of humans and of animals, and death-substances that caused pollution (*thīttu*). By performing these services the Paraiyars had functioned for the *Ūr* as intermediaries between higher beings, both human and divine, and demons (*pey-pisāsu*) that are mostly malevolent spirits of the dead. They removed pollution by scavenging dead cows, cremating the dead and guarding the village from evil spirits by drumming, and functioning as the village watchman (*kambukūṭṭi*). Because of this they were excluded from the *Ūr* and forced to live on the periphery of the village (Colony), near the cremation ground (*suṭukādu*). The Vanniyars and the other *Ūr* higher castes of Pappanallur defined their cultural identity as polluted and therefore as a group to be excluded from the *Ūr*. As Moffatt (1979: 111) rightly observed, in 'cultural semantics', the low status of the Paraiyars is defined by the services they carried out for the *Ūr* higher castes. In that way, to be a Paraiyar is to be necessarily associated with pollution, to be a polluted person is to be untouchable, and personally a Paraiyar is physically untouchable, economically dependent, politically powerless, and socially unable to relate with others: Dalits, cast out. However, though excluded from the *Ūr*, they formed a necessary and important part of the village in the sense that without them the purity and safety of the *Ūr* higher castes and the village would be endangered by pollution and evil spirits. In that way, the Paraiyars had the ambivalent status in the village of being excluded and yet included. As Michael, one of the drummers, said, they had been used like curry leaves (*kariveēipillai*) used to create an aroma in food but thrown away while eating; the person of the Paraiyar was an object to be used and when not in use to be relegated to the background. It was a case of objectification or commodification of persons. To extend it still further, being a

Paraiyar in the social framework of Pappanallur village was to be a person of 'thrown-away-ness' (Raja 2002: 127). Others defined them, from outside in, as polluted and polluting and their personhood was defined in terms of objecthood (Parish 1996: 7).

The objectification of the Paraiyar subjectivity or personhood was symbolised in concrete social institutions, events and objects, which helped the Vanniyars and the *Ūr* higher castes reinforce the low status in the minds of the Paraiyars themselves. Particularly the ritual occasions of festivals and funerals dramatised the objectified identity of the Paraiyars, in terms of the performance of their roles as pollution removers and polluters. In that sense, the symbolisation of untouchability had been a powerful way by which the definition of the Paraiyars' identity as low and polluted was kept alive for a long time, and helped the higher castes enjoy hegemony over them, because the symbolisation had ingredients of divine power assisted by tradition and history.

In this chapter, we will see that they reject this hegemony by rejecting the type of symbolisation of their identity by the higher castes. They attempt to define 'from inside out', and reject the definition 'from outside in': a transformative process from objecthood to personhood (Parish 1996). By doing so, they regain hegemony, not over the higher castes but over themselves in the terms in which they want to define themselves, and how they want to be seen by others. In other words, they are recovering their agency over self and society.

This they do by remembering the past in which they had the status of being an object and relive this mentally and repeatedly, while making efforts to change the very symbols of pollution into symbols of positive identity and culture. Put simply, they think that they need to know how they were made to be in order to become what they want to be. To that end they need to know their past and the events and stories about them are crucial for every effort they make to imagine their new life. Therefore, they constantly recreate and relive the past, in which they were given a polluted identity, and this gives them the energy and wisdom to imagine their new life. In addition to the memory of their past, what has sharpened their endeavour towards identity formation is the memory of their experience in the conflicts and the advantages gained from it; they are constructing their history through the dynamics of the conflicts they have had with the higher castes. In their efforts to re-form the symbols – the drum, beef-eating, land – they constantly relive their experience in the conflicts, because this remembering refuels and sharpens their initiatives to change their status and greatly helps the group unite for the same purpose. In doing this, the Paraiyars demonstrate that in the past, 'they' (the higher castes) defined 'us' and forced us to live according to that definition, but now 'we' define 'us' and imagine anew our culture and history.

The second observation is that the drum has been the foundational symbol, which contains all the other symbols considered in this study; it was the central symbol of the identity given to the Paraiyars by the *Ūr* higher castes. The symbol of the drum at once envelops and discloses the other symbols – beef-eating and land – and, more importantly, it 'summarises' and 'elaborates', following Ortner (2002), the life and character of the Paraiyars. Understanding the symbol of the drum is equal to understanding the thought and action of the Paraiyars. The very name, 'paraiyars', they got from the Tamil word for a drum (*parai*). The material the drum was made of, cowhide that indicated death, and the drumming, allowed only on inauspicious occasions, referred immediately to pollution and demons, thus defining their persons as polluted. This was the 'focal and fecund' symbol (Clarke 1998: 111) that was used repeatedly to reinforce the identity of the Paraiyars. The story of the drum will be a privileged vantage point from which one can grasp the character of the Paraiyars' culture and identity.

The *parai* is the antidote by which the Paraiyars chased away the demons and evil spirits of the people who died an unnatural death from the village, and which are attracted during ritual times of festivals and funerals, for they always have a thirst for bloody sacrifices. The sound of the drum served to frighten away the demons and spirits. Closely associated with this are the other services of cattle scavenging, cremating dead bodies, announcing deaths, and guarding the village. By removing the dead cow, which is holy in the Hindu ethos, the Paraiyars removed the pollution from the house where the cow died. Not only that, they also ate the meat of the dead cow, which the *Ūr* higher castes treat as most polluting behaviour, equal to eating pollution. Thus, for the *Ūr* higher castes, the Paraiyars became physically polluted beings. Similarly, the service of cremating the dead implicated not only the *Thotti* Paraiyar, but also all the Paraiyars in the Colony with death pollution. In the service of being the cremation attendant, the digging of the grave and the burning of the corpse, and the acceptance of the severely polluted clothes of the dead and the cooked food, the Paraiyars become more explicitly than in the other services associated with demons and evil spirits. The announcing of death (*vāriyan*), was also a polluting activity since the Paraiyar who took the news of death to the relatives of the deceased person, was considered to be polluted, even if not as intensely as in the case of the other services just mentioned. To that extent, the drumming, which is also associated with cremation and beef-eating, is performed in the realm of religion, much more expressively during festivals. The fifth service to the *Ūr* higher castes, the guarding of the village, is weakly associated with evil spirits. But it was strongly associated with land in the sense that the Paraiyar watchman, *kambukūṭṭi*, guarded the village and paddy fields at night from demons, evil spirits and thieves. He was the one who organised the Paraiyar labour force to work on the land of the Vanniyars and Reddiyars and other higher castes. In Mariamman festival, the watchman Paraiyar has in fact a very significant and a vital role in the conduct of the rituals. To this extent, the Paraiyars had ritual power in the village in the sense that without the watchman Paraiyar the festival will not be conducted, and if done without him, the whole festival will be considered incomplete. This is what the *Ūr* higher castes feel. Since 1997 the Paraiyars have abandoned their services to the *Ūr*.

The five *Ūr* services made them a people who removed pollution and laboured in the fields and therefore they were personally polluted and to be segregated to the periphery of the village. This, the Vanniyars and other higher castes reinforced by calling the Paraiyars by the names of the services and insulted and denigrated them: "drum-beating dogs", "beef-eating Paraiyars", "how can you be arrogant when you have no piece of land".[1] The *Ūr* services and their associated actions served as symbols to exclude the Paraiyars from the *Ūr* to the margins of the village (*kirāmam*). The Vanniyars made them or continued to keep them as landless labourers, as Arockiasamy, one of the *Vagaiyarā* leaders, said, "they used the sweat of our bodies for cultivation and our drum-playing talent for pollution removal rituals, but we were made to live in poverty". Yesumarian, a Jesuit lawyer, also of Paraiyar origin, says, "our people [Paraiyars] need to learn two histories, one is our history of oppression by the higher castes, second is the history of our leaders who fought this oppression, and every boy and girl of the Dalits should know the two histories if we ever want to redefine and assert our identity".

Therefore, the memory of their past when they were considered polluted, the impact of their conflicts with the *Ūr* and the key and foundational symbol of the drum are the factors needed to understand the discussion of the three symbols: the drum, beef-eating and land. Here, in this chapter, we will take up drumming, which will be followed by beef-eating and land in the next two chapters.

The Drum (Parai): From Servitude to Paraiyar Art Form

The drum, which was a symbol of pollution, the death-drum (*sāpparai*), is being transformed into a symbol of Paraiyar art and a political weapon, the war-drum (*pōrpparai*). More than any of the other four services, it was drumming that vividly defined the Paraiyars' low status and cultural identity. More sharply, drumming generated and communicated pollution so that the *Ūr* should be guarded pure and safe, and had been typical of the Paraiyars as individuals and as a community; around this their whole life was centred, at least, in the eyes of the higher castes of the village. Though the drum and act of the drumming had symbolised the core of Paraiyar subjectivity, and having been demonised as a polluting activity, it was imperative to be reinterpreted and given a positive meaning, thereby forming a new Paraiyar identity.

Therefore, in this section, I have four aims. First, I will describe how the drum is made, and look into the materiality of the drum. This will explain why the higher castes in the village treat the drum as a polluting object from its origin. Secondly, I will focus on two festivals – the Mariamman and Pongal – and funerals in which drumming has an important role. Since we have given in Chapter 2 a complete description of festivals and funerals in Pappanallur, here I will concentrate on the areas where drumming is involved and analyse the drummers' role in order to demonstrate how this service had become a symbol of pollution. Thirdly, I will discuss the ways in which the Paraiyars are changing the drum from being a symbol of pollution to being an art form.

In my discussion of this activity of the Paraiyars, I will constantly refer to cases and works beyond the village in Tamil Nadu and elsewhere where similar efforts are going on, in order to give wider validity to my argument and to argue that what is happening in Pappanallur is not an isolated case.

Drumming Service as Pollution

A *Parai* is large, circular, and one-sided; drum, the head is made of calfskin tightly strung on a circular wooden or metal frame. To have a better grip leather thongs are attached to the edges of the frame (Moffatt 1979: 198; Sathianthan 1998: 110). The process of making a drum is highly strenuous and time consuming; it takes more than two weeks. In addition, the calfskin gives off a revulsive stink on the second day of production which makes onlookers stand at a distance while the drum maker gets on with his job with the ease and concentration of a sculptor.

Arockiadoss, the drum maker, told me, while I was observing his work, that the sound of the drum in its final form should be like the roar of an angry lion. The drum as seen in

Pappanallur usually has a rope attached so that it can be tied around the waist or around the neck to allow the drummer to play with both hands. One hand holds a stick and the other open palm accompanies the stick's beat or rhythm.

The drum is not immediately used for occasions after it was made. It has first to be transformed into a ritual instrument through a ceremony, which was in earlier times elaborate with blood sacrifices and offerings for the gods (*pataiyal*). The ceremony is meant to make the drum and the playing it powerful enough to dispel evil spirits (*pēy*). Nowadays, they take the drum and place it facing in the direction of the god, *Sanīswaran* (*sanimūlai*) and offer a prayer that completes the ceremony. Finally, the drum is used for drumming on three occasions in the village: the Marriamman festival, which is called pouring porridge for the goddess (*kūḻūṭutal*); the Pongal festival; and at the funerals of the higher castes.

For the *Ūr* higher castes, pollution originates in the production of drums, which involves the drum-maker in handling the hide of a dead cow, which is treated as a holy animal when alive. Then this is carried on when the hide is touched with bare hands while drumming. In addition, this is why, as Pakkiri Gounder told me, the *parai* is meant to be played on inauspicious occasions. He went on to argue that if the Paraiyars had used any other animal's skin, they would not have been treated that way; in the case of the drums – *Uṭkkai* and *pambai* – which are made of goat skin, used by the Ambattan priests, these are not treated as polluted; instead they are respected by the *Ūr* higher castes. This the Paraiyars reject, as we shall see, saying that it is not their handling of the cow hide that made them polluted but that it was the intention of the Brahmins earlier, and is now that of the Vanniyars, to reduce the beautiful Paraiyar art to an object of pollution. Before we explain how they substantiate this argument, we will consider the drummers: who are they, which *Vagaiyarā* do they belong to, and how do they organise themselves?

Organising the Drummers

In Pappanallur, the drum band consists of five drummers, all of whom are male, from four *Vagaiyarās* – Michael of Theradi *Vagaiyarā*, Ambrose, Selvaraj and Uthariam of Thalaiyari, Meyyappan of Thotti. The *Thalaiyari Vagaiyarā* paraiyars are the ones who do most of the five traditional *tholil*. Among the cousins (*pangalies*, literally meaning sharer, but what is meant here are the families who share the common patrilineal descent of the Thalaiyari *Vagaiyarā*) they share the service (*tholil*). Every year one cousin holds two services – drumming and guarding the village. The main traditional service of the Theradi *Vagaiyarā* to the *Ūr* has been drumming and they have very talented drummers. From this *Vagaiyarā*, every year one person chosen from the cousins is sent to represent it in the drumming. From the Thotti *Vagaiyarā*, one represents them as a drummer, though they are mainly in charge of announcing death, cremation of the dead and scavenging dead cows, called *Vettiyan* work.

While they play, four of them play *parai* and the fifth plays on a bowl-shaped drum (*satti*) held horizontally and beaten with two sticks, whereas the *parai* is held vertically. The drummers organise themselves in sharing different services depending upon the occasion. In funerals, the drummer from the Theradi *Vagaiyarā*, who is in fact the leader of the five drummers, does not do any other work except drumming; instead, the Thalaiyari and Thotti drummers do the other services also. At the Mariamman festival, the Thotti drummer, Meyyappan, has organised the drumming from the 1950s until 1996, since he played the important role as the main ritual assistant. In the Pongal festival, the Theradi *Vagaiyarā* drummer takes the lead, as this has been the tradition in the village. The drummer who leads the drumming takes a double share of the money given in payment, mostly a mere pittance considering the time they spend drumming, and of the food given to them by the *Ūr* leader's family, if it is a festival, and by the family of the deceased, if it is a funeral. More importantly, the lead drummer begins the drumming and when the drumbeat has to change from one beat (*thālam*), to another, he gives the sign. He takes pride in this. There are twelve beats: four godly beats (*sāmi thālams*) at funerals, played during festivals, marriages, and life-cycle rituals, and eight death beats (*sāvu thālams*). Nevertheless, mostly, as Michael said, they do not always adhere strictly to the beats. Apart from this, very few can tell the difference. Everyone in the village generally thinks that *parai* drumming means the death drum (*sāpparai*), so the nuances mean very little to them. In addition, whether the drum is played in festivals or funerals, it is treated as inauspicious by everybody in the village, as associated with death and evil spirits. Even while drumming in festivals like the Marriamman festival and the Pongal festival the drummers were not allowed near the temple or the higher castes' area; they were supposed to stand drumming far away from holy places and sites of auspicious rituals. The only occasion when they were allowed at close quarters were funerals. Even then, they were not supposed to enter the house where the funeral took place. Put simply, by playing the drum, the Paraiyars had become personally polluted and lost the nature and character of human beings; in addition, the whole community in the Colony had acquired the pollution, and have become polluted persons. This will become clear when we look at the role of drumming and the drummers in festivals and later in funerals.

Drumming in Festivals

In Pappanallur, drumming in festivals is meant to guard against evil spirits that are believed to be capable of polluting the rituals. The beat the drummers use, the place where they stand, the way they are treated are more than enough for any one to realise that drumming is mainly for the removal of pollution. In Chapter 2, in the description of the festivals where I highlighted the drummers' role, I demonstrated clearly that though the drumming was considered to be a necessary and indispensable part of the rituals, the drumming and the drummers were treated with contempt.

Although we have seen in Chapter 2 the festivals and the role of the drummers in them, we need to recall the ways in which the drummers were involved in the removal of pollution by evil spirits. In the Mariamman festival, the drumming is fundamentally performed before the ritual offering to the goddess, and while the image of the goddess is taken in procession, the drummers go ahead chasing away the demons that are believed to be in the way. Later, all through the night, during which the *karakam* is kept in the Vannan's house, the drummers are forced to drum continuously. If they failed to do so they were beaten up. This is even confirmed by the Vanniyars who justified their action, saying that it was the drummers' job to protect the goddess from demons, or else an epidemic of smallpox would erupt in the whole village. Apart from these ritual participation, in terms of payments each drummer received, until 1996, only 60 rupees for the three days. This was very little considering the amount of work they did. Moreover, at the same time the more respectable Ambattan drummer was paid 150 rupees. In addition, to get their food, the drummers had to go from house to house. This is often referred to as demeaning by the Paraiyars. One of the Paraiyars, Xavier, told me that, "after having drummed the whole day when we went to the high caste houses they would send us away without giving any food. I used to ask myself: how long can we go on with this *thoḷil* [service]?" If the drummers had to suspend the drumming in order to heat the drums so as to retain the tension required for the proper sound, the Vanniyars would scold them in vulgar words. More cruelly, many a time the Vanniyars broke up the drums. Even today they recall these events vividly. Although they had an important role in that they got the ritual respect of *kappu* tied to their wrist on the first day of the festival and of leading the procession, every time they felt that they were not being treated humanly and were simply an object or a machine that removes pollution. Even their roles in the festival are mainly, once again, to safeguard the Vanniyars and other higher castes from evil spirits. They complained that even the *kambukūṭṭi* Paraiyar who has a main role in the festival is asked not to come near the image of the goddess while she is being carried in the procession. All this made them realise that whatever they do, Paraiyars are always Paraiyars, and are meant to serve. They are never treated with the respect they feel they deserve.

In the Pongal festival, the drumming is mainly to chastise the demons or spirits that are believed to cause illnesses to the livestock, and further to threaten bulls, cows, water buffalos and goats so that they run away from the cow shed, while the village crowd looks on with amusement. If the drum frightened the demons in the Mariamman festival, it threatened the cattle in the Pongal festival. Squarely, the drum acquired in time an image of an object involved with pollution removal and with frightening animals. Drumming in funerals further confirms this point.

Drumming in Funerals

Much more forcefully, the Paraiyars are made to realise their polluting status and identity during drumming at the funerals of the higher castes. From the time a high caste person dies until the body is cremated the drummers have to go on playing the drum. The drumming at the funeral is done for two main reasons. The first is to 'bid and contain the spirit of the dead person' (Sathiananthan 1998: 117). It is believed that the dead person's spirit hovers over their house, and that sometimes it may get into living persons unless it is driven away by drumming. This leads the spirit with its polluted nature contaminated from dead calf's skin to *suṭukāṭu*, the cremation ground that is believed to be the place for the spirits of the dead. The second reason is to keep away other evil spirits who are aroused by death. Drumming prevents malevolent spirits from entering the village. This type of drumming is used in referring to the cultural identity of the Paraiyars of Pappanallur, as it is generally the case elsewhere in Tamil Nadu. It directly associates them with death in two ways: the death of the high caste person and the drumming on dead calf-skin with bare hands, and in addition, in the two ways they deal with evil spirits.

Finally, a conflict in 1996 helped the Paraiyars transform the drumming, that had served as the cardinal symbol of their polluted identity, into a symbol of Paraiyar art. They did this in a way similar to the way they had done away with other institutions in which they were treated as Dalits. Indeed, this helped to cut the last and final link with the *Ūr* castes. Although the previous conflicts after 1941 led them to abandon the Hindu religion, to form their own council, to abandon scavenging dead cows, to found their own school, that gradually distanced the Paraiyars from the *Ūr*. Surprisingly, they continued the *thoḷil*, the drumming at festivals and funerals, guarding the village, and cremating dead bodies. However, the conflict in 1996 during the Pongal festival finally put an end to all of them, ultimately cutting the Colony off completely form the *Ūr,* and intensifying the Paraiyars' attempt to form a new image of their identity. For this reason, the discussion of the conflict and its consequences is important for our understanding of the process of identity construction, which is the central concern of this study. Therefore, in the remainder of this chapter, I would like to explain how the drum is being transformed from pollution to art. First, I shall describe the conflict of 1996 and discuss the changes the conflict ushered in. Secondly, I will try to explain the ways, by which the Paraiyars in Pappanallur are demythologising the drum, reconstructing its history and transforming its sound into fine music In doing this they are popularising the drum as their unique art form and a means of gaining their liberation.

Drumming as Paraiyar Art Form

Abandoning the Drumming Service

After the final conflict in 1997 the Paraiyars abandoned the drumming service to the *Ūr*. With that all the five traditional services of the Paraiyars were discontinued since the drumming was related to other services. Although they decided to give up the drumming service for the higher castes, they did not want to lose or give up their drumming talent.

After the conflicts they gradually dissociated themselves from many institutions – the Hindu religion, the Village Council, and the school – through which they had interacted with the *Ūr*. They also distanced themselves more sharply by forming their own institutions. With drumming, however, they have chosen a different method: drumming has not been stopped and substituted by something else. It has been accepted and owned as their own but it has been transformed from being seen as a demeaning activity into a respectable artistic talent. They did not get to this stage easily. They had to overcome many obstacles.

After they had stopped the drumming service for the *Ūr*, for quite some time they had no idea of what to do with the drums, and the drummers felt that they had been left jobless. Although some see drumming as merely a profession that brings material benefits, the dominant strand of thought in the Colony is that they should look at drumming in a symbolic sense. Once it was used to symbolise their low and polluted identity, now it should be used in a similar symbolic sense to redefine their identity in a positive way. This idea they began to form from the time of their conflicts with the Vanniyars. One only has to listen to what the Paraiyars, especially the drummers, feel after they stopped their services to the *Ūr* to see how they view themselves: "every time we went to the *Ūr* for drumming we felt deep within us that we were like the bullocks used for ploughing and later tied in the cowshed; but after we had stopped the service, we began to feel like human beings [*manushan*], with human dignity [*manitha mānbu*]" said Michael, one of the drummers. This does not reflect the language of the ordinary Paraiyars but reflects clearly how the drummers have learnt through their interaction with the Dalit activists to use discourses according to the people who ask them questions. However, what the ordinary Paraiyars told me was "when we were performing the services for the *Ūr*, we were shameful persons [*kēvalamānavrkal*), now after we have stopped doing the services, we have gained some respect for ourselves (*maṭippum mariyāṭaiyum*)".

Meyyappan, the former cremation attendant, said: "we must get rid of the devilish job for good."[2] They are becoming conscious of their neglected self that was often obscured by the interests of the welfare of the village; whatever was their low status and polluted existence they felt forced both by the coercion of the higher castes and the so-called 'divine plan'. The individual self, suppressed by a strong sense of the collective self, has been opened up to make the Paraiyars realise their past. This has made them ask questions like: why should we alone lie at the bottom of the hierarchy? And why should we alone burn the dead? One of the Paraiyars, who works as a coconut-tapper, Devandran, told me, "when we scavenge dead cattle or cremate a dead body we function like a doctor who cures our illness, and we should be respected like medical doctors; if they do not respect us in this way, let them do these jobs themselves". Ambrose, one of the drummers, said, "for the Vanniyars the drumming profession was looked upon as a very cheap and demeaning activity (*kēvalam*) and they treated us as not even equal to insects (*pulupōchi*). Now, we have shown them who we are. If they respect our drumming talent we will drum, otherwise we know how to deal with it".

This consciousness has been sharpened further, and they have become articulate about the symbolic significance of the drum through their participation in different seminars organised by the Dalit movements such as DCLM and DPI and their participation in the Dalit cultural festivals (*Dalit Kaḷai Viḷa*) in many places in Tamil Nadu. Before we examine the efforts of the Paraiyars of Pappanallur we should discuss these outside influences.

Reconstructing the History of the Drum

The Paraiyar youth, particularly those who hold membership in the DPI party, argue that the drum was once historically used as a war instrument to celebrate a victory – *pōrpparai;* it was also used as ritual music in temples. It was, as Arulappan said, the higher castes, and particularly Brahmins, jealous of their talent and culture, who reduced drumming to its polluted status. To substantiate their claims they show many pamphlets – for example *thamukku* – from the Dalit Resource Centre (DRC) in Madurai and magazines-*Dalit Murasu* – published by Dalit intellectuals in Chennai. In addition, they played audio cassettes, released by different Dalit groups in Tamil Nadu to explain the positive elements of drumming. More importantly, these youths learn about all this when they participate in the Dalit Cultural Festivals (*Dalit Kalai Viḷa*) conducted in Thiruvannamalai in northern Tamil Nadu, at Thanjavur in central Tamil Nadu and in Madurai and Palayamkottai in the south. For the purpose of the present study, I want to take three areas in the reconstruction of the drum: the drum in the history of Tamil Nadu, the drum as art and music, and the drum as a political weapon popularised through cultural festivals.

Clarke (1998) and Valarmathi (1999) (both are Dalit scholars) discuss the question of how drumming, which was once a respectable art of the Paraiyars, was made into a polluting activity of the Paraiyars by the higher castes.[3] Clarke (1998) uses data collected in a village of northern Tamil Nadu, and his central argument is that the drum is the symbol of Paraiyar cultural identity and Paraiyars should own it as such. Arguing along these lines, he provides three arguments – the cultural and economic association; the historical association; the etymological association. The drum, he says, is closely linked to the Paraiyars' cultural and economic life. His informants tell him that they refuse to treat the drum and beef-eating as 'degradation and debasement' rather it is a paradigmatic symbol of their economic and cultural situation, in which they had no alternative to depending on carcasses of dead cattle, eating the flesh and making use of the skin for drums. This is nothing to be ashamed of. Historically too, as viewed by Valarmathi, Clarke searches for roots in the fourth century Sangam Age of the Tamils during which the drum was called *murasu*, and was used for religious as well as political purposes. Quoting the Tamil scholar, N. Subrahmanian (1980), Clarke argues that the drum was a representation of the Divine and it was 'bathed in holy water, garlanded and worshipped' (1998: 120). Still further, in his etymological argument he was informed by one of the informants in his fieldwork that the term 'paraiyar' comes from parai (drum)+*aiyar* (priest or Brahmin), meaning 'priests of the drum' (1998: 122). One could certainly and easily contest this and all the other reinterpretations given above as far-fetched and unscientific.

Similarly, Valarmathi (1999: 4-6) a Paraiyar scholar, argues that the *parai* was used to announce war and declare victory and not for funeral drumming. She suggests that we should consider the drum as a *pōrparai* (war drum), not a *sāpparai* (death drum). Tracing the origin of *parai* to classic Tamil literature such as *Puranānūru*, which talks about the social and political life of ancient Tamils and *Ahanānūru,* which deals with ancient Tamil family life, she insists that it was a generic name for leather instruments of seventy varieties. More specifically, *parai* – *para+ai* meant primarily 'speak' 'talk' or announce and thereby the instrument was used to declare the victory in war in ancient Tamil society. When Tamil society was geographically organised into five types of land such as *kurinchi* (mountain), *mullai* (forest), *marutham* (fertile land), *neithal* (sea) and *pālai* (desert), and there was no caste divisions as seen later and now, *parai* was an instrument of honour and a symbol of celebration and relaxation. She notes carefully that the earlier drum was not made of dead calf hide; instead the ancient Tamils used hides of many wild animals without removing the hair to show their bravery (Ibid.: 15). Later Valarmathi, enumerating literary evidence, argues that the drum was used for highly sophisticated music played in temples.

Parai was a generic term used for all the music played in all the *ainthinai* communities (five communities), during which the Tamil society lived in five geographical areas. It had different names according to the place where it was used amounting to thirty-six kinds of drum, among them *udukku, salligai, karadigai, kanaparai, thannumai, thadāri, thudumai, siruparai, adakkapparai, pagam, thudi, thagunicham, perumparai* were mainly in use (Valarmathi 1999: 26). All these drums were called *muḷavu* (one of the ancient Tamil traditions) instruments.

Although all these reconstructions are helpful in the formation of a new identity for the Paraiyars, the question of how all this can be validated and by whom remains to be seen. Most of the Dalit intellectuals believe that it will be gradually accepted by all and we need to allow the reconstructions to sink into the minds of the people; and for this to happen they need to be repeated from time to time.

In addition to the reconstructive attempts – the creation of counter-stories and the reconstruction of the history of the drum – have gone a long way into transforming drum music into a fine art.

Demythologising the Drum

One major insight the Paraiyars have gained from the exposure and training has been that story telling (myths) is a powerful tool in forming one's identity. Manimegalai, who has taken part in more than twenty exposure seminars and rallies says, "in every meeting I attended I was told to recall stories that the higher castes and others told about us [the Paraiyars] and in some seminars I was asked to narrate them in front of thc participants. Then the Dalit scholars who conducted the seminars would tell us that all those stories were deliberately constructed by the higher castes and we should create counter-stories and tell them regularly to our children". Another woman who was standing near Manimegalai, said, "when we breast feed our children we have been asked to feed them stories". They say that they are convinced about this.

Every time they return to the village after their training or their participation in a rally and cultural festivals, the Paraiyars say that the whole Colony in their daily meetings and interactions would recall their past life in the village and show how they have come to realise that the old myths were told by the *Ūr* Vanniyars to justify their being treated as the Dalits. When the drummers made attempts in the past to stop their service, the elder Paraiyars persuaded them to accept the status quo by re-telling mythical stories. Selvaraj, one of the articulate drummers, said that his grandfather often told him that by not doing the *Ūr* service he would be taken ill and be cursed by the goddess Mariamman. Indeed, once when he refused to play the drum at a funeral in the *Ūr* he suffered from diarrhoea. It took him a long time to come to realise that this was all in his mind that had been fed with stories. The Paraiyars in Pappanallur feel that their identity as drummers and their polluted and excluded status were constantly reinforced by many myths that have been told and retold for generations. Such mythologising of drumming and the other services became innately imprinted in their minds, and defined them as Dalits. To undo this, they realised that they should invent new myths that would not demean drumming, and go through a process that I propose to call *de-mythologisation*.

Although there are many theories of the historical origins of the Paraiyars (Clarke; 1998: 65-70), the name 'Paraiyar' is a derivative of the Tamil word, *parai*, a drum; one who plays the drum was called a *parai*-yar (Thurston: 1975: 77; Aiyangar 1982: 78). And the myths of the Paraiyars' origin, collected and discussed by Mosse (1985: 242-4), Moffatt (1979: 120-26), Deliege (1999: 71-88)[4] explain more the origin of the Paraiyars' occupation and thereby their identity than their history. Therefore, I will first present the conventional myth that both the Vanniyars and the Paraiyars in Pappanallur village have narrated to me by way of explaining the reason for the Paraiyars' traditional services to the *Ūr*. Then, I will look at the way in which the Paraiyars now reject many aspects of the myth and are evolving a counter-myth, '*re-mythologising*', in their attempt to make drumming a positive art form and music.

The version of the myth about the origin of the drumming service in Pappanallur was first narrated to me by Elumalai Gounder in the *Ūr*, and was confirmed by Rama Kannappa Gounder, both Vanniyars.

The Conventional Myth: In the beginning, there was only one woman called *Āṭi Pārāsakti* (literally original cosmic power) and nobody else lived in this cosmic world. There was an occasion in which she felt that she could no longer survive without a man; the creative energy (*paṭaippu Sakti*), specific to women who give birth to a child, needed a man to actualise that energy. So *Āṭi* conducted *yukams* for three eras. A *yākam* is a sacrificial fire, from which emerged a handsome man, called Paramasivan. She married him in *Inṭralōkam* (heaven where all gods assemble in front of Indran, the King of gods, *Thevars*), where three billion gods showered blessings on them and sang songs of praise.

Then they lived happily and *Āṭi* gave birth to four children. When the children reached adulthood, to check their manliness, *Āṭi* made them cook beef, promising them if they cooked the beef well, they would be given charge of heavens. As was the custom, the eldest one was given the privilege of leading the cooking and all the other brothers helped him. When the meat curry was boiling, one piece fell from the vessel to the ground. Fearing a severe punishment from his mother the eldest threw the piece of meat into the fire. Seeing this, the other brothers accused him, shouting, *paraiyā maraikkāthe* (paraiyan, do not hide). They promptly went and informed their mother, who cursed her eldest son and ordered him to go away from the *Inṭralōkam*. Therefore, eventually he became a Paraiyan, living near the cremation ground, taking up works such as burning the dead, drumming, and working on the land for his survival.

This myth is often, even today, recalled by the Vanniyars to argue that the traditional services of the Paraiyars are divinely ordained and if they refused to do it, that would amount to going against God, probably inviting once again the curse of God. Even the elder Paraiyars in the Colony agree with, the account if not openly for fear of opposition from the younger Paraiyars. The Paraiyars for long rationalised their polluted status as an outcome of their ancestor's (the eldest son of *Āṭi*) blunder and so it is justifiable that they live a life of the Dalits. Barnabas, who has done drumming service for sixty-five years, now in his nineties, says, "because of the mistake of our *pāṭṭan* (ancestor, referring to the eldest son in the myth) we suffer even today". To that extent, the myth remained as the divine will and *Ūr* higher castes made use of this to legitimise the services done to them by the Paraiyars. What the Paraiyars now try to do is to deconstruct the myth, or de-mythify, and argue that the myth was a trick of the Brahmins and the higher castes to be played upon them for their own benefit.

At the time of my field study in the village counter mythical stories were being popularised. I will present one of these that are so popular that even Paraiyar schoolboys and girls are aware of them. The story that I recount here was told me by a seventeen-years old Paraiyar girl, who was under training to be a tailor.

> *Counter Myth*: there was a foreigner who went around the world researching in music. For one of his experiments he came to Tamil Nadu. He collected thirty women and made them plant paddy [*nāṭu naṭutal*]. While the women were working, in front of them he asked many musicians to play on their musical instruments. A church organ was first played. As soon as the women heard the organ, they began to yawn and stopped working. Then *miruthaṇkam*, [Brahmin music] was played and the women went to sleep; and later at the sound of *vīnā* [guitar like string instrument] music, the women snored [*koraṭṭai*] in their sleep. Then our men came with their *vaṭṭaṭappu* [circular drum] and as soon as they played all the women got up briskly and did their work well. In addition, the women began to sing folk songs [*nāṭṭupura pāṭalgal*].
>
> Being surprised at this, the foreigner asked our men, 'what is the name of the instrument?' They replied, '*ṭappu melam*' [parai music]. But the foreigner misunderstanding the word said, 'it is not tappu[5], it is right; it is a very nice instrument'. Immediately Iyer [Brahmin] who was the assistant to the foreigner said, 'it is

> not right, it is *ṭappu*. It is played only for *sāvu* [death]'. Then, the foreigner asked our men, 'why do you play beautiful music for funerals?' One of our men said, 'we play the drum in order to verify whether the person is really dead or has simply fainted; if the person has fainted he will get up'. But the foreigner insisted that the *thappumelam* [parai drum] should be treated as our *kalai* [art].

Similar stories are spread throughout Tamil Nadu by a pamphlet magazine called *Thamukku* (drum) in which there is a section named '*Paraṭṭayin Tāvu'* (Parattai stories). This is written by Parattai, a professor in the Tamil Nadu Theological Seminary (TTS), in Madurai to propagate the idea that the drum should be transformed into a respectable Paraiyar art form. In course of my interview with Parattai, he told me that it was the stories that had denigrated the drum and made its playing a polluting and demeaning activity, and this negative ideology had been imprinted in the minds of the Dalits. In addition, if it is to be reversed into an art form, similar stories have to be evolved. He further said that it was not the truth of the stories that is important; of course, they were to be taken as untrue accounts of non-events, but it is how the stories are told in a way that people are able to believe in them. A mythical account according to him is ideology cast in the form of a story, which produces a social order; it takes a counter story to redefine that ideology to evolve a new social order. More importantly, he argues that myths were used by the higher castes to get the consent of the Dalits to their having hegemony over them. In the production of a social system what is important is the domination of the group that produces the system, and this can only be done by the consent of the dominated either through coercion or persuasion. Parattai believes that the higher castes got the consent of the Dalits by both methods. But the creation and telling of myths was more powerful in persuading the Dalits to give consent than the coercive method by which the Dalits internalised the content of the myths that structured their lives, he added.

Such efforts of Dalit scholars (and other Dalit social movements), I argue, is localised in Pappanallur as in many villages in Tamil Nadu through Dalits' participation in workshops, seminars and agitations. More sharply, this is done in Dalit cultural festivals.

Dalit Cultural Festivals: From Death Drum (Sāpparai) to War Drum (Pōrpparai)

"Let us make Paraiyar art into weapons of Dalit liberation" has been the aim of the Dalit cultural festivals (*dalit kalai viḷakkal*). This has an enormous influence on the Paraiyars of Pappanallur. Very often during my field study, the youths in the Colony talked about it and narrated to me the details of the festivals they had been to. When some of them went to Madurai, one of the southern cities of Tamil Nadu, to participate in a festival conducted by the Dalit Resource Centre (DRC) I accompanied them to see how the festivals influence their actions in the village, particularly their refusal to play the drum at the funerals of the Vanniyars.

The festival started from around ten at night and concluded at five thirty in the morning. There were more than 45 drum troupes taking part. The whole festival began informally with a short introduction by the director of the Centre. In his speech he said, "we have come here to play on our traditional music drum. The music our drumming is going to produce will not be *sāpparai* (drumming for the dead) but it will be, should be *pōrpparai* (drumming for war/freedom)". Immediately, more than twenty women appeared on the stage drumming in beautiful synchronisation.

It is revealing to see that women, some of them university students, had learnt the music to the extent of playing on the drums in such festivals. The powerful rhythm of the drums and their dancing according to the rhythm not only demonstrated the centrality of the drum that had been elevated from pollution to an art, but more specially, how the polluted symbol had been taken up by Paraiyar women to demonstrate the uniqueness of the *parai* music. From then on different drum troupes, drawn from different parts of the state, performed drumming accompanied by songs, and speeches on the importance of making the drum a symbol of their culture. To reinterpret the drum as a powerful cultural symbol of the Paraiyars, in the plays they made fun of all the Brahminical epics and Vedas, which, they consider, were instrumental in degrading their culture and society, particularly in making the drumming a polluting symbol. They made fun in the plays of the customs of the Brahmins and portrayed them as dirty people (*asingampudichavargal*). For example, one skit was about beef-eating in which two men, one Brahmin and another paraiyar, play music, the Brahmin on *Miruthangam* and the Paraiyar on the *parai*. The Brahmin stopped playing, unable to continue further, whereas the Paraiyar went on playing for a long time. At the end, the Paraiyar told the Brahmin, "Do you know the secret of my energy? I eat beef daily. Your *sāmbār* (a dish of lentils, mostly eaten by Brahmins, who are vegetarian) is useless. Come, tomorrow I will ask the butcher to give you half a kilo of beef and a 250 gm bone". Similarly, throughout the festival they made a contrast between Paraiyar and Brahmin customs, making the former appear far superior to the latter.

Another important point is that the festival is deliberately conducted in the month of December-January during which in Chennai and in other major cities of Tamil Nadu, classical music concerts are conducted by different *Sabhas* (Karnatic Music Associations). It is intended to project the Paraiyar art as a counter-symbol to the classical music that is dominated by Brahmins. The *Mirudaṇkam*, a double sided drum used in classical, Karnatic music that is dominated by Brahmins and 'played' in a very mild and mellifluous rhythm, is the opposite of the *parai* which is 'beaten' and results in a heavy rhythm, which sometimes, when accompanied by song is very evocative as well as provocative. The professional drummers in the festival said that the heavy rhythm is used not only to distinguish them from Brahminical music but also to demonstrate their social anger towards the higher castes, particularly the Brahmins, who made them untouchables.

Similarly, many other Paraiyar/Dalit organisations conduct such festivals in other parts of the state. For example, *Makkal Kalai Ilakkiya Kalagam* (People's Cultural and Literary Society) conducts a similar but more elaborate festival in Thanjavur city. This also releases every year an audiocassette on the theme. In 2001, it was held on 6 January at Thruvalluvar Thidal attracting more than forty thousand spectators and there were more than sixty drum troupes. In the brochure the object of the festival was stated as: "it is our cultural struggle (*panpāṭṭuppōrāṭṭam*) against the destructive Brahminical music that spreads slavery, vulgarity (*kalivēri*) and oppression". Its official emblem depicted a drummer with a *parai* showing his angry face, underneath it was written: the drum is our art and it is a weapon of our freedom[6]. The festival conducted there was different from the one in Madurai. The festival of Thanjavur, which was organised by *mā.kā.ī.kā*, a Marxist Leninist group, drew many Dalit intellectuals drawn from the Tamil film world who spoke on the beauty and intricacies of drum music. After the festival these talks were published in a magazine, *Putiya Kalātccāram* (New Culture); one of the talks given by Maruthaiyan appeared in the magazine in February 2001 issue (pp.4-6).

Such festivals are conducted in other towns like Palayamkottai, in the deep south of Tamil Nadu, and in Thiruvannamalai, a northern town, after the festival in Madurai. In addition, no political rally of the Dalit groups in Tamil Nadu is organised without drumming. This strengthens the project of making drum playing an art form by providing it a political platform. The DPI leader Mr Thirumavalavan is an elected member of the state Legislative Assembly (MLA), who popularised these ideas thorough their political propaganda. On 1 May, 2001 DPI founded a society called *Parai Isaikalainkerkal Nalasangam* (Parai Artists' Welfare Society) in Thiruvannamali.[7] The society's main aim is to resurrect the *parai* music from its funeral associations and make it the traditional art of the Paraiyars. In addition, the society strives to make the *parai* a weapon to reclaim Paraiyar lands and history. The society on 12

April, 2002 organised a rally of one hundred thousand *parai* drummers in Chennai city demanding the state government to institute a separate *vāriyam*, a Board for the *parai* artists.

Much earlier, on 16 August, 1999, the Dalit Resource Centre in Madurai also had started a similar organisation for *parai* drummers called Madurai District Thappu Artists Association. A memorandum was submitted to the Madurai District Collector, in which they listed ten demands, mainly demanding the state government to recognise the *parai* drummers as folk artists. Apart from formal organisations for *parai* artists, in many villages in Tamil Nadu the cultural consciousness is making the drum playing into the art of the Paraiyars and of the Dalits in general as well. For instance, Reddipalayam village near Thanjavur city produced many *parai* artists to the extent that some of them have found an entry into the Tamil cinema world; in a recent film, *Sankamam*, the *parai* troupe called *Vīra Sōḷa tappāṭṭa kuḷu*, from the village, played on the drum to accompany a song. This has increased not only the popularity of drum music but it has also contributed to the common project of transforming drumming into a respectable art of the Paraiyars. The project is also strongly supported politically by the Dalit political parties, particularly the DPI party; its founder leader, R. Thirumavalavan, in his speeches encourages the Paraiyars to make drum music into their art and identity. Every Paraiyar in Pappanallur is proud to have a photo of the leader hung in his/her house along with the photograph of Jesus Christ and Ambedkar, and regularly listens to the speeches of the leader recorded in audio cassettes, which urges them to assert their identity.

The low and polluted identity of the Paraiyars defined negatively by their service of drumming in the village is now being given a positive meaning, although it remains to be seen whether this will be recognised by others. They have given up drumming at the funerals of Vanniyars, but not their talent of drumming. Instead, they resolve now to reverse the symbol of pollution into a symbol of identity. "Drumming should be considered as beautiful music, an art *kalai*" said one of the drummers, "it needs musical talent; ask the Vanniyans to play on the drum, they would not be able to even hold the sticks". They have decided not to play the drum for funerals and inauspicious occasions. "The drum that is not played for marriage functions is not a drum at all hereafter" say the *parai* drummers in Pappanallur. To treat it as an art form they have now decided to play it only for auspicious occasions like any other music, *tavil, natasvaram and mirutaṇkam*, the instruments used in Carnatic music, a classical music which is dominated by the Brahmins.

Michael, the leader of the Paraiyar *Vagaiyarā* council asked, "if we are part of the village and our role as drummers was important, why then are we not treated as persons as we respect the Vanniyars; in what sense are they superior to us?" He further said that what they did as a service helped to remove pollution and protected the Vanniyars' life from *pēi pisāsu* (evil spirits), but the Vanniyars had failed to respect them who were in fact guardians of life. In fact, the Paraiyars often say that if the drumming gives life only for the Vanniyars and keeps them pure from evil spirits but does not provide the drummers with a proper life, then they should give up such a service and make drumming something that will primarily give them life and a respectable social status. So the drummers have decided to play the drum only on auspicious occasions like marriage, and if they are invited to play it for festivals, they demand that they be paid in the same way as a professional music troupe is. Nor will they eat in the higher castes' houses and demand food from hotels in the nearby towns. Pushpa, one of the drummer's wife said that the drummers should be paid by the hour. To be a Paraiyar or drummer is no longer a shameful thing, rather drumming is and should be a source of confrontation and creativity; it is an art form unique to the Paraiyars.

From Parai Noise (saṭṭam) to Parai Music (isai)

In Pappanallur, the Paraiyars are trying to reconstruct the nature of drum music from sound that drives away demons to music that helps identify the Paraiyar community in a positive way.

'*Saṭṭam'*, the noise of the drum that was threatening and frightened bullocks and demons is being changed into '*isai*', music. This is done by giving finer nuances to the drumbeat. By doing this, the Paraiyars in Pappanallur, and elsewhere in Tamil Nadu, elevate the drum music to be equal to Carnatic music, the classical music of south India, mostly dominated by the Brahmins. To do this, the drummers of Pappanallur try first to make the drumming pleasant by changing the usual loud sound of the drum. Selvaraj, one of the drummers, observed that because of its mild and melodious nature the Carnatic music was respected as 'high music' (*uyarntha isai*). So he said that drum music must also be melodious music.[8]

Moffatt (1979: 198-201) and Clarke (1998: 113-18) have already explained the different beats or *thālams* of drumming. I do not intend to review all of them except Clarke's works, which I find useful for my focus in this chapter. Clarke suggests that there are six kinds of drumming: the processional drum, the divine grace-bestowing drum, the invoking and inspiring drum, the protecting and exorcising drum, the announcing drum, and the relaxing dance-drum (1998: 113-18). In Pappanallur, all this has been so far classed into three kinds: *sāvumēlam* (death drum), *nalla mēlam* (good drum, meaning that it is played for domestic auspicious occasion) and *koil mēlam* (temple drum). But these are being changed into a music to which they add new beats imitating Tamil film music and Carnatic music. In the parish festival in 2002, the drummers played mainly for film songs played on the clarinet. They try as much as possible to avoid using the beats they used to play for funerals. In addition to the traditional drums, they have incorporated band instruments such as trumpet, cymbals, tambourines and so forth. Even the dress of the drummers has also been changed. Earlier, one of the drummers told me that when they did the drumming service, they used to wear only dhoti around their waist and the higher castes did not allow them to wear even a shirt while playing on the drums. But now in the reformed drum band, they wear full multi-colour suit and shoes quite similar to an army band troupe. They have also modified the way in which they organise the drumming. The band is arranged according to the kind of instruments. The whole drum troupe is formed into three lines. Pipe instruments are kept in the first line followed by small accompanying instruments such as cymbals, tambourines, and the last line is formed by the main drummers on their traditional drums and band drums. In front of the three-line formation, there is a conductor, who normally is the leader of the troupe. The leader is also the one who gives training to new recruits on the new form of drum music. Apart from the three-line formation, there are four or five persons in the same dress who perform dances travelling in front of the whole troupe. All this order and beauty, as Xavier, one of the Paraiyars said, has elevated the demeaning activity of drumming to the status of an art that has to be respected and considered as the unique art form of the Paraiyars.

In brief, the Paraiyars are attempting to change the jarring noise of drumming played only for inauspicious occasions into a fine art: from noise to sound, which is popularised in and through the Dalit cultural festivals.

Notes

1. *mēlam adikkira nāyē, māttukkari thingira parapayalē, kāni nilamillatha unakku thimrā*
2. *intha saniyan puditcha tholilai vittu olikkanum*
3. The discussion of the works of the Dalit scholars should be in place to explain that what the Paraiyars of Pappanallur are doing is not an isolated case but the collective effort of all the Paraiyars of Tamil Nadu who are increasingly supported with researches on the art forms of the Dalits. For instance, in Pondicherry Central University, Dr Gunasekaran, a Paraiyar, who heads the Sri Sankaradass Swami school of Performing Arts is a well known scholar who has done researches on the Dalit arts and played a seminal role in transforming the drumming from a polluting activity to a distinct art form. See Gunasekaran (1995), (1999).

4. Many others, such as Thurston (1975), Aiyappan (1937), Berreman (1963), also discuss the Paraiyar myths of origin; see Deliege (1999: 71-85) for an in-depth analysis of these studies. I have chosen Mosse, Moffatt and Deliege, for they did their field studies in Tamil Nadu.
5. The word '*ṭappu*' in Tamil also means wrong and parai as well.
6. *Parai engal Kalai, athu engal viduthalai karuvi.*
7. See *Thai Mann* (Mother Earth), a monthly magazine published by DPI party, July 2001, p.34.
8. Valarmathi (1999: 52) refers to the history of *mirutaṇkam*, the kind of drum used in Carnatic music, how it was transformed from ordinary *parai* into holy and respectable music to the extent that it was the music played by gods when Nataraja Perumal, one of the forms of Shiva, danced *ānanta tāntavam*.

6

Beef-Eating: From Symbol of Pollution to Symbol of Social Custom

Beef-eating as a Symbol of Pollution

The Paraiyars feel that there were two ways by which the practice of beef eating was considered as polluting and they were identified with this that led to a life of servitude. One was telling myths about the Paraiyars' origin, and the second was the cattle scavenging they did as a part of their traditional services to the higher castes in Pappanallur village. The mythical discourse and the practice of cattle scavenging, the Paraiyars think, had defined them as low and polluted people.

In the daily discourse of the higher castes in the village, the practice of eating beef has always been associated with the Paraiyars, and it is this that defines them as polluted and untouchable. For a long time, the Paraiyars accepted this state of life as a divinely ordained life and felt that they had received their polluted status most of all by eating the carcasses of cows. Although the five distinctive *Ūr* services involved the pollution of death, eating beef was the powerful symbol by which the higher castes defined the polluted status of the Paraiyars. Often at the time of verbal feuds between the Paraiyars and the Vanniyars, the Vanniyars used to tell the Paraiyars, "you beef-eaters, what courage you have to fight against us." It meant, as one of the Paraiyars told me, that in the opinion of the higher castes, those who ate beef became less human and were meant to be slaves.

Mythical Origin for Beef-eating

As with the drumming service, the custom of eating beef too has a mythical origin that goes back to the origin of the Paraiyars, and which explained the reasons for their being treated by the higher castes as polluted and therefore to be segregated. The myth was to a large extent a powerful tool in terms of reinforcing the idea of pollution, not only in the minds of the higher castes but also among the Paraiyars themselves, who accepted their polluted status. In addition, they internalised the idea that the practice was the will of God and there was no way they could escape it. Barnabas, an elderly Paraiyar in his nineties narrated the myth to me when I asked him why the Paraiyars ate beef and not any other meat as their staple food.

> Adhi and Paramasivan had two sons. The elder had the duty of performing *pūja* to their parents who were the main gods of heaven (*Inṭralōkam*). Whenever he went to the temple to perform the puja a cow would appear from heaven for a blood sacrifice (*Iraṭṭapaḷi*). He would cut a piece of flesh from the cow and offer it to the gods. Then he would return home bringing with him rice and fruits (*prasādam*) for his wife. The younger son who had been watching this went and told his brother's wife, "your husband is eating beef everyday in the temple after the puja, but he brings only rice and fruits for you, next time you should demand that he brings some beef for you." One day when her husband came back from the temple she asked him, "I hear that you eat beef everyday in the temple, but you do not give me that. Since I am pregnant you should give me beef. If you do not give it to me I will commit suicide." Although he had never eaten beef, he was worried about his wife and decided to bring some beef for his wife. On the following day, he cut off a larger portion of flesh from the cow, but immediately the heavenly cow died. Seeing what had happened,

all the gods from heaven appeared in front of the elder son and told him, "you cruel man, you killed a sacrificial cow. Since you have killed it, take it and eat it. Hereafter you are untouchable, you are a beef-eater and you should live outside the village. You should never come to the temple. Go away". Therefore, he left the village with his pregnant wife. While he was going the village people asked him who would perform puja in the temple. He replied, "My brother (*thambi*) will look after the temple (*ēn tambi pāpān*)." Then the elder son lived outside the village doing all kinds of services to the village for which he did not demand any wage. He used to wait every time for a cow to die so that he could collect its meat for his meal and the skin to make a drum.

There are different versions of the same myth in which the central idea remains the same. For our purpose, it is not necessary to go into them, but we should focus on how the myth was used to portray and define the Paraiyars as polluted people as it is claimed by the Paraiyars. Such myths, the Paraiyars argue, were told and retold on different occasions, which the whole village heard them repeatedly. Festivals, village dramas (*kūtṭṭu*), and ceremonies at the temples were the times when such myths were recalled in the form of songs and *bhajans*. Vellupillai, a Vanniyar who was known for his histrionic talents in the village, sang some of the songs for me that he would generally sing in the village dramas, which had many references to the myths explaining the social hierarchy and divisions of the village. He told me, "when you want to know the history of the village you should listen to the stories I have. It will explain to you why we treat the Colony people as we do; we did not make up the stories, instead they were handed down by our forefathers."

He further said that it was God who had assigned the practice of eating beef as the Paraiyars' practice and that this was the way God wanted them to live their life in this world. How could they change this? If they tried to do so it would be like a black man trying to become a white man. This conviction is shared by most of the Vanniyars, but not by the Paraiyars. For the Paraiyars, the myths they were told by the village higher castes, particularly at the time of festivals and public gatherings in the village have been a conscious attempt to mark them out as polluted and segregated from the rest of the village. This realisation has come very late after their series of exposures to outside influence and their conflicts with the Vanniyars from the 1940s. But every Paraiyar accepts that earlier they had always thought that eating beef was their practice assigned by God, as narrated in the myths.

The Practice of Cattle Scavenging

Such myths are associated with an activity that reinforces some 'historical' claims. The discourse is translated into action. The practice of cattle scavenging and the eating of the meat of the dead cows are the practices that were born out of and sustained by the mythical discourse of eating beef.

Cattle scavenging by the Paraiyars was done in the following way. Normally, the higher castes send for a Thoti Paraiyar when a cow dies for any reason known or unknown, usually because of sickness. The Thoti Paraiyar calls together a few other Paraiyars who usually represent different *Vagaiyarās* and they go to remove the cow. They tie the four legs of the cow together and insert a wooden pole so as to be able to carry it, holding both ends of the pole. Usually, says Michael, one of the Thoti Paraiyars, "the higher castes inform us only after the cow has been dead for two days and its carcass is bloated with oozing blood and has a rotten smell". On every occasion, they had to put up with this sort of treatment and remove the dead animal to a place far away from the *Ūr* area. Then one of them, skilled in removing the skin, cuts open the dead animal and removes the skin. They share the meet among the *Vagaiyarās* equally. Mostly, there will be a fight among the *Vagaiyarā* Paraiyars about who gets what and how much. This also contributed to the contempt of the higher castes towards the Paraiyars; in their description of the Paraiyars, the Vanniyars told me in my field study, "they are like dogs fighting for a carcass that has a horrible smell".

The main reason, Lourduraj, one of the leaders of the Paraiyar *Vagaiyarā* Council, said, why the Paraiyars had to eat the meat from carcass of cows in the 1960s was that economically they were poor and landless labourers who could not afford chicken or mutton that was expensive, and they could not grow their own vegetables. The only way that they could have meat in their meals was by collecting it from carcasses from high caste houses whenever cows or calves died. Poverty, dependence, and debt had been fundamental features of the Paraiyars' life for a long time, and it was that which forced them to have practices such as meat from carcass eating and begging for food daily from the houses of the higher castes.

The eating of cow meat from carcasses confirmed the ideas of pollution and untouchability that was associated with their other services to the *Ūr,* most of these involving death. It confirmed the myths about the Paraiyars' identity. For the Paraiyars, it concretely reinforced the concept of untouchable identity, in the sense of making the idea (word) into 'flesh'. It made them feel it physically as well. Ambrose, one of the drummers told me that when they ate meat from carcasses in the old way it used to take on foul smell, and this aroused revulsion in the higher castes in their interaction with the Paraiyars, literally rendering them untouchable. Ambrose, who was the main person who cut up the carcass and divided it amongst different *Vagaiyarās*, said, "my wife used to keep herself away from me for months; and I felt the smell in myself as well". He further added that many times he used to feel that it was right to live outside the village.

At the same time, many Paraiyars agree that it was also their economic condition they had earlier that forced them to consume carrion. As seen in Chapter 2, these days the Paraiyars have economically improved themselves in various ways, particularly through their jobs in Chennai city. But when they were only landless labourers and many of them bonded ones for the *Ūr* families, during the summer months there was no cultivation, they had no work and had no option for survival but eating of carrion. In such desperate situations, a Paraiyar told me, they used to kill a cow or a bull of the *Ūr* higher castes while they were grazing in the field with the aim of being called to clear away the carcass and this would provide them with a good meal. This economic side of the practice of eating beef should not be lost sight of while we highlight the influence of myths in structuring the practice as one of the identifying marks of the Paraiyars.

In addition, some Paraiyars realise that by cattle scavenging they did have a kind of power and influence over the *Ūr* in that the higher castes were dependent on them. "Although we did ugly things, the Vanniyars needed us and our service and without it the *Ūr* would have become hell," a former member of the cattle scavenging group said. Many Paraiyars often recall the times when they were highly valued by the higher castes on the days of cattle clearing; their families were fed by the *Ūr* higher castes and treated as if they were medical men. "When we refused to clear away dead cattle, the *Ūr* higher castes would spend a whole day begging us to come. We used these occasions to lord it over [*athigāram*] the Vanniyars, telling them, "wait I will come". They [the higher castes] would get terribly irritated by this, but they could not show this in case the cattle would be left to rot and this they would never allow to happen," said Meiyappan. For the Paraiyars, the dependence the *Ūr* higher castes had on them gave them a hold over the village that they feel they have lost since abandoning the service.

Beef-eating as a Social Custom

As seen earlier in the case of other symbols, the starting point in the attempts at redefining the symbol of beef-eating is the conflict that was created by the Paraiyars, who had, gained political consciousness, both on their own realisation and by the involvement of priests, the Dalit political and social movements, and NGOs. Conflict helps re-form self-consciousness in the sense that a series of conflicts in addition to their exposure to the Dalit political uprising has persuaded them to become aware of the ways in which the practice of beef-eating defined them as polluted. More specifically, as a consequence of the conflicts, the Paraiyars say that they began to look at the way in which mythical discourse had the power in the hands of the higher castes to define them and they think that in a similar way they should redefine the practice of beef-eating now that they no longer do the cattle scavenging service.

Counter Discourses on Myths of Beef-eating

Thanks to the teachings of the Dalit movements through pamphlets, monthly magazines, and public meetings, the Paraiyars in Pappanallur have come to realise that one of the ways by which they were defined as polluted was the practice of beef-eating. Further they have become aware that the myths associated with the practice, that had been repeatedly told, had the power to reinforce the idea that pollutedness was the original identity of the Paraiyars. Therefore, they have concluded that in order to change this identity they needed either to abandon the practice of eating beef – completely or to do something to 'de-pollute' the practice.

They have come to this state of mind, not by a sudden turn of events, but through a long process of the conflicts that helped them become conscious of their identity and what defined it. There were many Dalit movements in the state that conducted seminars and workshops, rallies and protests in which they took part, and had furthered the awareness they gained through the conflicts. They did not have for a long time any definite way of dealing with the practice of eating beef. Some Paraiyars suggested that they should completely give up the habit, others said, they should continue eating beef since it was the cheapest way they could eat meat at all. A small group of elder Paraiyars were of the opinion that they should go on scavenging the dead cattle since they did not know any other way of living. This oscillation and difference of opinion among the Paraiyars went on for quite some time. In the mean time, the Paraiyar youth saw to it that no one resumed the service of scavenging. It was only in the 1980s that the Paraiyars started a new way of re-forming the practice of eating beef and thus redefining their identity. This was when the Dalit movements, like the Dalit Christian Liberation Movement (DCLM) and the Dalit political party, Dalit Panthers (DPI), became popular and took up the cause of the Dalits' liberation from untouchability. Such an atmosphere heightened their awareness and they wanted to assert their identity not by giving up the activities they had been doing, but by redeeming them from their polluted state.

In this way they realised that what defined the practice of eating beef were actually the myths attached to it; these made the practice a polluting act. To reverse this they thought that they should evolve counter-myths that would show the practice in a positive light and, more importantly, and would make the Paraiyars' own the practice positively as their own social custom, unique to their culture.

They began to spread myths counter to the conventional myths. Young Paraiyars who are involved in the Dalit movements and hold membership in the Dalit political parties have actively spread them among the Paraiyar school children, who later got into the habit of narrating the myths particularly before they began their evening study in Pappanallur village. Mostly the myths I found were in use in two places: in Loyola School that is exclusively meant for the Dalit children run by the Jesuits of Tamil Nadu, and in all the twenty five evening study centres called *Sēntalir*. Let me give below some of them:

> *Counter-myth 1:* There was a Brahmin in Thiruvannamalai. For more than twenty years, he had been suffering from tuberculosis. He went all over the place and consulted as many doctors as he could but no body could cure the disease. Even his family took him to Apollo hospital in Madras spending more than two lakhs rupees, but all in vain. One day he met a homeopathy doctor in Uthiramerur who suggested that he should take beef soup twice a day and it would cure him of his disease. The Brahmin said, "how can I, a Brahmin, do that". To this the doctor replied, "if you want to cure yourself of your disease you should have beef soup".

Realising that there was no other way of curing his disease he decided to do it. Faithfully, the Brahmin took beef soup for a week, and he was cured of the disease.

Counter-myth 2: When Dr. Ambedkar[1] was studying Law in London, there was a competition in which every student was asked to memorise a thousand pages of laws and recite them. Ambedkar did it in thirty minutes. Whereas many Englishmen and even the Brahmin students who had gone from India were unable to memorise even a half of what they were asked to. Then everybody in the university was surprised at this and asked our Ambedkar how he could do it. He replied: "I ate beef from my childhood, and that increased my memory. From that time onwards, the whole university ordered that all the students should be given only beef".[2]

Counter-myth 3: You know the cricket player Sachin Tendulkar is a Brahmin. As a good Brahmin he always used to eat *dal* (*paruppu*) at his meals. But in his school days he was not a great cricketer. One day Tendulakar was really upset and shared his inability to score high in matches with his class mate Vinod Kambli who was a Dalit. Vinod Kambli said, "do not worry, I have a solution for your problem". "what is your solution?" asked Tendulkar. "you should take half a kilo of beef everyday at your dinner", said Vinod Kambli. Tendulkar was afraid whether his parents would allow this since he came from a very ardent Brahmin family. At the same time, he wanted to become the best player in the world, so he decided to eat beef with his friend. From then onwards he scored high runs and got selected for the national team. Even today he takes beef regularly and particularly before important matches. This is why he bats well and is the best batsman in the world.

Counter-myth 4: (In the *Senthalir* centres and Loyola school in their lessons to the Paraiyar children aged between 4 and 12)

Question: What is the use of our teeth?

Children's reply: To bite beef bones.

Question: What makes your teeth strong?

Children's reply: Eating beef regularly.

Question: What dish of beef helps to strengthen your memory power?

Children's reply: Beef bone soup.

Question: How did our leader Ambedkar get his doctoral degree?

Children's reply: Since he ate beef daily.

When I asked for clarification about the details of the myths they always said that they did not know. Where these myths came from and who the author (s) was, nobody could tell me. One possible source that I could trace later during my visits to libraries in Tamil Nadu was a monthly pamphlet called *Thamukku* (the drum). In it I found a section devoted to *Paraittaiyin Tāvu* (stories of Parattai). Other sources I gather could be from the seminars, workshops and protest rallies the Paraiyars attend regularly. But when I told the Paraiyars of this, they refused to accept that they got their stories from the magazine, instead the Paraiyars who are the DPI party members claim that the myths were their own creation. And they were angered that I did not give them the credit, and argued that this had been the method of Brahmins who could never think that they were capable of creative abilities.

I told a young and articulate Paraiyar that most of the stories he told me were not true, for instance I said to him, there is nobody who has been cured from cancer by eating beef. He said, "it is true that the stories we tell are lies, this is a deliberate way by which we think we can change our life. It is because of our conviction that we became polluted Paraiyars mostly by the Hindu myths told to us repeatedly as if they were historical events that made the oppressive caste system and it was forced upon us as holy and divine *dharma*. Now we use the same method. That is all. If you could accept those *pāpān* [Brahmins] stories as true why can't you accept our stories against them as true; this means that Brahmins are intelligent and we are not". This young Paraiyar in fact is characteristic of the dominant voice in the village in Pappanallur and elsewhere in Tamil Nadu among the politically conscious Paraiyars. There are many Paraiyars in Pappanallur who do not attach much value to the myth making, all that they are aware of is that they have stopped doing all the services to the *Ūr,* and that they are freely eating beef without any feeling of shame or guilt.

Communal Celebrations of Beef-eating

Apart from the myths, eating beef is also done communally to celebrate important events in the life of the Paraiyars. Every Sunday two or three Paraiyars come together to organise a communal meal of beef in the village. On Saturday, they buy a calf or a cow from a nearby village and on the next morning, they butcher it and divide it equally among all the Paraiyar families. Adding beef to their meal brings a sense of festivity in the Colony. It looks almost as if they were celebrating the village festival. This should be seen in the context of the past when the Paraiyars kept the practice as a secret and when one asked about it they had always said they had never eaten beef because beef eating was the one major practice that defined the Paraiyars as low and segregated. What was considered once as a shameful act is now glorified as a custom unique to the Paraiyars, defining their positive identity.

The important element here is that after killing the cow they carry the flesh hung from a wooden pole through the streets of the Vanniyars, intentionally in a way of protesting against the higher castes who consider eating beef as a polluting activity. Whenever they have done that, invariably, I was told, it had led to a feud or verbal duel between the Paraiyars who organise the event and some of the Vanniyar men of that particular street through which the Paraiyars carry the flesh. One such conflict I witnessed during my fieldwork on 18 February, 2001, and it took more than a month to get it settled. Elumalai Gounder said, "these Colony people do this purposely every time to insult us, if they want to eat that ugly thing (*asiňkampudicca saniyaṉ*), they should do so in private, not like this in public. It brings the village into disrepute. Our relatives from other villages do not want to visit us on Sundays fearing that they will have to put up with the ugly thing. Because of this, I am more afraid that our caste people in other villages will one day stop giving brides to our village". But the Paraiyars say that what the higher castes treated as polluting they will redeem as good and healthy, and that this is a part of their identity as Paraiyars.

The inspiration for this also comes from outside the village. The practice of communal beef-eating is glorified in Loyola school, where thirty four Paraiyar children from Pappanallur study, and by the members of Ambedkar Centenary Movement in Chengalpattu in which many Pappanallur Paraiyars are members. In the school, which is meant exclusively for the Dalit children, every Sunday and on feast days like St Ignatius of Loyola (31st July), the founder of the Society of Jesus, the Jesuits who run the school say that the beef meal is deliberately organised to educate the children that eating beef is not a shameful act but it is a prestigious thing that defines them as Paraiyars. Every time the beef meal begins with a slogan, "we will eat beef, and live with dignity" (*māṭṭukkari thiṉbōm, mānatōodu vāḷvōm*). At the beginning of the meal, the students listen to reading taken from the lives of the Dalit leaders like Irattaimalai Sinivasan and Dr. Ambedkar. When I interviewed one hundred and seventy two students, both girls and boys, most of them said that beef-eating in public with proper instructions on the positive elements of the practice created the consciousness of their Paraiyar culture and they felt happy. In addition, they said, it removed the inhibitions they used to have earlier. Ramesh in the eighth standard said, "When I go home during holidays, I tell my mother eating beef provides good health." Some other students have no idea about it all. Twenty-four students (15 girls and 9 boys) said that it was not good to eat beef since it brings shame on them. Father Thomas, who himself is a Paraiyar and teaches history in the school for tenth standard students, said that it was largely the glorification of the practice of eating beef that had done a great deal in creating awareness among the students of the school that eating beef was a healthy habit, and was one of the fundamental elements of the culture of the Dalits in general and of the Paraiyars in particular. He added that they have asked the Paraiyars not to eat dead cow meat. The Paraiyar children who learn all this in school spread it in the village when they go back during their vacations.

Similarly, the Dr Ambedkar Centenary Movement, a movement organising the Paraiyars to reclaim Panchami land, organises communal beef-eating events that are more spectacular than the ones I found in Pappanallur village and in Loyola School. It is important to discuss the event since many persons from Pappanallur Colony take part in the activities of the movement, and this has an enormous impact on their lives. In addition, the movement and particularly, its leader Father Yesumarian, who is a practicing lawyer in the Chengalpattu district court, the Pappanallur Paraiyars say, had been of great support to the Paraiyars whenever they have conflicts with the Vanniyars of Pappanallur village.

The movement uses beef-eating in two ways: one is to celebrate their victories in their struggle against the higher castes and the state government; the second way is a weapon to assert their identity. When they forcefully occupy the lands that they consider belong to them and allotted to them, by the British, the first thing they do is to put up huts all over the land, install a statue of Dr Ambedkar, and finally in each hut they cook a beef meal. After that, they come together and listen to the leaders who give speeches on the theme of beef-eating, apart from other themes, as the culture of the Paraiyars and every Paraiyar should take pride in it. In one of such events, which I witnessed, three leaders told the audience that in the beginning it was a practice the Brahmins had, and later only they made it a polluting act to marginalise the Dalits. The pamphlets they distributed that day had quotations taken from different sources that explained that animal sacrifice was a Vedic practice and the Brahmins initially ate beef. The

Paraiyar women and men who took part in it believed in it. Later, all the Paraiyars shout slogans like, "let us eat beef and live with dignity"; "beef-eating Paraiyars are courageous Paraiyars"; "beef-eating is a social custom, there is nothing shameful about it". Bathinathan, who studies law in a college and has taken part in similar events, told me, "such occasions should be organised regularly to create consciousness among us about the positive elements of beef-eating, drumming and other rich cultural elements of the Paraiyars".

The second way in which they popularise beef-eating is that they use it as a weapon to assert their rights over places like village ponds and public facilities. What happened in 1999, in Ekatur village that is on the road to Old Mahabalipuram from Chennai city, is illustrative of this second way in which beef-eating is used. Mohan, president of the movement told me that for a long time the higher castes in the village refused to allow the Paraiyars to take drinking water from the village pond, one of the disabilities that the Dalits in general in the state have been experiencing. One day a twenty-five strong group of the movement organised an event in which they cooked a beef meal on the banks of the pond and ate together, at the end of it all of them washed their hands in the ponds, and some of them threw portions of beef into the pond. The higher castes complained to the police that the Paraiyars had polluted the pond, but the police did not take any serious action against them. Later the higher castes dug a well for the exclusive use of the higher castes.

In these ways, the members of the Ambedkar movement use beef-eating to redeem the practice from pollution and make it a weapon for their emancipation. This idea is very popular among the Paraiyars in Pappanallur who have become convinced of the idea that there is nothing intrinsic in beef-eating that pollutes them, but it was the thought that the higher castes have put into the practice and helped to define it as a polluting act. Therefore, by changing that thought through glorifying the practice as a positive act they think they can redeem the beef-eating practice and make it a respectable Paraiyar social custom. But the

Vanniyars refuse to recognise this, saying that Paraiyars will always be Paraiyars whether they change the beef-eating practice into a positive act or not. This refusal of recognition makes the Paraiyars feel often frustrated although they put up a brave saying, "we do not need their [higher castes] recognition, you will see one day what we do today will be recognised by society; we only sow the seed but our future generation will reap the fruits".

Notes

1. Some times instead of using Ambedkar, they use Irattaimalai Seenivasan, another local Dalit leader who hails from Koliyalam village, which is three kilometres from Pappanallur village.
2. I asked the Paraiyar boy who narrated the myth that even the English men also consume beef and how were they not able to memorise the laws as Ambedkar. To which he replied, "I was told that they eat beef without any addition of spice whereas we eat beef that is cooked in hot curry powder".

7

Land: From Symbol of Marginalisation to Symbol of Empowerment

Landlessness as Powerlessness

In the pre-colonial period, the Paraiyars of Chengalpattu had lived as labouring slaves (Anandhi 2000; Sivakumar and Sivakumar 1993). In the Colonial period the situation of the Paraiyars seems less different from the pre-colonial time. Even then, the Paraiyars had been kept by the *mirāsidārs*, who hereditarily owned and controlled the resources of the village: arable lands, wastelands, irrigation tanks, temples and cremation grounds. According to Lionel Places' report of 1789, the Brahmins and Vellala Mudaliyars were the *mirāsidārs* who owned eighty per cent of the land in the Chengalpattu area (Sivakumar and Sivakumar 1993: 20) and they had the Paraiyar community as their slave labourers living in abject poverty.

About Pappanallur Paraiyars we do not have any clear picture in the post colonial period except that most of them till today recall, and records and books give us some idea about this. The Paraiyars had been landless labourers in Pappanallur who worked on the land of the Brahmins in the early 1910s, later of the Reddiyars and the Vanniyars who managed the Brahmins' land. The Vanniyars think that the Paraiyars of Pappanallur were in fact brought by the Brahmins to the land that they received from the Chola kings as *brahmadēya,* as we have seen in Chapter 2. Many studies (Kumar 1965, 1992; Manickam 1982; Sharma 1997) inform us that in the then Chengalpattu area, one of the places in the Tamil districts as divided by the British administrators in the 1810s, the Paraiyars had been working as landless labourers who were either *paṇaiyāl* (permanent farm servant) or *padiyāl* (hired farm servant). Anandhi (2000: 4ff) gives an account of this. But the Paraiyars of Pappanallur have been mostly semi-bonded labourers (*adimai*) to the Vanniyar and Reddiyar houses who looked after the land of the absentee Brahmins. Every high caste house had a Paraiyar family as its serving family, and such semi-bonded labourer families were transferable from one high caste house to another; Kumar (1965: 44) refers to the Paraiyar families as the property of the higher castes. Such labour owning higher castes were called house-holders (*kuṭidanakārar*). The Paraiyar families who were semi-bonded labourers worked in the householder's fields and their children took care of the cattle. There were no wages given to these families, but they were fed daily, whether or not they had worked on that day, by the house-holders, and annually they were given clothes, mostly at the time of Pongal festival. Some of these families were made real bonded labourers to high caste houses from whom they frequently borrowed money for house building, marriage of their children and medical treatment, but they were unable to repay the money; and until they repaid the debt they remained bonded to the high caste houses.

Apart from these, there were other Paraiyar families – fifteen in number – in Pappanallur, who were only hired farm servants not attached to any high caste houses. In one sense, these families had a relatively independent life and were powerful since most of the higher castes depended on such labourers particularly at the time of harvest, in addition to the bonded labourers. There were times when these families, the Paraiyars recall, used to refuse to work on the higher castes' land, and demanded high wages. In doing so, the Paraiyars enjoyed some influence over the village by way of their negotiations with the high caste men who hired them for work.[1] One of the demands, they say, they made before the higher castes in Pappanallur was to pay their wages in cash instead of giving them in kind: at that time every adult appeared to have been given two *marakās* (two and a half kilograms) of unhusked paddy or millet per day, instead of this they demanded ready cash that could be used for various purposes. One more thing for which these hired farm servants had been known was that at the time out of monsoon or drought they stole paddy bags from the high caste houses.

Whether they were hired servants or bonded labourers, the Paraiyars say that they were not allowed to own any land. Even the Colony land in which they had their huts was owned either by the absentee Brahmins, or the Reddiyars and the Vanniyars. If they wanted to alter their huts they had to seek permission from the high caste owners. For instance, Asirvatham, in his nineties, recalled the incident in which he was beaten up by a Reddiyar for digging a foundation to rebuild his hut without the permission from the Reddiyar and he was asked to pay a fine of Rs 200. Since he was unable to pay, he became a bonded labourer to the Reddiyar family. Even the public land (*purambōkku*) of the village that is normally kept for village cattle grazing and to hold public events such as Pongal festival and drama, the Paraiyars say that they did not have any right to use, which rendered them totally a landless people, who were just a labour force and completely dependent on the *Ūr*.

Colony Land versus Ūr Land

The village of Pappanallur is divided into *Ūr* and Colony, the former is the residential area of the higher castes, and the latter the residential area of the Paraiyars. The *Ūr* territory is understood by the people of the village as sacred and pure, because it is the place where higher caste people live and temples are situated, whereas the Colony is seen as polluted and low, since it is the place the Paraiyars live and where lies the cremation ground or cemetery, and paddy field are situated. This is the area that is closely related to the services that the Paraiyars have to do: burning or burying the dead and labouring on the land. It is also a low-lying area, which gets flooded during the monsoon. Even the church, presbytery and convent in the Colony area are seen together with the Colony, from the point of view of the *Ūr* people, the church and its priests and nuns are placed on par with the Paraiyars. In my conversation with the *Ūr* higher caste people I came to learn that they associated Christianity only with the Dalits, it is for them a Dalit religion. During my fieldwork, I could hardly see anybody from the *Ūr* coming into the Colony. If there was some work to be done with the Paraiyars the person from the *Ūr* stood on the tar road before the first house in the Colony and transacted business and went away. This territorial division of pure *Ūr* and impure Colony has a bearing also on how the people are valued according to the space or territory they reside in. A *Ūr* person is valued highly and respected with human dignity; s/he has a proper household (*kuṭiyānavar*). But a Colony person is seen as polluted and is marginalised outside the village, considered not only lower than the *Ūr* people, but also sub-human, if not non-human. It is this relationship between the land and the people that provides personhood to people in the village; the substance of territory is closely linked to the substance of the persons who live in it (Daniel 1984: 79; Inden 1976: 59-61). The Paraiyars, who have sub-human identity according to their living space, are seen as innately unqualified to own land, instead they are only to be objects for the use of the higher castes in the *Ūr*. This objecthood, the Paraiyars told me, they internalised as theirs to the extent that even though there had been many chances to buy and own lands they gave up the idea simply because they, as the Colony people, felt diffident about owning land in the village. Barnabas narrated an incident. His maternal uncle, who lived in a village near Kanchipuram, after his death left him three acres of land. But Barnabas wanted to sell that land and buy land in Pappanallur. When he approached Elumalai Gounder, leader of the village at that time, he told him that owning land by a Paraiyar in Pappanallur is a bad omen to the village. Elumalai Gounder told

Baranabas, "why do the ploughing bulls need land?".[2] He further said that there was no occasion in which the Paraiyars felt that they should own land, and it was taken for granted that only *Ūr* people could own land and the Colony people are merely workers on the land. This false consciousness they dispelled through their land conflicts in Pappanallur and beyond.

The Service of Village Watchman (Kambukūṭṭi)

One of the ways that symbolised the Paraiyars' dependence and poverty is the service of village watchman (*kambukūṭṭi*), one of the five traditional services that the Paraiyars did for the *Ūr* higher castes. In many ways he symbolised the state of dependence and poverty in which the Paraiyars lived. The village watchman had many duties, among which four were important: regulating the water flow from the village tank to the land and guarding the paddy fields, taking messages of death and festivals to other villages where the relatives of the *Ūr* higher castes are, and guarding the village during major village festivals and cremating dead bodies. The village watchman and his relatives usually were responsible for water acquisition, guarding the supply channels to the village tank and the regulation of the water flow.[3]

The village watchman was mainly in charge of channelling water to the fields of standing crops according to the decisions taken in the *Ūr* council, and no farmer in the village was allowed to regulate the water to their fields. He had to do the duty at night to allow other farming activities to go on during the day. He was paid in grains most of the time or in cash some times on a per acre basis; when it was given in grains it was given in the form of paddy bundles (*kaṭṭu*). Although the work was hard and poorly paid, what made the watchman suffer was the internal conflict between the *Ūr* castes in terms of who gets the greater share of the water. The watchman had to bear the brunt of this conflict. During December usually the village decides on a system of rules for rationing water from the tank to the fields and asks the village watchman to regulate it accordingly. But most of the time, the

Paraiyars say, some Gounders would threaten the watchman and force him to give more water to their fields against the rules of the village. Meiyappan, who was until 1996 a watchman in the village told me, "every night before I went to the fields for my work of rationing water Gounders would come to my house and ask me to direct more water to their fields; if I said no, they would beat me up. And if I had yielded to their pressure, the *Ūr* would have punished me. I used to be beaten up by both sides. We were powerless labourers who were punished whether we did the right thing or not".

The service of the village watchman in Pappanallur had always been seen as a servile work (*adimai*) and considered less than human. This was reinforced in the ways in which the village watchman was treated. Not only was he not paid in proportion to the work he did but also he used to be given handouts (*pitchai*) such as grain, cloth and remainders of the threshing floor, given water by pouring it into his palms instead of in a glass; all this signified their subordination to the *Ūr*.

Nevertheless, the service gave the village watchman and his cousins who assisted him a significant power that the higher castes needed his help to get water. For this reason Vanniyars hesitated to antagonise the watchman and his cousins. There were times when the watchman withdrew his service of water channelling to the fields after conflicts between his men and the Vanniyars in terms of allotment of water. But this only outraged the Vanniyar leaders and resulted in punishment and sanctions for the watchman. Often the punishments such as beating and fines, the Paraiyars say, used to be given at village festivals and at the time of the Pongal festival, and at the threshing floor in front of many people, which, the Paraiyars think, demonstrated their state of subordination publicly.

Myth about Ownership of Land

The Vanniyars and the Reddiyars in the village are convinced that the Paraiyars are not capable of owning any land or any property.

They believe that there is something in the Paraiyars' blood that does not let them become owners; they are only suitable for being servants. "you give them pieces of wood and ask them to build a house, they would go and sell it and buy *arrack* with the money", said a Gounder. They say that this is not only their experience but it has been also the experience of many NGOs who tried to help them improve their life. Many Vanniyars recall an incident when an NGO gave them goats, many of the Paraiyars killed the goats and ate their meat. The Vanniyars have many stories like this to show that the Paraiyars are genetically incapable of ownership.[4]

In addition, there are also proverbs and sayings that reinforce this idea not only in the minds of the higher caste people but also in the minds of the Paraiyars. To give some examples, 'if a Paraiyar is seen in a joyful mood, it means he has his porridge in his pot'; 'you can believe it when you hear that donkeys own land but do not when you hear that Paraiyars own land'; 'salt thrown into the sea and money given to the Paraiyars are the same'; 'if Vanniyans say bullocks are for ploughing, Paraiyans will say they are for meat'; 'the relationship with a barren woman and the relationship with the Paraiyars without a piece of land cannot be fruitful'. Many of these proverbs and sayings basically portray the Paraiyars as people who are lazy, and incapable of holding any property and land, and that bullocks are more useful.

Apart from these there are myths told to me by both the Vanniyars and the Paraiyars to show why Paraiyars are innately incapable of owning land and should only be considered for manual labour.

> *Myth 1:* In the beginning, there were two brothers who were poor and had no land to cultivate; all the land belonged to the gods. They went one day to pray to God to give them land. But as a precondition God asked them to remove the carcass of a dead cow. The elder brother said *en tambi pāpān* ('My younger brother will do it'), but God understood that his brother was *pāpān* (Brahmin)[5]. From that day God made the younger brother a Brahmin who

owned land and the elder brother became a Paraiyar who worked in the land of the younger brother.[6]

Myth 2: In the beginning, God (*Parama Sivan*) conducted a competition for his two sons. They were asked to cultivate paddy on the land and whoever reaped the bigger harvest would win the competition. The elder one worked sincerely on the land day in and day out, and at the end, he brought three hundred bags of unhusked paddy to God. But God was not there to see the harvest so he went to rest. Later God came to the threshing ground to see the sons' harvest where he saw only the younger brother standing on the floor in front of the paddy of the elder son. Mistaking it for that of the younger son he awarded him the with land and when the elder son came, God asked him to go and work on the land of the younger son.

These myths, the Paraiyars feel, were used to justify their state of landlessness as something willed by God that they would not be able to change whatever they did to reverse the situation. The myths and proverbs, and the discourses repeated by the higher castes, the Paraiyars believe, made them internalise their state of landlessness as part of their genetic make-up and this was further strengthened by the life they lived for so long as labourers. The Paraiyars say that even when they asked the Brahmins and the Reddiyars to let them use their land when they wanted to leave the village for nearby towns, the Vanniyars persuaded them not to leave the land with the Paraiyars saying that they would leave it barren (*tarisu*). And so the Paraiyars have tried to buy and own land but have never been successful. All this has changed since their continuous conflicts after which they have gradually bought land and now, at the time of my field study, many Paraiyars own land, to the extent even of providing work for Vanniyars. They have achieved this both by their economic advancement as well as their cultural regeneration in treating the land as a symbol for power that once was used by the higher castes as a symbol of their powerlessness.

Reclaiming Land as Paraiyars' Empowerment

Three factors have been helpful for the Paraiyars to reconstruct their life and identity by their use of land. Their conflict with the higher castes over the *dargos* land in the 1930s, was the starting point of their whole project of identity – formation. Second, their active involvement in the Panchami land struggle, organised in the district, furthered their belief in the land as a way of reforming their life. The third factor was their creation of new myths through which they traced their origin in the village as original inhabitants who owned the land initially before it was appropriated by the higher castes.

The Impact of the Dargos Land Conflict

For the first time in their life the Paraiyars of Pappanallur had an experience of owning land conflict in the 1930s over the *dargos* land. Since we have already taken note of the conflict earlier, I shall focus on the impact the conflict made on the life of the Paraiyars.

First of all, it was through the *dargos* land struggle that the Paraiyars came to realise that they could fight against the higher castes. Prior to the conflict, they say, they would never have thought themselves capable of opposing the higher castes. The fact that they could beat up Vanniyar men gave them the confidence to begin their journey towards asserting their identity. The *dargos* land remains for them a symbol of their assertion of their strength against the higher castes. "For the first time we got strength (*tairiyam*) from that land conflict, and from then on we never looked back", said Michael, one of the drummers. It is important in the lives of the Paraiyars that they gained the courage to oppose the higher castes, and they often told me, it was like, 'getting up from the floor and sitting equal with them [higher castes] on a chair'.

Secondly, land for the Paraiyars remains a symbol of their new identity, and it is believed to be another source (complementing to the foundational symbol of the drum) from which they have drawn inspiration and energy to change other symbols as it had been their focus first, even before they had thought about the drum as the core of both their past low identity and also a new identity. "When we just think of the *dargos* land it brings up in our minds the history of our challenge against the *Ūr*, and it re-energises us in our fight against the Vanniyars", said Lourdusamy, one of the Paraiyar *Vagaiyarā* leaders. The Paraiyars had done some cultivation in the beginning, although in 2000-02 they did not cultivate anything since the Vanniyars refused to allocate sufficient water from the village tank and it was hard to get labourers. But for every Paraiyar land was a symbol that symbolised the beginning of their new status in the village.

Thirdly, the conflict gave them for the first time the power of social status that 'we too own land' in the village irrespective of their material gains from the land in terms of cultivation and earning. Barnabas told me, "I am unable to describe what a great feeling I had when for the first time I went to the piece of land and ploughed it. I felt like that I have given birth to a boy child". Like him many Paraiyars feel that the *dargos* land transformed them from just 'labourers' (*velaikāran*) to 'cultivators' (*vivasāyi*). It was further strengthened, the Paraiyars remember, when a local bank considered their application for a loan positively, since they had the land as security, though they did not have the title (*paṭṭā*) of the land. As a result, the Paraiyars say that they were no longer called '*parapayale'* (calling Paraiyars disrespectfully) by the Vanniyars, instead they started calling them only by their names.

In brief, the *dargos* land is a symbol of their struggle against the *Ūr* and the starting point of their identity formation.

The Panchami Land Struggle[7]

First let us discuss briefly the background of the struggle and the main event in which the Paraiyars of Pappanallur took part that cost them the death of one Paraiyar, Thomas, when the police fired on the protesters. Later we shall examine in what ways the Panchami land struggle contributed to their struggle against the higher castes in the village.

The history of Panchami land is traced back to the 1870s during which the missionaries from Scotland who established churches among the Paraiyars in Chengalpattu area and for the first time brought to light the plight of the Paraiyars (Oddie 1979). The campaign indeed had an effect on the British administration of this area when a report was published in 1891. On having learnt the abject conditions of the Dalits through a report by J.H.A Tremen Heere, then the District Collector of Chengalpattu, in March 1891, the British colonial government passed a law in 1918 in the British Parliament to assign land to them. Since the land was allotted to the Dalits who were called the fifth *Varna*, '*panchamas*', it was called '*Panchami land*'. The law said that the Dalits were strictly forbidden to sell or give it on lease within ten years from the allotment, and if they wanted to sell it after ten years of use, they could do so only to other Dalits. The Panchami lands should be Panchami lands and no one else could own them, possess them, or make claim over them by any means. The British Government knowing well the wily nature of the higher castes laid down strict terms and conditions, and one of the terms was that the lands could not be sold, mortgaged, exchanged, leased or gifted away to non-Dalits and, if done the transfer of land should bc trcatcd as illcgal (G.O.M.S 2217, dated 1 October, 1941). All these conditions were entered in the government records under the title 'Conditional Lands for Depressed Classes'. From 1930, the colonial government passed various orders in connection with the law to implement the scheme.

In 1933, 633 acres of Panchami land were, according to the government records, allotted to 300 Paraiyar families in and around Karanai village, near Mahabalipuram, in Chengalpattu district (Cf. G.O, District Collector, Chengalpattu, R/Dis. 5590, dated 19 November, 1933). In the 1950s, due to a severe drought and famine all over Tamil Nadu, many Paraiyars moved to other parts of the state for survival. According to Anthony Paul, a Paraiyar leader of Kuppayanallur village, who was one of the active members of the Panchami land struggle, the higher castes of the village, using that opportunity, allegedly had bought the land in exchange for food, a few measures of rice, ragi, millet and for a mere pittance, for instance Rs. 10 and forced the Paraiyars to imprint their Left Thumb Mark (LTM) on blank court stamp papers. In 1958 when the higher castes of Karanai, who went to pay taxes for the lands that they appropriated from the Dalits, the Village Administrative Officer (VAO) refused to accept the taxes since the transfer of Panchami lands was illegal. Later in 1977, then the state government of Dravida Munnetra Kazhagam party (DMK) sanctioned *paṭṭas* (ownership title) for 650 acres of Panchami land to all the Paraiyars, but the *paṭṭas*, the Paraiyars say, did not reach them, instead they went into the hands of the higher castes with the connivance of government officials.

One such case led to a serious conflict that actually became a major event in the Panchami land struggle. In 1989, Deepan Chakravarthy of Karanai village agreed to sell his Panchami land to one Sakunthala from Chennai city and took an advance of Rs. 25000. Even after several months that passed by, there had been no initiative on the part of Sakunthala to naturalise the transfer. This made Deepan Chakravarthy suspect a foul play. When he contacted the local revenue department officials he was told that the land had been transferred to Gowtham Chand, a north Indian moneylender and pawnbroker. Realising that the situation was getting out of control, he told me, that he, approached the Social Action Movement (SAM), a local Non-Governmental Organisation for legal advice. The SAM took it up, not as an isolated case but as an important case to mobilise the Paraiyars of that area to reclaim the Panchami land.

The Paraiyars of Karanai village, with the support of the Dalit organisations – Ambedkar Pasarai, Bagat Singh Pasarai, Dalit Sena, and International Ambedkar Centenary Movement – founded an association called '*Karanai Panchami Nila Pathukappu Kuḷu*' (Karanai Panchami Land Protection Group) and decided to repossess the lands. They jointly formed a committee called 'Save Panchama Land Committee', and during a meeting of the committee, they decided to install a statue in one corner of Deepan Chakravarthy land. On October 5, 1994, the

Paraiyars installed a statue of Dr. Ambedkar to indicate that they had reclaimed the lands in front of more than two thousand Paraiyars. But the very same evening the Ambedkar statue was knocked down by two sand lorries, allegedly removed and taken away by the police. In addition, Deepan Chakravarthy and fourteen others were arrested that night. This news spread all over the place like wild fire and the agitated Dalits gathered together from all over the district.

The Dalits and their leaders, numbering around 5000 people, 80 per cent of them were women, came from many villages in and around the area (from Pappanallur village alone fifty men and thirty women), they went to the Sub-Collector's office on October 10, 1994 and made two demands: 'hand the statue back to the Dalits, and give an assurance that the Panchami lands will be returned to us [the Dalits]'. The Sub-Collector refused to listen to their demands, and the Paraiyars in Pappanallur who took part in the protest and the negotiations told me, the Collector ordered the police to physically remove them from his office. The Dalits were enraged and resorted to *road-roko* (road blocks) in front of the Sub-Collector's office. All of a sudden, eye witnesses say, the police fired right into the gathering with no prior warning by tear gas or firing in the air and so on. The helpless Dalits ran helter-skelter. The Paraiyar women were brutally attacked by the police and two Paraiyar men, Ezhumalai from Kulippanthandalam village and Thomas, from Pappanallur, were killed in police firing. 118 Dalits, including 20 women were arrested and sent to prison.

This incident led to an aggressive confrontation between the Dalits and the police, and the Dalit organisations organised rallies all over the state to protest against the killing and the arrest of the Dalits during which many shops and buses were allegedly set on fire by the Dalits. Jeyagaran Joseph, General Secretary of the Dalit Sena with the support of other Dalit organisations founded an association called '*Panchami Nila Urimai Pathukappu Iyyakam*' (Panchami Land Protection Movement) with the aim to reclaim all the Panchami lands in Chengalpattu district and in other parts of Tamil Nadu.

The Karanai incident inspired the Dalits in many places in Tamil Nadu to reclaim Panchami land. The International Dr. Ambedkar Centenary Movement under the leadership of Yesumarian, a Jesuit lawyer, has effectively reclaimed the Panchami lands in Ekatoor, Kelambakkam, Rettaimalai Srinivasa Nagar, Thaiyur, Kazhipattur, Buddhama Nagar in Chengalpattu district, and in February 1995 the movement reclaimed 250 acres of Panchami land near Chengalpattu and now it is named '*Vīra Dalit Maa Nagar*' (Daring Dalit Colony). It is important to note the ways in which the Paraiyars have reclaimed the Panchami land. After they had taken the decision to repossess a particular plot of Panchami land, the first thing they did was to install a statue of Dr. Ambedkar to indicate that the land belonged to the Dalits, and secondly, they put up small huts and cooked a meal which was shared among the Dalits at the end of whole programme. In most of the places where Panchami land has been reclaimed, except Kazhipattur, 20 km from Chennai, where a school had been started for the Paraiyar children, lies unused, but remains a symbol of Paraiyar assertion of their power. For many Paraiyars, the Panchami land is to be taken as a concrete evidence of their ability to fight the higher castes.

More than any other Paraiyar village, the Panchami land struggle had a great influence on the Paraiyars of Pappanallur in their ongoing struggle against the Vanniyars of the village. Every Paraiyar of Pappanallur remembers the day (11 October 1994) when the police brought the body of Thomas to the Colony. The Paraiyars recall that the whole village was in such tension that many feared there would be a riot between the *Ūr* and the Colony. Three Vanniyar houses were set on fire, allegedly by the Paraiyars. But I was told that it was brought under control by a large deployment of police in the village.

The Panchami land struggle made an enormous impact on the minds of the Paraiyars of Pappanallur village, not only because one of them was killed in the incident, but also because of the success they achieved, that they could demonstrate their power against the state and the higher castes in Tamil Nadu. More importantly, the Paraiyars of Pappanallur felt for the first time the significance of their struggle against the Vanniyars in the village in a wider context that made them feel a sense of solidarity with other Dalits beyond their village. The incident the Paraiyars think, in many ways, helped them to intensify their challenge against the *Ūr*.

At the centre of the Colony in Pappanallur they have erected a monument for Thomas who was killed in the Panchami land struggle on which is inscribed, 'a martyr of the Dalit struggle'. Every Paraiyar in the Colony, including small boys and girls, has a version of the incident in which Thomas was killed that he/she narrates vividly as if she or he had taken part personally in the incident. This demonstrates the ways in which the killing has been imprinted in the minds of the Paraiyars. It also stands, as one of the Paraiyar women said, as a sign that the Paraiyars of Pappanallur would be ready to give up their lives in order to get what they want. In the Roman Catholic school (run by the nuns in Pappanallur), in the evening session and in every gathering of the Paraiyars the incident is invariably recalled either to sort out any differences among the Paraiyars or revive the fighting spirit of the Paraiyars against the *Ūr*. It is also a way by which they can recall, reassess, and retrieve their past to enliven their present. The dead Thomas in fact animates and guides the Paraiyars in Pappanallur in their struggle of imagining their life after they have distanced themselves from the *Ūr*. That is why the widow of Thomas, with a three-year-old girl child, disowns her husband and let the whole Colony own him for the purpose of the common good. "He is no more my husband, he is a martyr of our struggle. The blood he spilled on the earth will make every Paraiyar who lives rise against the oppression of the higher castes. Because of that, I always have a feeling he is alive more than the living", said the widow. The financial support she had received after her husband's death from so many Dalit organisations and the state government by which she had built a big house gave her the confidence to be so articulate. In addition, the fact that Thomas' family could improve its economic position from a state of being poor and landless to the state of owning land and a big house, the only house in the village that has three bedrooms, a toilet and a kitchen, gives the idea that a Paraiyar who gives up his/her life for the common cause will have more to gain than to lose. This is demonstrated in the ways in which the Paraiyar youth who are ready to die for the cause of the Paraiyars and the Dalits in Tamil Nadu.

Therefore, the *dargos* land conflict and the Panchami land struggle have been important events that made the land one of the key symbols of transformation, which they could imagine for their life to be in the village.

Counter Myths of Landownership

After the two events the Paraiyars in Pappanallur gradually started buying land from the Reddiyars who left the village after the 1970s and from the Vanniyars. One effective way they got the land was that initially they asked the absentee Reddiyars and Brahmins to let them cultivate their land, and later by negotiation they got their land for a low price and owned it. For this, the Paraiyars earned money from their work in the cities as coconut tree tappers, as factory workers and so on. At the time of my fieldwork, there were very few Paraiyars who did not own land. Aside this material sense, the Paraiyars have been evolving stories that they were the original inhabitants of the village who actually owned all the land; by the trick of the Brahmins and other higher castes their land was taken away from them and turned them into slaves. Although the story has no base, but most of the Paraiyars in their private conversations seem to believe it, the stories are popular among the younger Paraiyars, which the elder Paraiyars think will make them one day the landlords of the village.

> *Myth 1:* In the beginning, we [Paraiyars] were the original inhabitants (*pūrvīka makkal*) of Pappanallur. We lived in the beginning

as five *Vagaiyarās* happily and owned all the land in the village. From the village tank bund until the water channel at the end of the wetland we owned all the land. The Brahmins with the help of kings came into the village and took the land away from us cheating our grandfathers who put their thumbprint on *paṭṭa* papers. Later from them gradually the Reddiyars and the Vanniyars got the land as they are part of the high caste group. We were made merely slave labourers (*adimaikal*) by manipulating our ignorance (*ariyāmai*), simplicity and innocence. So, we should reclaim our land.

Myth 2: In the beginning there was no proper village tank, only the village had a small tank that did not collect much water during the rainy season. It was only Father Neelapanar who asked us to deepen the tank to make it a proper tank by giving us wheat and bulgar imported from America. Seeing our work, he awarded us more than fifty acres as our *dargos* land, and Father (*sāmiyār*) told our leader Barnabas, "Barnabas, it is your Panchami land and do not give it to anybody and promise to me on the Bible". Our leader promised that he would not give the land to any higher castes. Then on that land for a long time our grandfathers cultivated millet, ragi and corn. Our grandfathers used to tell us that they harvested more than a hundred bags of ragi. Then the higher castes by some trick took the land away from our grandfathers and made it for the use of the *Ūr*. Later, the village started using the land as public land (*purampokku*). We got some parts of the land after the first conflict and we will soon one day own the entire land.

These myths and other myths similar to these on land the Paraiyars try to spread among the young generations although they do not take it very seriously. Some elderly Paraiyars burst into laughter when I told these myths to them. One of them said, "it is a *pithalattam* (a dance of a mentally retarded person), the stories are only stories they could not be true (*nisam*). These young ones (*ilanthāripasangal*) do not know what they are doing, do not believe them". Similarly, the Vanniyars say that whatever the Paraiyars do to change their life they will always be considered as low people (*kīltharamāmanavargal*), "can you straighten a dog's tail?", they ask. For the Vanniyars, the myths of the Paraiyars are the work of only a few people instigated by the Christian church and its priests, which would make no impact on the village as a whole.

But the young Paraiyars, who are mostly members of the DPI, asked me, "don't you accept the Hindu stories and epics (*purānam*)? If you believe them, then what prevents you from believing our stories". These young Paraiyars, who have a more regular exposure to the Dalit movements in the state than any other Paraiyars, are convinced that by evolving new stories counter to the conventional stories they can one day change their state of 'untouchableness' and assert their power. They believe strongly that their polluted and low identity as beef eaters, drummers and landless slaves was engendered by such discourse of stories, and by the same method they think they can and should transform drumming, beef-eating and land as their positive social custom. In spite of opposition from within and without, the young Paraiyars claim to represent the change that is taking place in the Colony. They argue that it has indeed already taken place by showing one of the evidences that the beef is openly sold in the towns like Uthiramerur and every restaurant sells beef *briyani* (a rice dish with beef) that is consumed by every caste person. I did find during my field study that there were five restaurants that had beef *briyani* on their menu. However, it is an exaggeration to say that all castes eat the beef dish in the restaurants, even if a few might do so secretly. What I can say is that no Paraiyar I met and talked to told me that eating beef is a polluting act, instead most of the Paraiyars want the practice to be redeemed from its polluting image to a respectable social custom.

Notes

1. See Kumar (1994: 85-9) and Washbrook (1999) for details of how the Dalits in general and the Paraiyars in particular made important contributions to agriculture and the British administration.
2. *Uḷavu māttuku ethukku nilam?*
3. Mosse (2003: 158ff) gives us an account of water management in southern Tamil Nadu and the different roles of the Dalit groups' duties in regulating water from the tanks to the land. He tells us that the Dalit men who perform such roles are called *nīrppāccis* or *nīrvettiyāns* (water cutters) and *kudumban*.
4. Contrariwise, Washbrook (1999) informs us that the Paraiyars in Chengalpattu area had some kind of ownership of land in the sense that they had at least the right to cultivate the land and he considers the late nineteenth century a 'golden age of paraiyar'. And my visit to Kodangipatty village in southern Tamil Nadu between the towns of Podi and Theni has also given a contemporary example that the Paraiyars for a long time have owned more land than the Thevars (one of the high caste groups) in that village.
5. The word, *pāpān*, has two meanings in Tamil: one is 'look after' and second is Brahmin.
6. Deliege (1999: 73) gives a similar myth in his discussion of myths of origin of the Dalits but the myth does not have any reference to land.
7. Although I took part personally in the final day of the struggle in 1995, when the police fired on the crowd, for the present study I draw on the pamphlets and bills published by the Dalit organisations and from the interviews, during my field study in 2001-02, with Yesumarian, a Jesuit-lawyer, the founder-leader of the International Dr. Ambedkar Centenary Movement, seventeen women and twenty-five men who had taken part in the struggle and went to prison on account of it. In addition, I visited Karanai village where the main struggle for the *panchami* land took place and met people from the higher castes and the Paraiyars.

8

Re-symbolisation and Re-identification: The Epistemic Status of Paraiyar Identity

Ambivalences in Symbolic Reversals

What we have discussed above may give the reader the impression that the Paraiyars have accomplished their identity formation without any problem. It is not so in the village. It is just a beginning of the process by which they try whatever means they have to imagine their life in a new way. Not every Paraiyar accepts the ways in which the Colony so far has proceeded in their assertion against the *Ūr* and its higher castes. There are some who feel that they should not have abandoned the services to the *Ūr,* particularly the service of drumming. By the drumming, these Paraiyars feel, they had some kind of ritual power that gave a space to them in the village institutions. "During the village festival time, the whole village would wait for me [*kambukuṭṭi* Paraiyar] as if he was the leader of the village. I used to have feeling of pride [*pērumai*]. Now I have lost it. See me now, I have no work and no money to pay the school fees for my children studying in Kuppayanallur", says Meiyappan. If he were given the choice, he would prefer to resume his former service for the *Ūr*. But the same person had also told me, on another occasion, that he felt greatly relieved from the 'ugly work' (*asiṇkam*) and it made him humane. In the same way, Ambrose, one of the drummers told me that wanted to resume his drumming at funerals of the *Ūr*. One day late at night, during my fieldwork, I witnessed an incident that remains with me. I saw him holding his drum in his hand and shouting at and scolding the Paraiyar leaders that he was deprived of his work as a drummer and would go to the *Ūr* and tell the Vanniyars of his willingness to resume his drumming. But the very next day when I reminded him of the previous night's incident, he said, "Oh, that was because I had consumed *arrack* [country liquor], do not take that seriously. I will never take up the work [drumming] for the Vanniyars".

Apart from that, some older Paraiyars consider the life they lived before being part of the *Ūr* as much more peaceful, and that is for them a real and orderly life in which each had a role to play for the functioning of the village, although they had to do the menial jobs. They see the caste system as something that gives a sense of security and a feeling of community. "When we went to Uthiramerur or Vedanthangal those days, if anybody from other villages challenged us, we used to feel that our *Ūr* leaders would support us. But now that feeling is gone. The only security we have now is that our parish priest will take care of us. But he is not always with us and they get transferred every two years". Arockiasamy, in his seventies, said, "nothing wrong in being an untouchable. What do you mean by equality? Show me a society where there is equality between people. There will always be master (*andān*) and servant (*adimai*) in some form or other". But the same person tells me that in his next life he wants to be born as a high caste person. More importantly, the changes the Colony have seen after the conflicts and the symbolic reversals, according to these elders, will never be able to change the stigma of untouchability.

Such contradictory voices, some young Paraiyars consider, as a transient phase in the process of change of their life. Some others see it as the real situation of the Colony, and they are pessimistic about their future. In my mind, the ambivalence and contradictions should be seen as a part of the process of change in a society that had a strong hierarchical and well-knit community, whose ideologies were internalised by all in the system for centuries. It will be hard to change it all on a sudden. It will take time during which one will hear and experience such ambivalences and contradictions.

And the Paraiyars have not yet replaced the institutions completely that they had rejected, though they have tried and are trying with their imagination. But the time they spend at a certain point of their efforts causes anxiety. It is the insecurity and anxiety, which make them speak of their life in ambivalent terms. I find it hard to see this as a lacuna, or a failure in their project of identity-formation, instead it should be considered as a state in the process of change.

Thirumavalavan, founder leader of the DPI party, said, "we [the Dalits] are breaking our century-old chains that bonded us to slavery and oppression; breaking the bonds some times may pain or the sound of breaking may terrify us; in that fear we may shout, 'stop, stop, I would rather be in chains', but, I tell you, from my heart they want only to be freed from untouchability". That liberative desire, he thinks, they suppress because that was what they had been forced to do for a long time and to consider it as the nature of human life. I agree with him because it was also my experience with the Paraiyars of Pappanallur. Thirumavalavan requested me further that I should focus on and write about the signs of change among the Paraiyars, not the temporary oscillations the Paraiyars go through in their struggle. If I made much of the latter, he said, the former would be obscured, and that would not be fair on my part as an anthropologist.

Keeping this in mind we should examine the signs of change that are at work in the Colony and in the *Ūr* of Pappanallur village. Particularly, in the following sections, I will theorise on the three symbolic reversals to understand the Paraiyars' way of identity-making.

'De-identification' and 're-identification' with the Symbols

The basic process at work in the three symbolic reversals discussed above is the identification of the Paraiyars of

Pappanallur with the symbols of the drum, beef-eating and land. The first act is that they 'de-identify' the symbols that had a meaning of pollution that defined the Paraiyars as low and polluted. By implication, this means that they had identified with the symbols of pollution. The Paraiyars would argue that they did not identify with the symbols on their own but they were forced to do so. At that time they say that they were in a state of false-consciousness in which they believed the negative identity as positive. The conflicts fear the false-consciousness and make them understand the reality and reject the symbols of pollution. In this, they do not reject the symbols as such but only the meanings given to these symbols. The second act in the process is that they inject a new meaning into each symbol in a way that it can redeem them from pollution to the positive characteristics of the Paraiyars. Then they positively re-identify themselves with the symbols that have had their meanings changed. In that way, de-identification and re-identification are the two phases of the Paraiyars' way of coming out of their low status and forming a new identity. As we have seen in Chapter 3, the act of identification is a crucial factor in identity construction (Jenkins 1996; Barth 1981; Cohen 1985; Giddens 1984; Laclau 1994). It is important to consider Laclau (1994: 3) who is instructive in this context. For him, the key term to understand the process of construction of identity is the "psychoanalytical category of *identification*' (emphasis is in the original) with its explicit assertion of a lack at the root of any identity: one needs to identify with something because there is an originary and insurmountable lack of identity". In the case of the Paraiyars, before their conflicts with the *Ūr*, they did not lack identity, in fact they had an identity, although low and polluted but they had internalised that identity. But what they lacked was the consciousness of the ways in which their identity was given, which they come to achieve in and through their conflicts, and then consciously and actively identify themselves with the symbols whose meanings are changed. In this I find two kinds of identities and identification: the polluted identity and de-polluted identity, false identification with the former and positive identification with the latter.

The de-identification and re-identification help them to form cultural differences that make for their identity, which Appadurai calls 'culturalism'. Appadurai (2000: 15) defines culturalism as "the conscious mobilisation of cultural differences in the service of a larger national or transnational politics", more clearly, he says that it is "identity politics mobilised at the level of the nation state". In this identity politics what is important is the dimension of difference, not a substance, which a group insists on for an articulation of identity against nation-states. In the case of the Paraiyars, the higher castes of the *Ūr* should be understood as a nation-state against which they naturalise a set of differences they form by changing the meaning of the symbols. Earlier the same symbols exhibited a set of differences but they were used negatively to define them as low and polluted, and they did not own those differences. I call this difference an oppressive cultural difference. Now the differences they make through the symbols help them define themselves positively and they do positively own them. It is a transformative difference. In this mobilisation the Paraiyars are self-conscious of their differences in terms of what they provide them with.

Hegemony through Symbolic Discourse

The main result of the process of identification is that the Paraiyars are able to recover their agency they claim to have had before and by which they realise their right to define themselves now after the conflicts.[1] Thus far they had been passive, allowing themselves to be defined by others, but now they become active by giving themselves a name of their own. Although they gain their agency starting from the time of the conflicts to the time in which they transform their symbols. What gives an epistemic status to the symbols is only when they use the mythico-symbolic discourse to change their meanings. Their former identity is, they realise, given to them by the same type of discourse, which they use now to give themselves a new identity. The Paraiyars believe that if myths formed their former identity they can now help them form the new identity that they want to have. As seen in our theoretical framework (mainly in Kearney 2002), the counter-myths the Paraiyars evolve help them (i) design (plot) the ways they want to reform and imagine their new life, (ii) recreate the past in which they lived as low and polluted people that has (iii) a kind of cathartic power to heal their wounds and evoke a response in terms of their future life, and (iv) have a wisdom for understanding the life they lived and the life they want to live. What is the core element in all this is the kind of discursive formulation that has the power to give a definition of themselves, to structure or de-structure a society (Torfing 1999: 85-93; Laclau 1993: 413-7).

The final outcome of the method of mythico-symbolic discursive formulation is that by such discursive practice, the Paraiyars achieve hegemony over their life and over the village institutions. The concept of hegemony is understood as the system of meanings and values and experienced as daily practices that are 'constitutive and constituting' a sense of reality that gives a group or individual an identity (Williams 1983: 110; also see Crehan 2002: 172). Hegemony of a group in that sense is a result of articulation of a discourse, which is, according to Laclau and Mouffe (1985: 105), "a practice establishing relations among elements such that their identity is modified as a result of the articulatory practice". Hegemony is a set of discourses that help form a dominant idea of social life and activities. In Gramsci's (1971) words, such hegemony is transformative and expansive in that it changes from one state of existence to another by negating the unhelpful, and deepening the helpful elements. The articulation of the mythical discourse, by and of the Paraiyars, has the power to give them a status of hegemony by which they rejected the village institutions and formed their own and changed the meanings of the symbols to form their own identity. Discourse and hegemony have been two important factors in the political construction of the Paraiyar identity.

Identity through Symbolic Interactions

Both the new and old identity of the Paraiyars are formed and re-formed in and through their interactions with the *Ūr,* in which the symbols remain the means of communication. If life is understood as a communicative act, my field study has helped me to see that this is done through symbols in Pappanallur. This, as I have discussed earlier, is informed by Blumer's (1986) theory of symbolic interactionism, according to which a society functions on three basic premises: (i) human beings act towards different things, places, persons and events on the basis of the meanings they have for them; (ii) such meanings are born out of the social interaction one has with others; and (iii) these meanings are then modified by the interpretative process one uses in interactions. The symbols we discussed above have been the means by which the Paraiyars communicated with the *Ūr* when they were part of the *Ūr* before, and now outside it. The communication is more intense and evocative now than before not only in terms of the Paraiyars' conscious interaction with and through the symbols but also in terms of the higher castes' realisation that the symbols are and were the locus of identity.

Epistemic Status of Paraiyar Identity

The question of identification, which is the basis of the Paraiyar identity, explains also the two dimensions of it: who they were/are and who do they think they are/want to be, the former is 'ontological', and the latter, 'epistemological'. There is a dialectic between these two, and such a dialectic seems necessary to strengthen the one by the other (Chakrabarty 2003: 2ff). The present study is concerned with the epistemological dimension more than the ontological. This does not mean that the latter has no place in the discussion of the former. 'Who they are' has in many ways to be a part of 'who they think they are', in the sense that the discussion of the symbolic reversals we realised that they constantly recalled the experience of their past life in order to structure their future life properly. And the 'who they are/were' was greatly shaped by what the other people defined the Paraiyars and the dimension of 'who they think they are' was either disguised by the force and enormity of the former dimension or did not exist for them at all. Alcoff (2000: 334-5) calls these two dimensions *public identity* and *subjectivity*. The public identity is the one that is seen by others, how the public sees them to be; the subjectivity is not in the sense of 'bias' or 'interested perspective' but merely the sense of one's lived self, one's own sense of self. Both the dimensions of identity are needed to make the identification complete. As we have seen, the Paraiyars reject their public identity and form their identity by evoking their own sense of self, waiting for others to recognise it as seen by them. But ultimately, in the case of the Paraiyars, what is important is who they think they are or want to be, not what others (particularly the higher castes) see them to be.

In this, experience seems to be the basis of their knowledge of their identity. As it was observed in our theoretical framework, the postmodern critique dismisses this subject-centred knowledge that is based on the relationship between experience and identification. Because experience cannot give objective 'truth' since it is mediated by language, in which meaning is relative; in this sense subjectivity does not exist outside grammatical structures that guide human thought (see for more on this Mohanty 2000; Moya 2000). So identities are basically fictitious and can never be fixed. But the case of the Paraiyars demonstrates that identity can only be formed by their experience of the past in which they had a low subjectivity, and of the present in which they have gained an assertive and positive subjectivity, both the experiences yielded a knowledge that was real. If they had not had the two experiences then it would have been hard to define themselves, not only now but equally also before. Their experience in the conflicts definitely yielded knowledge of their sense of what others see them to be and who they think they are and want to be.

Therefore, contrary to the postmodern critique, the reality of experience is a constitutive factor in the formation of identity. As Mohanty (2000: 57ff) has said, I find the identity of the Paraiyars both as constructed (both socially and theoretically), and real in the sense that it refers to the outward reality, and in this way identity becomes dynamic, variable and negotiated, not fixed by the caste system and pollution rituals and practices. In addition, the marginalised do have 'epistemic privilege' in that they demonstrate in their focus on the change of meaning of symbols to form their identity, and by that they show how they think of what they want to be. It is this epistemological dimension that matters most for the Paraiyars in their act of identification with the symbols.

Is this identification being recognised by others? What role does the dimension of public identity – what others see them to be – play in their identity-making? Because identification and recognition are the two sides of identity, and it is the latter only that gives legitimacy to and provides a complete picture of the former. Therefore, we need to answer the question: does the *Ūr* and the higher castes in Pappanallur recognise the self-formed identification and identity of the Paraiyars?

Resisting the Change: A View of the Elites

The higher castes in Pappanallur village, by and large, refuse to recognise the Paraiyars' rejection of the traditional village institutions and the symbolic construction of their identity. In their view, they look at whatever the Paraiyars do to assert themselves as a futile exercise and are convinced that it will never be able to remove the stigma attached to the them. "The Colony people should be Colony people and the *Ūr* people should be *Ūr* people and we will never allow them [the Paraiyars] to dominate us", say the Vanniyars.

If the *Ūr* people do not recognise the new identity of the Paraiyars, how are they going to succeed in their efforts, even if they give no value to what the *Ūr* people think about them? As

Jenkins (1999: 21) notes, "it is not enough to assert an identity. That identity must also be validated (or not) by those with whom we have dealings. *Social identity is never unilateral"* (emphasis is original). The Paraiyars can go on re-defining themselves by reversing the symbols, but that definition needs to be recognised by the *Ūr* higher castes, not because the higher castes are the high priests who confer identity to people, but because their recognition in some way or other is needed for the Paraiyars to internalise their own self-definition. Because identity making is a collective act in which the central questions are: who defines what against whom, and by whom, and how is this validated? The self-image should also become the public image to have the self-image naturalised. There is a dialectic between self-definition and definition by others in any social interaction through which one gains ultimately an identity. Barth (1969, 1981) sees identity-making in terms of giving and receiving messages: it is not enough to send a message; that message must be received by significant others. In this sense, identities are constructed in the process of an interaction between the groups, which are in conflict (Cohen 1985; Jenkins 1999). As Deliege (1999: 199) notes sharply, "untouchability is above all the expression of a set of social relations, of the relationship between different social actors and that is where the shoe pinches. Although one of the partners in the relationship seems to have changed, this is not true of the rest; among the higher castes, in effect, little in their basic conception of untouchability seems to have changed".

Therefore, the Paraiyars' identity formation has to be placed in the context of the non-recognition of and resistance to it by the *Ūr* people. We need to examine the question, why the higher castes do not recognise the Paraiyars' new identity. The answer to this will possibly provide a better understanding of the present study. In anthropological studies, the study of elites is a marginal area except for a few (Cohen 1981; Marcus 1983; Shore and Nugent 2002). In many studies, the elites are included but their perspectives are not; they are hardly studied in their own right.

Often we study either the domination of the elites (thesis) or the resistance of the subaltern (antithesis) but rarely do we try to understand both together (synthesis). In this sense, our understanding of the Paraiyars has to be mediated by an analysis of the *Ūr* higher castes, particularly the Vanniyars. This will give us a better grasp of the processes of both domination and resistance.

Therefore, although my principal focus was the Paraiyars, I spent three months staying in the *Ūr* during which I attempted to acquire a perception of the Vanniyars' view of the Paraiyars by observing, not their institutions, but their daily practices, individual relationships and their discourse about the Paraiyars through which their political power was exercised; how they continue to succeed and reproduce their domination over and stigmatisation of the Paraiyars. In this I follow Marcus (1983) and Shore (2002) who suggest directing anthropological analysis away from institutions and the institutional basis of power to biographical lives of elites that perhaps can help us better grasp the reality of power and domination. Power is not in institutions and in laws but in people's practices and discourses, more sharply, in elites' strategies that are embedded in rituals, personal relationships and social interactions. That power has to be uncovered if we really want to understand the culture of dominance. The study of elites should focus on the disclosure of a network of domination.

An ethnography of higher castes is beyond the scope of the present study. Instead I restrict my discussion to biographies of two Vanniyar leaders and four social and religious practices by which I hope to understand what they feel about the Paraiyars and their new life. I have chosen Elumalai Gounder, who is in his eighties, and Pakkiri, in his forties, to represent the Vanniyar elites. Elumalai Gounder was the unopposed leader of the village for more than five decades and there has been no event of the village in the past, and even recently at the time of my fieldwork, that does not have his intervention or involvement. Even in his old age I found him very articulate about the situation in the village. Pakkiri, whom I call a twentieth century model of higher castes, is the husband of the present (2002-03) leader of the Village Panchayat, Karpagam. He has an intimate knowledge not only of the reality of the village, but also of the politics of the state; more importantly, he knows the inner networks of the Colony and he often uses this to sustain his domination over the whole village. I lived in the homes of the two leaders, had meals with them and talked to them everyday about their lives. The following sections are part of the result of my interactions with them.

(a) The Vanniyars of Pappanallur

(i) Elite Story 1: Elumalai Gounder

Elumalai Gounder is married with four children, three sons and a daughter. The three sons live with him, his daughter is married to a man of a nearby village. He owns twenty-seven acres of wetland but I was told that he owned another twenty acres illegally under *binomi* (false) names. Although his three sons manage the cultivation and the administration of the house, Elumalai Gounder is still in charge of the money matters and takes the major decisions in his house.

Elumalai Gounder belongs to the Goundan *vittu Vagaiyarā* that traditionally holds the leadership post in the village. From the 1910s, after the Naidus, Reddiyars and Brahmins left the village, Elumalai Gounder has been the unofficial leader of the village and even the Village Panchayat, the lowest unit of the state government, has not in any way altered his power and domination. Even before he gets up in the morning three or four people will be in front of his house from the *Ūr* or from the Colony with problems to be sorted out by him. But he does not come out to meet them until he gains sufficient knowledge about the cases and the persons who have come to meet him with their problems. This he does by asking a daughter or a son of one of his own sons to enquire into the details of the cases. Once he has had the required information, he comes out in his white dhoti and sacred ash (*vibhūthi*) applied on his forehead and meets the people who have come to see him. All those who were sitting on rope cot, stand up in respect to him. He does not ask them immediately about their problems but he offers them tea or coffee; sometimes he asks them to have a meal with him. One of his daughters-in-law told me that every day about ten people from the village either have a meal or take coffee/tea with him. While having coffee Elumalai enquires about the problems. If the problem is a minor one he sorts it out, basing his decision not on his hearing of both parties but on his judgement of the persons involved in the case. He would say to one person, "I know you too well, you must have made the mistake. Better make peace with him". If the person hesitates to heed this advice he warns him of the dire consequences of taking the case to the *Ūr* council. Sometimes he beats up the person whom he thinks has done wrong or asks him to do some work in his house, such as supplying straw feed for the cattle or working in his fields. When I asked the persons who did such work or whom Elumalai had beaten, they said, "Whatever he does, Gounder [Elumalai] has always been just and considerate to the poor. And his family has the divine authority (*kadavul varam*) to find solutions to our problems. We believe him and obey him more than the Village Panchayat or the police".

Elumalai told me that his *Vagaiyarā* people and particularly his family have been given him the authority by God to be arbiter in the village. He told me the story of how his family came to be the natural leaders of the village. "once upon a time, there was a very big problem (*thagarāru*) between two *Vagaiyarā* people in the *Ūr*. An *aither vīttu Vagaiyarā* man murdered an *aitham vīttu Vagaiyarā* man. This started a riot between the different groups. No leader could settle the dispute and the leaders from other *Vagaiyarās* made every effort to calm the situation, but nothing could prevent the conflicting groups from killing each other. At that time, one of our grandfathers, called Lakshman Goundar, seeing the plight of the people in the village went to Periapalayathamman temple and prayed before the goddess. The goddess said to him, 'you have my power to settle disputes and before you listen to the warring parties you should take a bath and apply my sacred ash and vermilion (*kungumam*) on your forehead. If anyone does not respect you and refuses to obey you, curse him in my name'. Strictly following the instructions of the goddess, our Lakshman Gounder came back to the village, assembled the two *Vagaiyarā* people and settled the dispute. Miraculously the people who so far had been aggressive suddenly became submissive and obeyed our Gounder. From then on our family was ordained by God to be arbiters (*nāttāmai*) of the village".

After narrating the story, he told me further that whatever he said during his arbitrations in the village had never come from himself but from that special gift of God given to his family. He reasoned that his knowledge of the Hindu epics, the *Mahabharata* and the *Ramayana* and the power of his argument all came, not from his formal education that in fact he never had, but mainly from the special gift of God to him and his family from the beginning. This discourse of ritual and political power Elumalai repeats often in some form or other when he is settling disputes. When some people do not believe his judgement he tells them, "what I am telling you does not come from me, it is from Amman [goddess]. Do you remember the special gift given to our family?" Alternatively he starts telling the story to them. Immediately the people believe him and follow his advice. The Paraiyars too still have great respect for Elumalai Gounder, although they have much less to do with the *Ūr* and the higher castes. Many Paraiyars readily oblige Elumalai whenever he requests them to do work for him; they do this out of respect for an elderly person who is 'full of wisdom and experience' (*arivāli, anubavasāli*). At the time of my field study it was only on the land of Elumalai Gounder that some Paraiyars still went to work. But the Paraiyars who work for him are treated in the same way as they were treated before their conflicts and giving the traditional services up to the *Ūr*. No Paraiyar is allowed to enter Elumalai Gounder's house and every time the Paraiyars who work for him and come to meet him stand in front of him out of respect and remove the sandals from their feet and the towel from shoulders. Asked why they still behave like this, the Paraiyars told me that they did not regard Elumalai Gounder as belonging to a high caste (*mēlsāthi*) but only as a respected leader (*periyavar*). But the Paraiyar youth see this as a subtle form of maintaining the status of a high caste, disguised by the talk about a 'gift of God'.

Elumalai Gounder has strong opinions about the caste system and insists on the importance of the principles of the caste system. For him, if a village is to be a village it should have higher castes and low castes and should be divided geographically into *Ūr* and the Colony. "If there is a master who orders things, there should be a servant to take his orders. This is natural. In every system (*amaippu*) some things will be on top and some others are at the bottom. How can everything and everybody be on top? If all are kings who will be ministers?" he argues. According to him, divisions are important for a village to be in order. He told me that before the Paraiyars went away from the *Ūr*, although they had divisions as higher castes and low castes, as a village there was unity and happiness, but now after the division the Paraiyars have created there is only disunity and disorder. For him, what the Paraiyars have done is in fact divisive but not the hierarchical division they had before.

"We did not ask God to make us higher castes after our birth, we were born higher castes. They [the Paraiyars] were born low caste people. It is not our plan, but God's plan. As real human beings we should abide by God's plan" he argues. It is one's *karma* that he is born into a high caste or a low caste and he should abide by this; only by the proper adherence to one's *karma* can anyone reap the benefits of this life in his next life. Further he said that there was no evidence in history of any low caste person becoming high caste or vice versa by any human efforts. When asked if he would be willing to be born if God were to make him be born in a Paraiyar's house, he said, "no, God will not make me low like that. Since God has made me a high caste once, He will never hereafter make me a low caste". When I told him about the change that the Paraiyars have brought about in the village through their conflicts with the *Ūr*, he said that nothing was going to change, neither the status of Paraiyars nor that of the higher castes. He says that he could believe it if someone told him that the Vanniyars have become more pure and high (*uyarnthavargal*) like Brahmins, but he would never believe that the Paraiyars have become pure. In addition, he says that the Paraiyars' giving up of their polluting services has not made any change in their continuing to be polluted and polluting Paraiyars. "Look at the way they speak, all foul language, and look at the way they keep their houses in spite of the support they receive from the parish fathers [Roman Catholic priests]; if you give a pocketful of *arrack* and briyani they will do anything for you. God has written it in their head that they should live like this and nothing will change this" said Elumalai Gounder.

These thoughts Elumalai Gounder repeatedly disseminates among the people in the village during major functions such as village festivals, and particularly, he often makes a point of telling this to the very few Paraiyars who go to him for help. This is quite effective because the kind of discourse that Elumalai Gounder develops and disseminates sometimes blunts the Paraiyars' aggressive campaign against caste discrimination and discourages many of them. In addition, Elumalai Gounder remains the personification of the system that will never allow changes in the village; even if some Vanniyars are willing to make concessions to the Colony people, Elumalai Gounder persuades them to reject their positive attitude.

Repeatedly Elumalai Gounder stressed the idea that life in the village is the order of God (*katavulin dharmam*) in which higher castes and low castes are not to be seen as unequal statuses but an order. This 'cosmological order', given to them in birth, can never be changed by any attempts of any groups that reside in the order. In this way, Elumalai Gounder prevents change in the village and remains a power that sustains the domination of the higher castes. To my mind, central to this is the way in which he mobilises mythical history, 'the divine plan', tradition, 'village order and unity' to shroud themselves and their domination with a veil of legitimacy and to define the boundaries between the *Ūr* and the Colony, in spite of the efforts the Paraiyars make to change their low and polluted identity. By successfully portraying the status quo, the caste hierarchy, as the stable and divine order, the elite status is confirmed and maintained, albeit grudgingly by the Paraiyars.

(ii) Elite Story 2: Pakkiri Gounder

Pakkiri Gounder is forty-three years old, educated until higher secondary (advance level) and is now reading history for an undergraduate degree through distance education. He belongs to *aitham vīttu Vagaiyarā*. He made his wife, Karpagam, win the election to the post of Village Panchayat president in 2002 as Pappanallur had a Panchayat place reserved for women. He has two children, one seven years old and the other four. Pakkiri presents himself a modern version of Elumalai Gounder. Like Elumalai Gounder he has the same ideas about life in the village but he is diplomatic in expressing them and he has a good rapport with the Paraiyars. He interacts with the Paraiyars so closely that some times it is not easy to differentiate him when he is standing beside them. He was one of the few who studied in the R.C. school that was meant only for the Paraiyar children in the village. He has a few friends in the Colony with whom he often associates freely unlike any other Vanniyar. Later, after his marriage with Karpagam, he got a job as a noon-meal scheme organiser in the R.C. School. This facilitated a close interaction with the Catholic nuns who ran the school for the Madras-Mylapore Archdiocese. This gave him the opportunity to get to know the church and the diocese. He has used this association in securing scholarships for some of his relatives, and he has got jobs for three Vanniyar girls in Chennai city with the help of the nuns. Some Vanniyars think that Pakkiri has gained materially more than the Paraiyars from the Church. He also has good rapport with government officials in the district headquarters in Kanchipuram that, many Paraiyars think, he has succeeded in making himself appear before government officials as a person acceptable both in the *Ūr* and in the Colony. He functions as a contact person between the state and the village and he has influence in the sanctioning of government schemes for the village. In 2000, he allegedly used his contacts in high places to divert a scheme meant for rural poor women's development of the Colony to the *Ūr* high caste women and made his wife its leader.

The language and the idiom he used were close to the ways in which the Paraiyars would speak about their emancipation. He said, "I like the way in which the Colony people fought against our people [Vanniyars]. I support the idea that the Paraiyars should be treated equally with our people. Tell me in what way are they less human than the higher castes? I strongly advocate caste equality". Many Paraiyars, particularly Paraiyar women, are mesmerised by such talk. Some articulate Paraiyars feel that Pakkiri uses the familiarity he enjoys among them to prevent Paraiyars from being elected president of the Panchayat consistently from the 1980s, though there had been every prospect of victory for the Paraiyars, if allowed to stand united. Despite the Paraiyars being numerically stronger in three villages in the Pappanallur Panchayat – Pappanallur, Theresapuram, and Thiruvenkatapuram – they have so far been unable to win the elections.

The main reason why, the Paraiyars think, this is so is that Pakkiri close to the date of the poll divides the votes of the Paraiyars in these villages. At the time of the last election (October 2001), Paraiyars told me that they had decided in their *Vagaiyarā* council to field their candidate Angela Mary, wife of K. Charles for the post of president. But Pakkiri Gounder came into the Colony on the eve of polling day, and allegedly distributed light bulbs, sarees for the women and money for some Paraiyars to go and buy a drink. This created disunity among the Paraiyars and some sections of Paraiyars voted for his candidate, his wife, Karpagam. This happens in every election.

Asked why he does not allow a Paraiyar to become president of the Panchayat, he said, "I have no problem in their becoming president. But this would not be good for the village. In the meetings of the Panchayat no Vanniyar member would listen to a

Paraiyar president. A Paraiyar president would find it hard to speak to officials in Maduranthagam and in Chennai to secure benefits for our village, because most of the officials being high cast people would not listen to a Paraiyar. Ultimately we would all be the losers". He further showed me some newspaper clippings to give me evidence about how Paraiyar presidents in the Panchayats of southern Tamil Nadu were not allowed to function by the higher castes in those Panchayats. Deep down he strongly believes that the Paraiyars do not have any innate quality to be leaders. His definition of a leader is one who gives to people, not one who receives from people. He sees Paraiyars as people who have an innate quality to receive from others. Because, he says, "they have lived so long as servants in our fields and houses and this has made them slaves whose main objective in life has only been food; to get this they will do anything; they would even sell their wives to the Vanniyar who gives them a bowl of porridge. How could such people become leaders for our village?" he asks. Whenever he expresses strong opinions about the Paraiyars, diplomatically he peppers them with saying, "of course, the Colony people are very good people, I want them to come up in life". I told him that there is evidence of Dalits who have been great leaders such as Ambedkar, who was once the Law Minister of India and the principal architect of the Indian Constitution, and K.R. Narayan who was President of India. To which he said, "let us talk about Pappanallur village, why do you bring those cases that have no relevance for our life here".

Pakkiri Gounder does another thing that further truncates the rise of the Paraiyars. Although moneylenders come from the nearby town, he is the local organiser of money lending to the Paraiyars, and in this he sees to it that many Paraiyars are indebted to him all the time. Even when some Paraiyars go to him to repay the money he would sometimes ask them to use the money for some other purposes and return the money later. Many Paraiyar women see this as a gesture of generosity to them. But what they fail to see is that he exercises his domination in subtle ways. The Paraiyars who received money on loan are the people who would never dare to go against him. If anyone were to go against him, he would demand the money back within a day, which would be hard for a Paraiyar to arrange. Therefore, many hesitate to oppose him for any reason. This is also even the case with the most articulate Paraiyars who have links with the DPI party. "All their revolutionary ideas will surrender to my money", said Pakkiri Gounder.

If Elumalai Gounder considered the Paraiyars as permanently polluted and low people who have no choice except to be 'untouchables', Pakkiri Gounder would say that the Paraiyars should improve their status in a world of democracy, but they do not have the natural ability to do so. In that sense, both seem to have the same ideology in terms of their attitude towards the Paraiyars. Both of them believe that they, the Vanniyars, can continue to keep the Paraiyars in servitude and can still maintain their domination over the Colony even though they are no longer part of the *Ūr*. To that end, both believe, as every Vanniyar does, that political power should never be given to the Paraiyars. Using every means available to them the Vanniyars want to keep the Paraiyars always at their mercy. There are always ways of maintaining their hegemony in the village. The difference between then and now is that in those days the Vanniyars and other higher castes used coercion to have their design prevail over the village life, whereas now they persuade the Paraiyars with a different kind of discourse to consent to their ideologies. The discourses we have just noted in the two elite stories once again prove the point that the core to identity-making is discourse, for discourse should be seen both as a consequence and a cause of hegemonic articulation. More sharply, "it is the play of meaning within discourse and the subversion of discourse by the field of discursivity that provide the condition of possibility of hegemonic articulation" (Torfing 1999: 102). Put simply, in Pappanallur the hegemony of the higher castes still continues, only the form it has taken on a new idiom and it differs from the earlier traditional caste hierarchy within which the higher castes dominated the Paraiyars. Now the same higher castes monopolise the sources of mobility provided by democratic politics and have the edge on the flow of benefits from the government to the people.

At the same time, we cannot simply deny that in some areas the Vanniyars have lost their hold. For instance, recently the Vanniyars have been forced to bury their own dead and to celebrate the Mariamman festival without the crucial rituals carried out by the *kambukūṭṭi* Paraiyar, which made them experience the domination of the Vanniyars. Every time, the Vanniyars talk about this they get very angry and say, "if they [the Paraiyars] do not do their work they should leave the village. We will bring Paraiyars from nearby villages". As we have seen earlier, the Vanniyar men who have done the work of burying the dead twice in the village feel totally helpless and fear that very soon they too will be rendered 'untouchables'. In a sense, these Vanniyar men experience directly the impact of the Paraiyars' new status in the village. In this, what is frustrating for them is that they are left with no means of controlling the Paraiyars or forcing them to return to their traditional services for the *Ūr*, because the Paraiyars no longer depend on the *Ūr* for anything, neither financial nor social. They are independent of the *Ūr*. Therefore, they are compelled to come up with different structures and practices of domination.

(iii) Everyday Life of the Vanniyars

A study of everyday life needs an elaborate description of repetitive activities of the day and a discussion about it. That is not possible within the focus of the present study. So a brief discussion would be enough to explain one of the dimensions of the cultural character of the Vanniyars.

I privileged the street in the *Ūr* as the primary location for my study of everyday life of the Vanniyars. There were many other public locations – tea shop, fields, the Panchayat board building etc – and private locations – home, family interactions, and individuals' everyday life – by studying which I could have understood the daily routine of the Vanniyars' life. But my central questions in the study of elites were: Does the everyday life of the Vanniyars provide a training ground for their treatment and resistance to the Paraiyars' assertive efforts? Do everyday activities reveal the underlying attitude of higher castes to the caste hierarchy of the village? To answer these questions I preferred the street as the primary locus of analysis although I may discuss some other locations to strengthen and complement the findings.

Each street is assigned to one *Vagaiyarā* where that particular *Vagaiyarā* has built their houses and the streets are named after *Vagaiyarā* names. The *Goundan vīṭṭu Vagaiyarā* holds leadership of the *Vagaiyarās* in the *Ūr* on hereditary basis and even the president of the Panchayat board is elected from this *Vagaiyarā*. Every morning starts with the *Ūr* women coming into the streets to go to the water pipes to collect drinking water, while the men are busy in arranging fodder for their cattle and some others gathering at the teashop for morning tea. In the teashop men talk about Tamil Nadu politics, the cinema and the incidents that happened on the previous day. Invariably their conversation is directed towards the Colony and their interactions with the Paraiyars whom they think have become powerful since they failed to control them. Most of the conversations among the women centre on their anxiety in collecting water before the supply is stopped. There is a long queue of pots near the water taps from early morning. Women complain about the partiality of the Panchayat president who arranges to allow water run for a long time in the pipe, which is located in the street where his house situated, and they accuse the Colony people of filling more water than the *Ūr* people, which reduces the time that is allowed for the *Ūr*. Such conversations are interrupted often by a brawl over who gets water first in the queue. After the collection of water, the next activity that fills the streets with people is when they are going to the bus stand to catch the mini-bus to different places for work, shopping and other purposes. This is where the *Ūr* people come into contact with the Paraiyars who also go to catch the bus. No Vanniyar talks to a Paraiyar there. The Vanniyars mostly board the bus through the front entrance and the Paraiyars through the back entrance. But once they are inside the bus all of them choose any seats available. But there is no conversation or interaction between them. Instead the Vanniyars talk to other Vanniyars and the Paraiyars confine their conversation only to Paraiyars. This produces a volatile situation in which often there is either a verbal duel or violent brawls between the two groups over the issue of seats. But there is cooperation among the Vanniyars that is shown in the way in which the persons who go to the bus early reserve seats for other Vanniyars and they offer their seats to other Vanniyars, particularly the older Vanniyars. There is a gap in common activities after the mini-bus leaves the village bus stop. Later around ten o'clock two other activities fill the street: the *Ūr* cattle herder (*Ūrkāli*) gathers the cattle from each house to take them to grazing fields and men and women prepare to go to work in the fields. The streets become busy with every house untying the cattle from the cow shed and the cattle herder trying to organise the unruly cattle. Suddenly the cattle herder takes a dominant role in the village, and all the Vanniyar families try their best to be kind to him lest their cattle will be left behind. He begins his cattle gathering from *Goundan viṭṭu Vagaiyarā* Street. While this goes on women and men start leaving for their work in the fields. From noon onwards until the evening the whole *Ūr* becomes quiet except for some old people here and there who commute between teashop (or water pump) and their houses. The quietness of the place is interrupted by the mini-bus that comes from Uthiramerur and by the women who clean the streets and collect cow dung, which used to be done previously by the Paraiyar women. Then the returning of cattle from the grazing fields recreates the scene similar to the morning and it signals the arrival of evening. The people from fields return home and this also causes interactions between people in the streets, which lasts briefly. Then people settle down in their houses for dinner that brings the *Ūr* into a lull. Now the atmosphere becomes very different from what it was during the day. It is quiet in the streets but noisy in different private locations. Men assemble in three places. Youngsters who mainly belong to the youth wing of the PMK political party assemble at Panchayat board hall. Their conversation focuses mostly on the Paraiyars and their DPI party and how they should be united to fight against the Paraiyars. Apart from this, they also talk about the failure of the Vanniyar leadership in the village in ensuring welfare programmes from the state government. Older Vanniyars assemble in front of the Vinayagar temple to spend time in gossip and playing card games. At the house of Elumalai Goundar (which is also the house of the Panchayat president) a group of *Vagaiyarā* leaders are seen to hold an informal discussion on different issues of the village at large. In that meeting, invariably somebody brings up the issue of the Paraiyars that leads into recalling their past conflicts with the Paraiyars.

In such daily interactions and relations, there is both conformity and resistance. There is conformity within each *Vagaiyarā* and among the Vanniyars as a whole. But there is resistance between *Vagaiyarās* to *Ūr* leaders and to the Paraiyars. The locations of conformity are inside each street in sending their cattle for grazing, organising labourers for their fields, collecting water and within the boundary of the *Ūr* until they come in contact with the Paraiyars. Resistance is constantly shown in their daily interactions between the people of different streets and to the leaders of the *Ūr*. This resistance suddenly dies down and conformity is surfaces among them as soon as they reach places like the bus stand where they come in contact with the Paraiyars. Secondly, as Goffman (2002) has said, there are two regions in their daily life and interactions: the back region and the front region. The actions of people differ from one region to the other. The back regions are the houses, drinking water tap, the Panchayat building, the Vinayagar temple and so on where the Vanniyars openly criticise the village leaders, particularly, the president for their failure to contain and control the Paraiyars, but in the regions (front regions) such as the street and meeting at Elumalai Gounder's house they show high respect for the leaders as if they had a separate self for each region. Thirdly, the hierarchy of the *Vagaiyarās* is tacitly observed in everyday activity. The *Goundan viṭṭu Vagaiyarā* is given priority in every distribution of the *Ūr* sources such as drinking water and labourers for work, and it enjoys higher status among the other *Vagaiyarās*. The *Goundan viṭṭu Vagaiyarā* leaders continuously reproduce forms through which they maintain their high status. The *aidar viṭṭu Vagaiyarā* is the subaltern group in the hierarchy of the Vanniyar *Vagaiyarā* organisation that enjoys very little privilege in the daily interactions. This principle of hierarchy is also followed in daily relations between the people. They form their conduct and behaviour according to the *Vagaiyarā* people they happen to meet in the street or in public places. Boundaries of high and low between *Vagaiyarās* are constantly drawn and redrawn in their daily interactions.

Fourthly, in the everyday life of the Vanniyars there is spontaneous and temporary leadership. For example, the cattle herder becomes the focus of attention of the *Ūr* for an hour everyday. All the Vanniyars suddenly elevate him to a high status and abide by his 'orders' and everybody hates to hear him say, "I cannot wait for a long time, either send the cattle immediately or you bring your cattle to the grazing fields. Do not treat me like the Paraiyar who took the cattle to the grazing field". The cattle herder's job was earlier done by one of the Paraiyars. When they stopped their services to the *Ūr* the cattle herding was also stopped. They remember every time how they suffered until they had one of the men from *aidar viṭṭu Vagaiyarā* to do the cattle herding. But the same cattle herder at other times of the day enjoys no respect from others. He has to wait for that one hour next day to take on his role that is respected by all.

Finally, the locations of paddy fields, cattle herding, and cleaning the streets after the cattle are taken to the grazing field (partially, the meeting of youngsters at the Panchayat building and the informal meeting at Elumalai Goundar's house) are the locations that make the Vanniyars feel the absence of the Paraiyars and recreate the memory of the ways in which the Paraiyars fought with them. I call them *memory locations* that keep the animosity between the *Ūr* and the Colony alive on a daily basis. In brief, the everydayness of the *Ūr* is regulated by and structured on principles of conformity-resistance, and hierarchy of *Vagaiyarā* relationship, and such everydayness keeps alive their animosity to the Paraiyars. This everyday nature of life is furthered and strengthened by other social practices evolved after the Paraiyars broke off their relationship with the *Ūr*.

(iv) Reproducing Practices of Dominance

There are some simple yet powerful practices in Pappanallur that seem to me potent tactics and methods the elites use to sustain their domination and to resist the rise of the Paraiyars.

As we have noted earlier, since 1997 there has been no proper celebration of the village Marriamman festival due to the Paraiyars stopping their traditional services of drumming and *kambukūṭṭi*. Many Vanniyars told me that they did not want to conduct the festival because every time they did so the absence of the *kambukūuṭṭi* Paraiyar was acutely felt by the *Ūr* people. In a way they see it as a proof of their incapability now to 'control' the low castes. This feeling is intensified because most of the elderly Vanniyars do not consider a Marriamman festival without the presence of the Paraiyars as complete, since the role of the Paraiyars had been important for the removal of pollution and providing protection from demons during the festival. Therefore, the last two years (2001-02) the *Ūr* has devised a new kind of festival in which a day of *puja* is conducted in the village Vianayagar temple. This replaces the rituals for which the Paraiyars were needed. All the other usual ceremonies of the Mariamman festival are of course carried out.

The Vanniyars have now reorganised their annual pilgrimage (*pātayātrai*) to the Thirupathy Venkatesa temple in the nearby state of Andhra Pradesh, two hundred miles away from Pappanallur village. Previously it was a very small event in which a few Vanniyars joined people in Chennai city who went on pilgrimage. The Vanniyars who were the organisers of the pilgrimage in the days before setting off engaged five Paraiyars to clean the temple area every day and bring water from the village overhead tank for washing the temple outer area. The Paraiyars were paid a daily wage of Rs 100 in addition to the food they received from the offering (sweet Pongal rice, bananas, coconuts, and oranges). However, the Paraiyars who helped out in the ceremony were not allowed to go near the sacred spaces of the temple, instead, after their cleaning and washing jobs had been done, they had to wait standing outside the temple to collect their food and wages. Before the pilgrims began their journey they put aside their old pilgrimage clothes, which were collected by the Paraiyars. Two Paraiyars accompanied the pilgrims on their journey, carrying their bags and food; they were paid Rs. 75 daily with free food and the fare for the return journey.

The Paraiyars feel that although the Paraiyars are no longer engaged in the religious ceremonies of the pilgrimage, as they used to be when they played the drum in the Mariamman festival earlier and performed their other traditional services, the services they perform during the puja is but a reproduction of their traditional services in a different form. They have rejected the Mariamman festival in which their low identity was actualised every time. However, events like the pilgrimage replace that and re-enact the Vanniyar domination; the boundaries of purity and impurity are being redrawn. The pilgrimage helps the Vanniyars to maintain their 'purity' of caste by keeping the Paraiyars for the cleaning services in the temple. The Paraiyars continue to be shown as 'polluted' and 'impure' through their menial jobs during the pilgrimage.

But the Vanniyars see the situation differently. "We give them [Paraiyars] work by allowing them to help us during the pilgrimage puja, and it is in no way true that we treat them as untouchable Paraiyars", said Kuppusamy Gounder, the chief organiser of the pilgrimage. When asked why the Paraiyars are not allowed into the temple, he said, "Oh, that we cannot do". He said that even if he wanted to allow this, other Vanniyars would not permit him to do so.

There are numerous other subtle ways in which the Vanniyars assert their dominance over the Paraiyars. For instance, the village bus stop is located in the *Ūr* rather than the Colony, compelling the Paraiyars to walk to the *Ūr* area. By the time they arrive there all the seats in the bus are deliberately taken by the Vanniyars, who refuse to allow any Paraiyar to sit even when seats become available after a few stops. Similarly, the Paraiyar members at the Village Panchayat meetings are routinely asked to vacate their chairs. Most of the time the Paraiyars are forced to stand throughout the meetings. One of the Vanniyars said, "how could we allow *parai* dogs to sit with us equally? It is already our generosity that we allowed them to attend the meetings". Therefore, despite the assertions of the Paraiyars, the Vanniyars continue to finds ways of reminding the Paraiyars of their low identity.

(b) The Church Elites[2]

Whenever I told the Vanniyars about their continuance of untouchability practices, every one of them invariably told me, "they [the Paraiyars] should ask their Christian brethren to treat them equally and then come and demand us to do that". In fact there are recent evidences that the high caste Christians in the Catholic Church discriminate the Paraiyars in Chengalpattu area. Before we examine the cases in Chengalpattu area that have direct impact on Pappanallur village, we should briefly locate the issue of caste practices in the Church in the wider context of Tamil Nadu.

Among the Christians of Tamil Nadu sixty five per cent of them are the outcaste Christians (Paraiyars, Pallars, Arunthathiyars and Valluvans, under these four divisions there are seventy-eight sub-outcastes), and the rest are high caste Christians, Vellalars, Gounders, Udaiyars, Mudaliars, to name but a few, (Grafe 1990: 138; TNCBC 1987-88: 66)[3]. We should note here that these outcastes who converted from Hinduism to Christianity continue to be treated in Christianity as 'outcastes'. Many reports and studies state the fact that change of religion has not in any way changed the stigma of the outcastes (Raj 1992a, 1992b, 1995; Stanislaus 1999; Sivasubramanian 2001). Caste practices such as two chapels, one for the high caste Christians and other for the outcaste Christians, separate seating arrangements within the chapels, two separate cemeteries that demonstrate the reality of the outcaste Christians in the Church of Tamil Nadu. The clergy, many studies have stated (Stanislaus 1999; Raj 1995; Fernandes 1993; Amaladoss 1994), directly and indirectly encourage the discriminative practices in the Church and in Religious Congregations.

The high caste Christians in Kanchipuram district and in Madras-Mylapore Archdiocese refuse to treat the Christian Paraiyars equally. To give but one example, in four village parishes – K.K. Pudur, Manambathi Kandigai, R.N. Kandigai, Thatchur – the churches remain closed for the last five years (1998-2003) due to conflicts between the Christian Paraiyars and the high caste Christians such as the Telugu Naidus and Reddiyars. It is significant a matter for the Paraiyars of Pappanallur as they have relatives in these villages. They do not have discrimination among themselves in Pappanallur parish, since all are only Paraiyars and there is no high caste Christian family. Had here been high caste Christians in Pappanallur parish, perhaps in Pappanallur too, there would have been caste discrimination among the Christians. In the three parishes mentioned above, the main issue around which whole problem seemed to have started was that the Naidus and Reddiyars had refused to allow the Paraiyar Christians to read the *Bible* at the alter, to be part of the choir, and during the annual parish festival, they refuse to let the car procession be taken to the Colony area, which the Paraiyars seemed to have demanded. It appeared to have led to a violent clash between the two communities resulting in the closure of the churches in those parishes.

The case of R.N. Kandigai would be helpful to understand the mentality of the high caste Christians, and in that sense, the attitude of the elites in the Church towards Christian Paraiyars. The Paraiyars of Pappanallur have relatives in R.N. Kandigai village, and have given brides to the village, which makes them to interact with the Paraiyars of R.N. Kandigai. So whatever happens to R.N. Kandigai Paraiyars has a bearing on the Pappanallur Paraiyars.

R.N. Kandigai village is situated at a distance of twenty kilometres from Pappanallur village. The two hundred families of Telugu Naidus live around the church, and whereas the one hundred and fifteen families of Paraiyars live outside the village as it is mostly the case elsewhere in Tamil Nadu. The Paraiyars are only landless labourers and the Naidus own most of the lands. The parish history begins from 1889 when the church was built. From the beginning, although there had been regular parish priests, the Naidus appeared to have taken the dominant role in conducting church activities. One reason for this, Philomen (1999: 9-10) says that until 1994 all the parish priests came from the Naidu caste, who allegedly have taken side with the Naidus of the parish. Only in 1995, when the parish priest, Father Eucharist, announced during a Sunday Mass that he wanted to treat all the parishioners equally, the problem seemed to have begun. After the Mass, the Naidus had beaten the priest, and later the church was closed to liturgical activities, since Father Eucharist left the parish for the archbishop's house. After three years, another priest, Father Amaladoss, was appointed parish priest to R.N. Kandigai. On 7-8 December 1998, when he tried to celebrate the parish festival giving equal place to the Paraiyars and the high castes, the Naidus not only boycotted the festival but also tried to prevent the parish priest from performing his duties. In spite of all this, the priest managed to celebrate the festival which the Archbishop, Aruldass James presided over the festive Mass. The Naidus, as planned, boycotted the festival and only the Paraiyars took part in it. But after the celebrations, when the Paraiyars were returning to their Colony, they were attacked by a group of people who were armed with knives, sticks and stones. Then the state police sealed the church until the problem was sorted out. Until the time of my field work the church remained closed.

What is important here to emphasise is the attitude of the elites in these parishes. During my visits to R.N. Kandigai village and other three villages I talked mainly with the Naidus and Reddiyars. Most of them said that they would never allow the Paraiyars to be treated equal to them in the church activities. Apparently the reason they give for this opposition is that they were the ones who built the physical structure of churches with the money collected as tax from the Naidus, and the land on which the church buildings stand belongs to their grandparents. To explain and justify it they have stories of the Naidu caste origin in Chengalpattu area. They feel proud that they had stood by the Catholic Church in difficult times in the past, if their support had not been there the church would not have grown to the stature it has now. Therefore, the Naidus and Reddiyars argue that it is unfair on the part of the Paraiyars to demand equal status in church activities. However, there is a small minority of the Naidus who feel that in the church all should be treated equally. But this voice of equality is hardly heard in the din of the voices of hierarchy. Most of the high castes in the four villages want the church of Madras-Mylapore Archdiocese treat them higher than the Paraiyars. If not, they would go to the extent of legally claiming the church building and the church land as theirs.

Rajaratnam, a Naidu leader of R.N. Kandigai, said, "if they [the Paraiyars] want, let them build their own church and they can do there whatever they want to do, who cares. But if they try to acquire equal status in our church, we will never allow it to happen. Our people [the Naidus] are ready to shed their blood for the cause". Asked how he and his caste people could control the church activities that are supposed to be the job of the Madras Archdiocese, he said, "who is the church? We are the church. Even if the Pope wants to enter our village he has to ask our [the Naidus] permission". He further said that he was extremely angry with the Archbishop, Aruldass James, who was born of outcaste parents, supported the Paraiyars of R.N. Kandigai. From the point of view of the Naidus, it seems that they have the right to have dominance over the Paraiyars in terms of church activities, because they were the original owners of the church properties. But the Paraiyars see it unjust.

Mostly the high caste leaders are very careful not to be seen as people who discriminate the Paraiyars as 'outcastes' for fear of legal proceedings against them under the Untouchability Offences Act. But the Naidu women and children I spoke to openly expressed their contempt towards the Paraiyars. One elderly Naidu woman, a retired school teacher, said, "those parai dogs should be taught a lesson, I think what they got in the last festival was not enough. They should keep their mouth shut and eat what we throw to them. How can they dare to go to the altar to read the *Bible*?" When I said that Jesus died for people like the Paraiyars. She said, "No, that is a false propaganda of the Paraiyar priests, go and talk to our [Naidu] priests they will tell you the truth. Don't ever tell this to our people, if you do, many would become Muslims. They would not be ready to worship an 'untouchable' God. Then Christianity would become religion only for the Paraiyars".

The attitude of the Naidu children is the same. They have always been told that the Paraiyar children are 'low people' (*thālnthavargal*) and 'ugly people' (*asingampudithavargal*). It is strengthened in the school where the Paraiyar children and the Naidu children are treated differently, and have separate seating arrangements. Among more than thirty children I talked to during my visits to the four villages, not a single child said that he/she would like to treat the Paraiyar children equal to them. The idea of 'high casteness' is deeply internalised by these children and they will never be able to stand when a Paraiyar girl goes to the altar to do a reading during a Mass. In brief, the high caste Christians have a strong opinion that the Paraiyars cannot be treated equally with them. Even in Christianity it should be so, caste discrimination in it should not be merely tolerated but should be treated as natural. If the church administration takes side with the outcastes, which it has done so recently, many high castes whom I met would prefer to have their own church. This they would not say openly, but they will shroud it with all other reasons that would not easily betray their caste mindset.

Hierarchy as Justice

The core of the elites' thought and attitude to the Paraiyars of Pappanallur in particular, and the Dalits in general, in Tamil Nadu, is that their high status is just, natural, and divinely willed. They say that they are born higher castes and therefore they are entitled to be treated as higher than the Dalits; this is justice. Being born as higher castes is for them an award given by God for the good deeds they had done in their previous life and the status of the Dalits is a punishment of God for the bad deeds that the Dalits had done in their previous life. "We did not ask to be born as higher castes, it is God who has made us higher castes", they say. It is divine justice (*kadavulin tharmam*). By implication, life is not made by any human power but purely given by God, and it has to be lived as given by Him. The essence of a human person is set by the community in which one is born, a Dalit has the essence of pollutedness and a high caste has an innate purity. The human person just exists and lives according to his/her birth; the high caste lives as high caste, and the Dalit as Dalit. There is no way of becoming something else, but only of being what is ordained by birth; high caste cannot become low caste and vice versa. Economic advancement and cultural and political mobilisation can make, Dalit rich and powerful, but he cannot become morally higher than a high caste, he would still be considered a Dalit. A Paraiyar may have become a medical doctor, but in his village he would not be allowed to enter a high caste's house. For most of the higher castes in Tamil Nadu, the essence and totality of human life is hierarchical, mainly in the moral sense.

In my conversations and living with the higher castes, they sometimes seemed to use the concept of hierarchy in the sense of difference, not in the sense of 'high' and 'low', 'pure' and 'impure'. They say that they are created by God different from the

Dalits (*viṭṭiyāsam*). To substantiate this, they direct our attention to the difference in food habits, language, and works between them and the Dalits. A Vanniyar put this simple question to me: "Why from birth in the Colony do people eat beef with such ease, while we just cannot stand the smell of it?". It is, he argued, because of the nature and essence with which God has created them. The difference does not need to be seen as something holy or high, or in the case of the Dalits polluted and low, simply different from each other, what Dumont has called *substantialisation*. Basically, they have no problem in agreeing with the idea that as human beings both the higher castes and the Dalits are equal. But do they behave that way in their daily social interactions? Mostly they do not. What they tell you as difference is mostly actualised in terms of high and purity. Because here difference is not to be appreciated but to be used to define the 'other' and 'us'.

Put simply, both the idea of hierarchy and difference are embedded in the life of the higher castes. Three elements of caste ideology – *karma* and hierarchy and social status – have been deeply internalised by the higher castes, and so imprinted in their minds for such a long time that they find it extremely hard to understand the idea of equality suggested by the Dalits and the symbolic reversals of identity-making by the Paraiyars.

(c) Unbroken walls of 'Cosmological Order'

However, the thoughts of the higher castes just discussed are not those that one will often hear in public. Instead, this is mostly for private discourse. If you ask a high caste person in public when he stands with a few others, particularly when he is with Dalits, 'how do you treat the Paraiyars?' he will say, "we are all brothers and sisters of one another (*tāyāpiḷaiyā*)". But the same person will tell you in private how he hates the Dalits. In Tamil Nadu, as is the case in most of India, public discourse is different from private discourse. Caste practices may be denied in public discourse by the higher castes, but in private they consciously promote them. What they believe deep within themselves seems to be totally different from what they openly say. Such ambiguity often precludes clarity of vision and understanding of the reality of the caste system in India. In our study of the elites we are required to examine what lies behind public discourse and search for the normative understanding in their private discourse that is complex and complicated (Fuller 2000: 27; Parish 1996: 101-141). It is because of this, I believe, that what we have seen in this study, the fact of the Paraiyars trying to identify with the symbols, whose meanings are reversed from pollution to culture, is less likely to be recognised by the higher castes with whom the Paraiyars interact daily. This is not to suggest that the Paraiyars should totally abandon their project of identification simply because this does not get the recognition. Nor do I believe that the Paraiyars will do so. I consider that recognition of any new practice is always a process, it takes time and therefore it needs perseverence on the part of the people who want a change in society. Sharing this opinion, Thirumavalavan, the leader of the DPI, declared: "whether the higher castes recognise our assertions or not, we will go on doing what we are doing. Because this is meaningful to us. It gives us the feeling of becoming human and realising our human dignity (*maniṭa māṇbu*). The benefits of any revolution are reaped by the successive generations, not by the people who work for it. We nourish it with our blood and our future generations will enjoy the fruits. It is absurd to abandon our work today, because we, the present generation, will not enjoy the fruits of our work. Wherever I go, I tell this to our people". An aggressive version of this is told by Pama, a Paraiyar woman activist, "we hate to depend again on the higher castes' recognition of our new identity. Why do we need the Vanniyars (and the higher castes) to confer an identity on us as if the higher castes are the sole authority of identity? We don't need to live at their mercy, it is our life and we will do whatever we want with it". It remains to be seen whether the Paraiyars (and the Dalits) will be successful in eking out their new identity without the recognition of the higher castes in Tamil Nadu.

Notes

1. By the term 'agency' I mean simply an intentionally acting agent. Interested readers should see Torfing (1999) especially chapter 7 pp. 137-154.
2. The focus is on the Archdiocese of Madras-Mylapore. Similar cases of caste practices are still followed in the church all over Tamil Nadu. Particularly, in the recruitment for clergy it is evident that the candidates from outcaste families are rejected in subtle ways. Even the outcaste candidates, who get past this stage and become nuns and priests, are treated with contempt by the clergy with high caste family background, and they are not favoured for high positions in the church. My visits to four seminaries in Tamil Nadu and meeting with outcaste candidates during my fieldwork confirm this. In Pappanallur itself, there were two boys and four Paraiyar girls went to join religious congregations but they were rejected before they were about to be inducted formally. The Paraiyars of Pappanallur seem to believe that the authorities who were in charge of selecting candidates came from high caste families.
3. There are sixteen Catholic Dioceses and seven Dioceses of the Church of South India (CSI). The ratio between Protestants is 2:1. In the total population of Tamil Nadu (55, 858, 946, according to Census of India 1991) Christians comprise 5.69 per cent.

9

Conclusion: The Paraiyars' New Identity and Its Implications

I do not think that I can make any definite statement on the basis of the five diverse chapters I have written so far. First, for it is too early to draw any firm conclusions. The Paraiyars' new identity formation has only just started and is in a process that will probably take a long time to achieve its end completely. As we have seen, they are at a transitional phase between what they had been in the past and what they intend to be in the near future. This produces some ambivalence in their thought and action and diversity in their grasp of the situation both inside the village and beyond. In such a situation, it is not easy to provide one single totalising and essentialising idea about their identity formation.

Therefore, by way of looking back I want to make just one observation on the direction in which I think the rise of the Paraiyars (and of the Dalits more generally), is moving at present and the implications of this. To anticipate this briefly, the direction is the 'ethnicisation' of the Paraiyar identity.[1] Here I will try to provide the reader with my final ideas about the object of the Paraiyars' way of forming identity.

Through their symbolic reversals the Paraiyars are trying to form an ethnic identity of their own. The motivation for this kind of identity-making they derive from their creation of and participation in the conflicts with the *Ūr* (Chapter 4). As noticed earlier, the starting point of the whole identity – formation is conflict, which provides a new self-consciousness and an ability to oppose and challenge the higher castes. This self-consciousness leads to a realisation of how and why they were defined by the symbols and symbolic practices, and they have come to realise how mythic and symbolic discourse had the power to define them as low and polluted. They are now trying to use the same discursive formulation to deconstruct the identity given to them and construct their own. Instead of mobilising themselves to move up in the hierarchy, by what is called *sanskritisation*, and make themselves as pure and high, they stay where they are in the hierarchy but make it the true locus of their selves and community. This gives them an identity they have made for themselves. The problem they faced earlier was that others provided the locus in which they existed, but this gave them an identity of objecthood that they wanted to negate and construct their own personhood. Therefore, they needed to transform this locus by removing those elements they did not want. In this process, they realised that if they wanted to transform the locus they would have to redefine the symbols and practices that were embedded in it. In the process of redefinition, they first of all abandoned the symbolic and social practices, the institutions in which they were once treated as low, and they changed, not the symbols but the meaning of the symbols by the same method of myth-making through which they were earlier defined as polluted and low, which we have examined in Chapter 5. They do not change their location of identity; on the contrary, they transform the character of the location of their identity by purifying its elements so as to suit their new imagination of their life and activities.

The identity formation of the Paraiyars is (i) the deconstruction of their identification with symbols given by the others, (ii) the reconstruction of their identification by reversing the meaning of the symbols, and (iii) the repossession of the transformed symbols and re-identification with them. Therefore, in the

The Paraiyars' Way of Constructing Identity

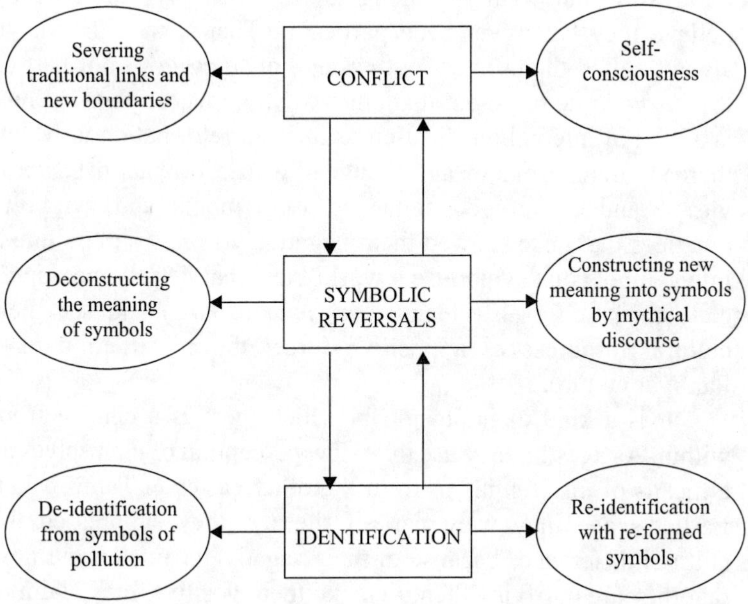

whole process conflict and symbol are the two important phases that the act of identity-making goes through, the former being the starting point of the other two phases. Our study has shown that conflict is the necessary condition for the identity-making by the Paraiyars, and equally important is the employment of symbolic resources in the redefinition of identity.

I call this horizontal integration as opposed to vertical mobility done through *sanskritisation*. By considering the drum, beef-eating and land as symbols of their identity and culture, they form a caste identity of their own: from 'Dalits' to 'caste'. I must note here that 'caste' is used not in the sense it is used in the caste system, in which purity and impurity are the basis of hierarchy, but it should be seen in the sense of a separate and distinctive community that has an identity of its own; they define this not against the caste hierarchy but against the definition that they were given by the caste hierarchy. I do not think that any Paraiyar would want to belong to the hierarchy, nor do they believe they have ever been part of it. That is why they have always called themselves 'out-castes', or '*avarna*' – not part of the *Varna* system. To put it another way, the whole phenomenon is a kind of internal purification or internal reformation in which there is a transformation and change of values, orientations, world views, and of attitudes attached to symbols and symbolic practices that once showed them negatively as low and polluted, into symbols that symbolise a world view that helps them appreciate their self (self-esteem – *suyamariyāthais*) and see their cultural resources as a positive force: the construction of a Paraiyar culture.

It is a kind of implosion in which there is a change from within. As a result, they use their new perception of themselves as a means of differentiation from the other castes in Tamil Nadu. Earlier when they were part of the *Ūr*, they suppressed the cultural differences because of their negative character, but now that they are purifying them to make them positive, they claim to own their cultural differences; they say, "I am a drummer, so what?" and "yes, beef is our staple food, what is wrong with that?" Is this difference to be understood along the lines of differences of racial, linguistic ethnicity? Probably not. If that were so, we should be able to recognise some racial or linguistic differences between the Vanniyars and the Paraiyars. If you make them stand together, they would look the same, you cannot tell the difference. But the difference the Paraiyars are trying to make is not an ascribed one but one constructed conceptually within their given location. This construction I do not think of as fixed and rigid but flexible, having a certain degree of openness for the addition of similar differences. It is not aimed at displacing or marginalising others' identities, not something like the hierarchical relation where you have two ends of a spectrum, pure and impure, in which the pure Brahmin has identity only when there is the impure shudra/Dalits.

But what the Paraiyars are trying to do is simply a repositioning of their identity in a positive manner, which, according to Hall (2003: 94), is a shift in ethnicity that is "predicated on difference and diversity". Such cultural differences are mobilised to form an identity in order to gain space and power in politics in the state and the country and ultimately to be recognised and respected as a community, what Appadurai (2000: 15) called 'culturalism'. This is exactly what I think is being done by the Dalit political parties in Tamil Nadu, and in other states in India, by asserting their power that cannot be easily ignored in the political formation in India (Jaffrelot 2003; Shah 2001; De Souza 2000; Vivek Kumar 2002).

By such a 'culturalising' process through the reversal of symbols the Paraiyars distance themselves from the methods of the state that used positive discrimination to reserve places for the Paraiyars in education and in government jobs. The economic approach of the state in the empowerment of the Dalits has in the past led to a dilution of the Dalit mass movements. The co-optative method that the Brahmin-dominated political parties used included welfare programmes in their ideology and policy and it caused division among the Dalit leaders. The result of this was that the Dalits could not remove the stigma of 'untouchableness' (Jaffrelot 2003). Because the economic approach to Dalit empowerment has only made the Dalits advance their economic status but they have continued to remain 'untouchable rich', an 'untouchable medical doctor' and an 'untouchable engineer'. The stigmatising tag was always added. But the methods of the Paraiyars of Pappanallur demonstrate a cultural approach to the social change of the Dalits that could possibly succeed in removing the stigma of 'untouchableness'. The economic approach tends to focus on the 'politics of demand' that only addresses the material aspects of life, but the cultural approach focuses on the 'politics of command' that transforms the world-view of the people (Aloysius 1998: 87). The latter approach is a better suited to change one's identity, if not the best.[2]

The reader may well ask: is this act of ethnicising what the Paraiyars see themselves as intending or aiming at? My answer would be, yes and no. No, in the sense that they never mentioned to me in my fieldwork, "we are making an ethnic identity of our own". Yes, in the sense that they often told me that they wanted to change their low status and be respected as human beings and as a community that has its own unique culture and history. They believe strongly that men and women (the higher castes) made their low identity; therefore, it could be unmade and rewritten so as to make them feel that it is 'our' identity, 'we' constructed it, and we possess it on our own. More than all this, they repeatedly told me, "we will never be the slaves of the Vanniyars again". To achieve this they created conflicts and stopped their traditional services to the *Ūr*, and they are trying to make their life more respectable and positive by re-forming their symbolic sources, a manifestation of the kind of social imagination that the Paraiyars have or have come to recognise in themselves.[3] They in fact "develop [a] discursive theoretical knowledge regarding the underlying rules and assumptions" about their life, which Baert (1998: 204) calls a 'reflection of the second order'.[4] A fourteen-year-old Paraiyar girl demonstrated such a knowledge when she said to me, "they [the higher castes] made us low castes purely by stories, and now, we will tell you stories about ourselves". The Paraiyars I spoke to and lived with are creative, talented and intelligent, they try every means available to make sense of their new life in Tamil Nadu.

This does not mean that they have the theory of ethnicity that I am discussing in this section. This is my understanding (theorisation) of the social change that is taking place in the lives of the Paraiyars: the process of identity formation – conflict: symbolic reversal: identification with symbols – I have discussed these as terms of my own understanding of the Paraiyars' action and thought. The location of the Paraiyar ethnicity is in my mind, not in the mind of the Paraiyars, the subjects of my study (Banks 1996: 183-87). This is my way of thinking about the Paraiyars' way of doing and thinking. Whether the Paraiyars agree with my theory or not, is another issue but they will surely agree with me that they are in a process of identity-making, in which their focus is on symbols and discursive reformulations that will possibly give them a new and positive identity, different from the one they had in the past. I view this as an effort of the Paraiyars to re-conceptualise their personhood from 'pollutedness' into 'respectfulness' (*suyamariyāthai*), from a fixed and rigid concept of person in the caste system to a concept of person as one who has the capacity to change, remake and improve his/her status (cf. Vincentnathan 1993).

In all this, my concern is whether the Paraiyars will be successful in achieving the new identity recognised by the elites, if the identity is really to be naturalised. As we have seen in Chapter 6, the Vanniyars in Pappanallur refuse to give any value to the efforts that the Paraiyars have been making to imagine their life. The only option that the Paraiyars have now is, what Michael, one of the drummers said, "we will do what we think best for us and for our children in the future, we hope one day the world will recognise our efforts and allow us to live as people with human dignity (*manitha mānbu*)". In this context it is instructive to learn from the history of Afro-Americans in North America, from 1500 until 2003, who have been by and large successful in their efforts of reconstructing and asserting their identity as Afro-Americans, and getting this recognised by the white Americans (Taylor 1999; Pérez-Sarduy and Stubbs 1995; see also http://www.pbs.org/wnet/aaworld). Black pride has achieved a respectable status through different methods from the beginning, and the presence of the Afro-Americans is felt today in every realm of American life. I cannot fail to hear the echo of "say it aloud: I am black and I am proud" of the Afro-Americans in the Paraiyars assertion: "Say with pride that you are a Paraiyar, and hold your head high". Therefore, this inclines me to think of the Paraiyars' future positively.

Finally, there are many implications of this change, not only for the life of the Paraiyars but also for the *Ūr* and beyond. One immediate result that has been realised already is that, as seen earlier, the Vanniyars have started taking up the Paraiyars' services such as burying the dead and the *kambukutti* work, although not in the same way in which the Paraiyars did it before. Does this mean that the Paraiyars are no more Paraiyars, and the Vanniyars are no more Vanniyars, as they ought to be? By implication, if purity and impurity are no longer attached or fixed to one group in the spectrum of the caste system, what sort of caste system is being developed there? Will the change of roles and status alter the caste hierarchy in the village? Will it make the Vanniyars who do the roles of the Paraiyars be seen as Dalits? If the process started by the Paraiyars of Pappanallur is successful in the years to come, could we take this as signalling a beginning of the end of untouchability? To provide any conclusive answers to these questions, I believe, we need more of such cases to be repeated in the state of Tamil Nadu and in India in the future, something every Paraiyar in Pappanallur hopes to see happening sooner rather than later.

Notes

1. In the context of the present study I use the term, 'ethnic' in a broad sense, because the case of the Paraiyars in terms of their identity formation is unique. I use the term in the sense suggested by Varshney (2002) and Eriksen (1993). Varshney (2002: 5) defines ethnicity as "the larger set to which religion, race, language, and sect belong as subsets". In these subsets I place the kind of ethnic identity the Paraiyars are constructing. Similarly, I think that Eriksen gives more clarity to the definition of Varshney. For Eriksen, ethnicity "refers to aspects of relationships between groups which consider themselves, and are regarded by others, as being culturally distinctive" (1993: 4). The 'ethnisisation' that the Paraiyars are doing arises from the fact that they are making the ascribed status of pollution, 'Dalitness' into a status of culture and identity in a much more positive sense. See also Banks (1996: 4,5) for a set of definitions on ethnicity.
2. In one sense, it is a substantialisation of castes, which Dumont recognised as one of the main aspects of modern change in the caste system and what others saw it as transformation of "vertically integrated

hierarchy" into "a horizontally disconnected ethnic array" (Fuller 1996: 26). But what is new and original in the present study is that firstly it is the first time that an Dalit group, the Paraiyars, in their approach to change of their status is concerned with their cultural identity, and secondly it focuses on symbols and myths for ethnicising their identity.

3. Parattai, an Dalit scholar at Tamil Nadu Theological Seminary in Madurai city, who disseminates the counter myths through his writings and audiocassettes, says that the Paraiyars for centuries had been culturally creative people in terms of music and art. All this, he believes, has been blocked out by the Brahmin-dominated media in Tamil Nadu and stigmatised their cultural talents as polluted and low culture and marginalised them far away from the main stream.
4. 'Reflection of the first order' is what takes place when people talk about the meaning and effects of their actions as opposed to 'reflection of the second order', which is theoretical and discursive knowledge of their actions (Baert 1998: 201-6).

Appendix

Conflicts between the Paraiyars and the Vanniyars

1. In 1951, on a Pongal day, while a Paraiyar was decorating the house of a Gounder he was alleged to have entered into the room where the Gounder's wife was taking a bath. She went and complained to her husband who with his brother beat up the Paraiyar. Later it led to a brawl between the Paraiyars and the Vanniyars in which one Paraiyar woman sustained minor injury. That year excepting the drummers all the other Paraiyars did not take part in the cattle procession of the festival in protest against the Vanniyars.
2. As usual on the eve of the Pongal festival, in 1953, a Paraiyar boy was accused of stealing a mike from the *Ūr* temple where a sound system had been hired for the festival from Uthiramerur town. Although the boy denied that he had stolen it, he was beaten up by a Reddiyar, which resulted in a violent clash between the *Ūr* and the Colony. Two Vanniyars were injured and later hospitalised. Five Paraiyars were arrested by the police and later released without any charges.
3. In 1951, during the preparations for the Pongal festival, a Gounder asked a Paraiyar, who regularly worked for him, to take his bullocks for a wash in the village tank. The Paraiyar

instead of taking the bullocks chased them into the paddy fields of another Gounder. Not realising that it was the mistake of the Paraiyar, the Gounder, the owner of the field, went to the house of the Gounder whose bullocks was in his paddy fields and shouted at him. Later when both of them came to know the truth, it became a big issue that was brought to the attention of the village leaders. The Paraiyar was fined and he and his family were forbidden to work on the land of the Vanniyars.

4. During the Pongal cattle procession in 1954, a Paraiyar youth was alleged to have teased a Gounder woman that led to a verbal duel and halted the procession. Later that day the Gounder woman's brother manhandled the Paraiyar youth's younger sister while she was returning from Vedanthangal. The Paraiyar *Vagaiyarā* men to which the youth belonged took it up in the Colony *Vagaiyarā* Council that banned all Paraiyar services to the Gounder family.
5. A drummer during his drumming on a Pongal day in 1957, had his sandals on and it angered some Gounders who felt that it was disrespectable on the part of a Paraiyar to have his sandals on in front of them. They challenged the drummer and asked him to remove the sandals. But the drummer refused to obey since he felt that it was his freedom to put on his sandals, while it was too hot to stand on bare feet. What started as verbal duel spiralled into a major conflict between the two groups and resulted in the boycott of all the drummers in that year's Pongal festival.
6. In 1964, Paraiyar women during their paddy threshing work for a Gounder drank water using a glass from the Gounder's house; this was treated as a polluting act by the higher castes. Usually the Paraiyars were supposed to drink water that is poured into their palms by a high caste person. The women who broke this code were admonished by the Gounder. This led to a strike by the Paraiyar women for that particular Gounder.

7. Instead of five drummers there were only three drummers on a Pongal festival day in 1962. Two other drummers refused to join the drumming as there was a gradual awareness that the Paraiyars should stop drumming for the Vanniyars. Some Gounders questioned this and warned that if the other two drummers did not join the drumming, all the drummers would have to face serious consequences. Paying no heed to the warning the three drummers went on drumming, which angered the Gounder leaders. One of them beat up two drummers using sandals and their drums were broken. In protest, the drummers threatened to boycott drumming for the festival. But later Gounder leaders intervened to settle the dispute.
8. In 1984, More than ten Paraiyar women from the Paraiyars Women's Association in one of their programmes against the sale of *arrack* in the village went to the place near the paddy fields where a Gounder illegally distilled *arrack* and destroyed all the containers. And the women made a formal complaint to the police about the illegal sale of *arrack*. The police arrested the Gounder and a case was registered against him. This caused a great tension between the Vanniyars and the Paraiyars. To avenge the arrest the Vanniyars stopped the daily supply of drinking water from the overhead tank in the *Ūr*. In retaliation, all the Paraiyar women boycotted their work in the fields of the Vanniyars that for lasted six months. The Vanniyars had to get workers from other villages on higher wages.
9. During the Marriamman festival in 1970, the *kambukūṭṭi* Paraiyar, who was supposed to abstain from drinking alcohol and consuming meat since he was to perform sacred rituals, not only took alcohol but also slept in his house without guarding the statue of Mariamman goddess (*karakam*). This the higher castes considered as an act that would bring a curse by the goddess on the village. When the Paraiyar was questioned he said that he was a Christian and so he did not follow Hindu religious rules. This led to a violent brawl

between the Paraiyars and the Vanniyars when the Vanniyars on the organising committee beat up the *kambukūṭṭi* Paraiyar. Later this turned into a serious conflict in which the Jesuit parish priest intervened and defended the *kambukūṭṭi* Paraiyar. The Vanniyars seemed to have had a plan of turning this into a religious conflict. But later the Vanniyars did not pursue the matter as they realised the strong support of the Church.

10. There was a minor conflict, in 1975, due to some Paraiyar women entering the inner rooms of a Gounder's house during their cleaning work on a Pongal festival day. The Gounder family considered the act as having polluted the house. The Paraiyar women justified their act saying that if the Vanniyars considered them polluting they should not have been invited to clean the Gounder's house in the first place. This made the Gounder's wife angry and she pushed one Paraiyar woman who fell down against a stone pillar and sustained a head injury. She was taken to hospital for treatment. Although there was every chance of this incident becoming a big conflict, it was sorted out by the Gounder who accepted to pay the medical bills.
11. On a Pongal day in 1992, when the cattle procession was taking place a Paraiyar youth who was an active member of the DPI sexually harassed a Vanniyar woman who complained to her husband. This resulted in a major brawl between the Vanniyars and the Paraiyars. Since the Paraiyars were well prepared for this, they started attacking the Vanniyars with sticks and stones. The Vanniyars who were taken by surprise ran into the *Ūr* to escape the attack. This not only disrupted the events on that day of the festival but also led to a spiralling of events for more than a month.
12. In 1993, while the drama (*kūṭu*) was going on the last day of Marriamman festival. Some Paraiyar boys hiding themselves at the top of Tamarind tree threw stones at the site where Gounder women who were watching drama (*kūṭu*). Two young Vanniyar girls were injured. This led into

a confusion and panic among the people. But nobody could find out from where the stones came. The Vanniyars blamed the Paraiyars and vice versa. Although this did not lead to any further conflict but made them cancel the show.

13. In 1990, a Paraiyar girl fell in love with a Vanniyar boy, both of them were studying in a higher secondary school (year twelve). They were seen together in cinema theatres in the nearby towns by Vanniyars who informed the parents of the Vanniyar boy. The parents of the boy punished the boy and warned the parents of the Paraiyar girl to admonish the girl. A few days after that the boy eloped with the girl to Chennai city. That year the Pongal festival was used to settle the score. While the whole village had gathered in front of the temple some Vanniyars beat up the father of the Paraiyar girl. It led to a clash between the Paraiyars and the Vanniyars. Later this was taken up in a meeting of the Panchayat board and the Vanniyars were fined.
14. In 1988, the drummers refused to drum for the cattle chasing for a Gounder on Pongal festival who refused to employ the Paraiyars for work since they demanded high wages. This caused a brawl between the drummers and the Gounder.
15. In 1991, a Paraiyar youth snatched the booty tied around a bull of a Goundar before the bull was chased. This led to a verbal duel between the Paraiyars and the Vanniyars. But it was quickly sorted out.
16. Conflict was erupted when some Paraiyars set the Goundar's (president of the Panchayat) motorbike on fire because he did not give the Paraiyars their share of saris and dhotis, allocated by the state government as Pongal prize to all the villages. This led to a conflict between the Colony and the *Ūr*. The president refused to do anything until he was compensated for his bike. But the Colony decided to boycott drumming for the festival until they received their share of the Pongal prize.
17. On a Pongal day in 1990, A Vanniyar woman attacked a Paraiyar woman while they were travelling in a bus. The

Paraiyar woman stamped on the feet of the Vanniyar woman, which became a brawl between them, leading to a tense situation in the village even after the festival.

18. In 1988, a Paraiyar walked into the *Ūr* with his towel on his shoulders and wearing sandals, which was considered disrespectable to the higher castes. The Vanniyars forced the Paraiyar to carry his sandals on his head and paraded him in the streets of the *Ūr*. The Paraiyars were planning to file a case against the Vanniyars. A month after this incident, on the night of a Pongal festival the Paraiyars beat up those Vanniyars who were involved in making the Paraiyar carry his sandals on his head. This case was taken to the RDO of Madurantagam who sorted out the issue by talking to the elders of the Vanniyars and the parish priest of the Paraiyars.
19. In 1989, a conflict arose over the sale of firewood belonging to the village. The Paraiyars complained that the money from the sale was not accounted for by the Vanniyar members of the Panchayat board. The Paraiyars took the case to the Panchayat Union which ordered the Vanniyars to set the records straight.
20. In 1991, a Paraiyar girl was manhandled by a Vanniyar youth for not dismounting from her cycle when she travelled through the *Ūr*. She spread the rumour that she was raped by the Vanniyar youth. This created communal tension in the village. On a Pongal day some Paraiyars of the DPI party asked Paraiyar women and girls to ride on cycles through the streets, waiting for the Vanniyars to challenge it. But the Vanniyars kept quiet about it.
21. In the morning of the second day of three-day Pongal festival in 1992, which was devoted to the cattle, the Paraiyars killed a cow for meat outside the village and carried the dead cow through the *Ūr*. The incident angered the Vanniyars. Later the Vanniyars refused to allow the drummers inside the *Ūr* for drumming. Instead, they hired drummers from a nearby village for the festival. But the Paraiyars persuaded the drummers to abandon the drumming. Finally, in a peace

meeting in which leaders of the two groups took part the issue was peacefully sorted out.

22. During the ceremony of chasing the cattle on a Pongal festival in 1986, a Vanniyar woman shouted at a Paraiyar, 'Parai dog' since he by mistake touched her. The Paraiyar in return called her 'Palli bitch'. This created a brawl leading to the withdrawal of all the Paraiyars from the festival.
23. Someone tied sandals and broomsticks with the flag post of the DPI party in the Colony on a Pongal day in 1995. The Paraiyars blamed the Vanniyars who belonged to the PMK party. To avenge the act, on the night of the Pongal day some Paraiyars cut down the flag post of the PMK party in the *Ūr*. There was almost a chance of it spiralling into a political clash between the DPI and the PMK. But this was averted by the involvement of the Vanniyar elders who persuaded the Paraiyars as well as the Vanniyars not to further the issue.
24. In 1994, a Vanniyar forced the drummers to drum in front of his house for a longer time than usual during the cattle chasing ceremony of the Pongal festival. The drummers refused to do so. Immediately, the Vanniyar yelled at the drummers, "you, carcase eating dogs, how dare you disobey me" and broke one of the drums. This led to complete withdrawal of all the drummers from that year's festival.

References

Documents

Chengalpattu Giramappura Membattu Sangam. *Annual Report 2000-2001 (in Tamil).*

Chengalpattu Rural Development Society. *Annual Report 1996-7.*

Chengalpattu Rural Development Society. *Sanga Arikkai* (Society's Annual Report in Tamil). 1990-1991.

Chengalpattu Rural Development Society. *Annual Report 1996-1997.*

Dalit Christian Liberation Movement (DCLM). *Statement of the Tamil Nadu Catholic Bishops' Conference (TNCBC)* Madurai. (1987-88).

Government of India. Ministry of Home Affairs. *The Report of the Commissioner for Scheduled Castes and Scheduled Tribes*. New Delhi. (1991).

Government of India. *Report of the Commissioner of the SCs/STs*. New Delhi: Ministry of Welfare. (1987-88).

Government of India. *Report of National Commission for Scheduled Castes and Scheduled Tribes, Atrocities on Scheduled Castes and Tribes, Causes and Remedies*. New Delhi. (1911).

Government of Tamil Nadu. Tamil Nadu Legislative Assembly. *The Gomathinayagam Commission Report on Caste Clashes in Southern Districts of Tamil Nadu*. Chennai. (1999).

Government of Tamil Nadu. *The Bellie Commission Report on Police Firing in Front of Sub-Collector's Office, Chengalpattu.* Chennai. (1996).

Human Rights Watch. *Broken People: Caste Violence Against India's 'Untouchables'*. London. (1999)

National Campaign on Dalit Human Rights. 2000. *Dalit Human Rights Violations: Atrocities against Dalits in India. National Public Hearing, Case Papers: Summary Jury's Interim Observations and Recommendations*. Vol. 1. Ahmedabad: National Campaign on Dalit Human Rights.

National Council of Applied Economic Research. *India: Human Development Report*. 1999. New Delhi: Oxford University Press.

National Council of Applied Economic Research. *South India: Human Development Report* (2001). New Delhi: Oxford University Press.

Tamil Nadu People's Forum for Social Development. *Tamil Nadu Social Development Report 2000*. Chennai.

The Association of Sarva Seva Farms. *Silver Jubilee Report*. Madras. (1994).

Viduthalai Siruthaigal Kolgaiyarikkai (Election Manifesto of Dalit Panthers). 2001.

World Bank Country Study. *India: Reducing Poverty, Accelerating Development*.

Books and Articles

Abbasayulu, Y.B. 1978. "Scheduled Caste Elite: A Study of Scheduled Caste Elite in Andhra Pradesh". Hyderabad: Osmania University.

Ahearn, L. M. 2001. "Language and Agency". In *Annual Review of Anthropology*. 30: 109-37.

Aiyangar, S.M. 1982. *Tamil Studies: Essays on the History of the Tamil People, Language, Religion and Culture*. New Delhi: Asian Educational Services.

Aiyappan, A. 1937. *Social and Physical Anthropology of the Nayadis of Malabar*. Madras: Bulletin of the Madras Government Museum.

—. 1945. *Iravas and Culture Change*. Madras: Bulletin of Madras Government Museum.

—. 1965. *Social Revolution in a Kerala Village: A Study of Culture Change*. Bombay: Asia Publishing House.

Alcoff, L.M. 2000. "Who's Afraid of Identity Politics?" In Moya, P.M.L. and Hames Garcia, M.R. (eds.). *Reclaiming Identity: Realist Theory and the Predicament of Postmodernism*. Berkeley/Los Angeles/ London: University of California Press. pp. 279-311.

Alexander, K.C. 1998. "The Neo-Christians of Kerala". In J. Michael Mahar (ed.). *The Untouchables in Contemporary India*. New Delhi: Rawat Publications.

Allen, N.J. 1990. "On the Notion of Structure". *Journal of Anthropological Society of Oxford* 21: 279-82.

—. 1999. "Hinduism as Indo-European: Cultural comparativism and political sensitivities". In Johannes Bronkhorst and Madhav M. Deshpande (eds.). *Aryan and Non-Aryan in South Asia: Evidence, Interpretation and Ideology*. 1999. Cambridge: Department of Sanskrit and Indian Studies.

Alm, B. 1996. "The State and Caste Conflicts, Two Cases from Tamil Nadu". In N. Jayaram and Satish Saberwal (ed.). *Social Conflict*. pp. 113-29. Delhi: Oxford University Press.

Aloysius, G. 1998. "Dalit Empowerment: The Lessons from History". In *Religion and Society*. Vol. 45. No. 4. pp. 81-88.

—. 1999. *Ayothidasar Sinthanaigal*. Vols. I and II. Palayamkottai: Nattar Valakkatriyal Aivu Maiyam.

Althusser, L. 1971. "Ideology and Ideological State Apparatuses". In L. Althusser (ed.). *Lenin, Philosophy and Other Essays*. London: New Left Books.

Ambedkar, B.R. 1948. *The Untouchables: Who Were They? And Why They Became Untouchables*. New Delhi: Amrit Books.

Anandhi, S. 2000. *Land to the Dalits: Panchami Land Struggle in Tamil Nadu*. Bangalore: Indian Social Institute.

Anderson, P. 1998. *The Origins of Postmodernity*. London: Verso.

Appadurai, A. 1981. *Worship and Conflict Under Colonial Rule: A South Indian Case*. Cambridge: Cambridge University Press.

—. 1977. "Kings, Sects and Temples in South India, 1350-1700 A.D". *The Indian Economic and Social History Review*. 14 (1): 47-73.

—. 2000 (1996). *Modernity at Large: Cultural Dimensions of Globalisation*. Public World Series. Minnesota: University of Minnesota.

—. 1986. "Is Homo Hierarchicus?" *American Anthropologist*. 13: 745-61.

—. 1991. "Global Ethnoscape: Notes and Queries for a Traditional Anthropology". In Richard G. Fox (ed.). *Recapturing Anthropology: Working in the Present*. New Mexico: School of American Research Press. 1991.

Archer, M.S. 1988. *Culture and Agency: The Place of Culture in Social Theory*. Cambridge: Cambridge University Press.

—. 2000. *Being Human: The Problem of Agency*. Cambridge: Cambridge University Press.

Arendt, H. 1958. *The Human Condition*. Chicago: University of Chicago Press.

Asad, T. (ed.) 1973. *Anthropology and the Colonial Encounter*. London: Ithaca Press.

Attridge, D., Bennington, G. and Young, R. (eds.). 1987. *Post-Structuralism and the Question of History*. Cambridge: Cambridge University Press.

Augustin, P. "Conversion as Social Process". *Religion and Society*. 28 (1981). pp.31-57.

Ayoorkuzhiel, A. 1990. "The Ideological Nature of the Emerging Dalit Consciousness". In *Religion and Society*. Vol. XXXVII. September. 1990.

Babb, L. 1975. *The Divine Hierarchy: Popular Hinduism in Central India*. New York: Columbia University Press.

Baert, P. 1998. *Social Theory in the Twentieth Century*. Cambridge: Polity Press.

Bakhtin, M.M. 1993. *Toward a Philosophy of the Act*. Austin: University of Texas Press.

Bal, P. "Driven to the Wall: Dalits Under Shiv Sena-BJP Rule". *Economic and Political Weekly*. August 2, 1997. pp. 1948-50.

Balakrishnan, G. 2002. "The Age of Identity?" In *New Left Review*. 16 July/August. pp. 130-42.

Banks, M. 1996. *Ethnicity: Anthropological Constructions*. London and New York: Routledge.

Barnard, A. and Spencer, J. (eds.). 2002. *Encyclopedia of Social and Cultural Anthropology*. London: Routledge.

Barth, F. 1960. "The System of Social Stratification in Swat, North Pakistan". In E. Leach (ed.). *Aspects of Caste in South India, Ceylon and North-West Pakistan*. Cambridge: Cambridge University Press.

—. 1969. Introduction. In Frederik Barth (ed.). *Ethnic Groups and Boundaries: The Social Organisation of Culture Difference*. Oslo: Universitetsforlaget.

—. 1981. *Process and Form in Social Life: Selected Essays of Frederik Barth*. Vol. 1. London: Routledge and Kegan Paul.

—. 2000. "Boundaries and Connections". In Anthony P. Cohen (ed.). *Signifying Identities: Anthropological Perspectives on Boundaries and Contested Values*. London: Routledge. pp. 17-36.

Barthes, R. 1973. *Mythologies*. Translated by A. Lavers. London: Paladin.

Bayly, S. 1999. *The New Cambridge History of India: Caste, Society, and Politics in India from the Eighteenth Century to the Modern Age*. Cambridge: Cambridge University Press.

Beck, B. 1981. "The Goddess and the Demon: A Local South Indian Festival and its Wider Context". In *Puruṣārtha*. 5: 83-136.

Beck, B.E.F., 1976. "The Symbolic Merger of Body, Space and Cosmos in Hindu Tamil Nadu". In *Contributions to Indian Sociology*. NS 10: 213-43.

Benedict, R. 1967. *The Chrysanthemum and the Sword*. Cleveland and New York: World.

Bénéï, V., and Fuller, C.J. (eds.). 2001. *The Everyday State and Society in Modern India*. London: Hurst and Company.

Berreman, G. 1963. *Hindus of Himalayas*. Berkeley, CA: University of California Press.

—. 1971. "Brahminical View of Caste". In *Contributions to Indian Sociology*. NS. 5: 16-23.

Berreman, G.D. 1979. *Caste and Other Inequities: Essays on Inequality*. Meerut: Folklore Institute.

Beteille, A. 1966. *Caste, Class and Power: Changing Patterns of Stratification in a Tanjore Village*. Bombay: Oxford University Press.

—. 1969. *Castes: Old and New – Essays in Social Structure and Social Stratification*. Bombay: Asia Publishing House.

—. 1998. "Pollution and Poverty". In J. Michael Mahar (ed.). *The Untouchables in Contemporary India*. New Delhi: Rawat Publications. pp. 412-3.

Bhatt, C. 2001. *Hindu Nationalism: Origins, Ideologies and Modern Myths*. London and New York: Berg Publishers.

Blumer, H. 1986. *Symbolic Interactionism: Perspective and Method*. California, London: University of California Press.

Blunt, E. 1969. *The Caste System of Northern India with Special Reference to the United Provinces of Agra and Oudh*. Delhi: S. Chand & Co. (first edition 1931).

Bolton, L. and Weiner, J. (eds.). "Using Multi-Sited Ethnography: Investigations of a Methodological Proposal". *Canberra Anthropology*. Vol. 22. No. 2. October 1991.

Bordewich, F. 1997. *Killing the White Man's Indian*. New York: Anchor.

Bourdieu, P. 1969. "Intellectual Field and Creative Project". In *Social Science Information*. 8: 89-119.

—. 1977a. *Outline of a Theory of Practice*. Cambridge: Cambridge University Press.

—. 1990. *The Logic of Practice*. Cambridge: Polity Press.

Bowman, G. 2001. "The Violence in Identity". In Bettina E. Schmidt and Ingo W. Schröder (eds.). *Anthropology of Violence and Conflict*. London, New York: Routledge.

Breckenridge, A., and Appadurai A. "The South Indian Temple: Authority, Honour and Redistribution". *Contributions to Indian Sociology*. NS. 10. (1976). pp. 187-211.

Bruner, E.M. 1986. "Experience and Its Expressions". In Victor W. Turner and Edward M. Bruner (eds.). *The Anthropology of Experience*. Urbana and Chicago: University of Illinois Press.

Burland, C. et al. 1970. *Mythology of the Americas*. London: Hamlyn.

Butler, C. 2002. *Postmodernism: A Very Short Introduction*. Oxford: Oxford University Press.

Byron, R. 2002. "Identity". In Barnard, A. and Spencer, J. (eds.). *Encyclopedia of Social and Cultural Anthropology*. London: Routledge.

Calhoun, C. 1995. *Critical Social Theory: Culture, History, and the Challenge of Difference*. Cambridge, MA: Blackwell.

Camus, A. 2000 (1953). *The Rebel*. London: Penguin.

Carrithers, M. et al. (eds.). 1999 (1985). *The Category of the Person: Anthropology, Philosophy, History*. Cambridge: Cambridge University Press.

Cassirer, E. 1955. *The Philosophy of Symbolic Forms*. Volume 1: *Language* Translated by Ralph Manheim. New Haven and London: Yale University Press.

—. 1955. *The Philosophy of Symbolic Forms*. Volume 2: *Mythical Thought*. Translated by Ralph Manheim. New Haven and London: Yale University Press.

—. 1985 (1957). *The Philosophy of Symbolic Forms*. Volume 3: *The Phenomenology of Knowledge*. Translated by Ralph Manheim. New Haven and London: Yale University Press.

Castells, M. 1998 (1997). *The Power of Identity. The Information Age: Economy, Society and Culture,* Vol. II. Oxford: Blackwell Publishers.

Chakrabarty, B. 2003. "Introduction". In Chakrabarty, B. (ed.). *Communal Identity in India: Its Construction and Articulation in the Twentieth Century*. New Delhi: Oxford University Press. pp. 1-50.

Champakalakshmi, R. 2001. "Reappraisal of a Brahmanical Institution: The Bramedeya and its Ramifications in Early Medieval South India". In Kenneth R. Hall (ed.). *Structure and Society in Early South India: Essays in Honour of Noboru Karashima*. New Delhi: Oxford University Press.

Charsely, S. and Karanth, G.K. (eds.). 1998. *Challenging Untouchability: Dalit Initiative and Experience from Karnataka. Cultural Subordination and the Dalit Challenge.* Vol 1. New Delhi: Sage Publications.

Charsley, S. 1996. "'Untouchable': What's in Name?" *Journal of the Royal Anthropological Institute.* 2(1): 1-24.

Chatterjee, P. 1993. *The Nation and Its Fragments*. Princeton, New Jersey: Princeton University Press.

Chaturvedi, V. (ed.). 2000. *Mapping Subaltern Studies and the Post Colonial*. London: Verso.

Cheater, A. (ed.). 1999. *The Anthropology of Power: Empowerment and Disempowerment in Changing Structures*. London: Routledge.

Chittan, G. 1993. *Tamil Ilakkiyathil Pallar (Mallar) Devendhra Kula Velalar (adipadai sandrukal)* (Basic evidences of Pallar (Mallar) Devedndhra Kula Velalar in Tamil Literature). Coimbatore, Tamil Nadu: Devedhra Mandram.

Chomsky, N. 1989. *Necessary Illusions: Thought Control in Democratic Societies*. London: Pluto Press.

Clifford, J. and Marcus, G.E. (eds.). *Writing Culture: The Poetics and Politics of Ethnography*. Berkeley: University of California Press.

Clough, J. E. 1914. *Social Christianity in the Orient: The Story of a Man, a Mission and a Movement*. New York: Macmillan.

Cohen, A.P. 1981. *The Politics of Elite Culture: Explorations in the Dramaturgy of Power in a Modern African Society*. Berkeley: University of California Press.

—. 1985. *The Symbolic Construction of Community*. London: Routledge.

—. 1998 (1994). *Self-Consciousness: An Alternative Anthropology of Identity*. London: Routledge.

—. 2000. *Signifying Identities: Anthropological Perspectives on Boundaries and Contested Values*. London: Routledge.

Cohn, B.S. 1988. "Representing Authority in Victorian India". In Hobsbawm, E. and Ranger, T. (eds.) 1988 (1983). *The Invention of Tradition*. Cambridge: Cambridge University Press.

—. 1987. *An Anthropologist among the Historians*. Delhi: Oxford University Press.

—. 1985. "The Command of Language and the Language of Command". In Ranajit Guha (ed.). *Subaltern Studies IV: Writings on South Asian History and Society*. Delhi: Oxford University Press.

—. 1984. "The Census, Social Structure and Objectification in South Asia". In *Folk* 26: 25-49.

Comaroff, J. and Comaroff, J.L. 1997. *Of Revelation and Revolution*. Vol. 2. Chicago, IL: University of Chicago Press.

Coser, L. 1956. *Functions of Social Conflict*. Glencoe: Free Press.

—. 1968. *Continuities in the Study of Social Conflict*. New York: Free Press.

Cox, C.O. 1970. *Caste, Class and Race*. New York: Monthly Review Press.

Crehan, K. 2002. *Gramsci, Culture and Anthropology*. London: Pluto Press.

Culler, J. 2002. *Literary Theory: A Very Short Introduction.* Oxford: Oxford University Press.

Cuthbertson, G.M. *Political Myth and Epic.* East Lansing: Michigan State University Press.

Damasio, A. 2000. *The Feeling of What Happens: Body, Emotion and the Making of Consciousness.* London: Vintage.

Daniel, E.V. 1984. *Fluid Signs: Being a Person the Tamil Way.* Berkeley: University of California Press.

Davidson, D. 1980 (1971). "Agency". In D. Davidson (ed.). *Essays on Actions and Events.* pp. 43-61. Oxford: Clarendon Press.

Davies, B. 1991. "The Concept of Agency". In *Social Analysis* 30: 42-53.

De Souza, P.R. 2000. *Contemporary India: Transitions.* New Delhi: Sage.

Dean, M. 1998. "Questions of Method". In I.Velody and R. Williams (eds.). *The Politics of Constructionism.* pp.182-199. London: Sage.

Deleige, R. 1993. 'The Myths of Origin of the Indian Untouchables'. *Man* (NS). 28 (1993). pp. 533-49.

—. 1999. *The Untouchables of India.* London: Berg.

—. 1992. "Replication and Consensus: Untouchability, Caste and Ideology in India". *Man* (NS). 27 (1992). pp.155-73.

—. 1997. *The World of 'the Untouchables': Paraiyars of Tamil Nadu.* Delhi: Oxford University Press.

Deshpande, J.V. "Behind Dalit Anger". *Economic and Political Weekly.* August 16-23, 1997.

Diani, M. and Donatella Della Porta (eds.). 1999. *Social Movements: An Introduction.* Oxford: Blackwell.

Diehl, A. 1977. *Periyar E.V. Ramaswami.* Bombay: B.I. Publications.

Dirks, N. B. 2000. "The Crimes of Colonialism. Anthropology and the Texualisation of India". In Peter Pels and Oscar Salemink (eds.). *Colonial Subjects. Essays on the Practical History of Anthropology.* Ann Arbor: The University of Michigan Press. pp. 153-179.

Dirks, N.B. 1994. "Ritual and Resistance: Subversion as a Social Fact". In Dirks et al. (eds.). *Culture, Power, History. A Reader in Contemporary Social Theory.* Princeton, New Jersey: Princeton University Press.

Dissanayake, W. (ed.) 1996. *Narratives of Agency: Self-Making in China, India and Japan.* Minneapolis: University of Minneapolis Press.

Dobres, M.A. 2000. *Technology and Social Agency: Outlining a Practice Framework for Archaeology.* Oxford: Blackwell Publishers.

Dolgin, J.L. et al. (eds.). 1977. *Symbolic Anthropology. A Reader in the Study of Symbols and Meanings.* New York: Columbia University Press.

Doniger, W. 1991. *The Laws of Manu*. London: Penguin.

Douglas, M. 1970. *Natural Symbols*. London: Cresset.

— 1999. *Implicit Meanings. Selected Essays in Anthropology*. London: Routledge.

Dubois, J. 1906 (first edition 1806). *Hindu Manners, Customs, and Ceremonies*. Oxford: Oxford University Press.

Dumont, L. 1970. *Religion, Politics and History in India*. Paris: Mouton.

—. 1980. *Homo Hierarchicus. The Caste System and Its Implications*, trans. (complete revised edition). Chicago and London: University of Chicago Press.

—. 1986. *A South Indian Subcaste: Social Organisation and Religion of the Pramalai Kallar*. New Delhi: Oxford University Press.

Durkheim, E. 1982. *The Rules of Sociological Method, and Selected Texts on Sociology and its Method*. London: Macmillan.

Eagleton, T. 1991. *Ideology: An Introduction*. London and New York: Verso.

Eck, D. 1983. *Banaras: City of Light*. London: Routledge and Kegan Paul.

Eliade, M. 1958. *Patterns in Comparative Religion*. London: Sheed and Ward.

—. 1989. *The Myth of the Eternal Return, or, Cosmos and History*. translated by W.R. Trask. London: Arkana.

Eriksen, T.H. 1993. *Ethnicity and Nationalism: Anthropological perspectives*. London: Pluto Press.

Erikson, E. 1968. *Identity: Youth and Crisis*. New York: Norton.

Evans-Pritchard, E.E. 1940. *The Nuer*. Oxford: Oxford University Press.

—. 1967. "The Nuer Concept of Spirit in its Relation to the Social Order". In John Middleton (ed.). *Myth and Cosmos: Readings in Mythology and Symbolism*. Garden City, New York: The Natural History Press.

Fabian, J. 1983. *Time and the Other: How Anthropology Makes Its Object*. New York: Columbia University Press.

Fanon, F. 1965. *The Wretched of the Earth*. New York: Grove Press.

—. 1967. *Black Skin, White Masks*. New York: Grove Press.

Fardon, R. 1999. *Mary Douglas*. London: Routledge.

Fawcett, T. 1970. *The Symbolic Language of Religion*. London: SCM Press.

Feldman, A. 1991. *Formations of Violence: The Narrative of the Body and Political Terror in Northern Ireland*. Chicago: University of Chicago Press.

Fernandes, W. (ed.). 1996. *The Emerging Dalit Identity: The Re-assertion of the Subalterns*. New Delhi: Indian Social Institute.

—. 1993. Dalit Christians in Tamil Nadu (Unpublished manuscript).

Fernandez, J.M. 2000. "Peripheral Wisdom". In Anthony P. Cohen (ed.). *Signifying Identities. Anthropological Perspectives on Boundaries and Values*. pp.117-44. London: Routledge.

Feuer, L.S. 1975. *Ideology and the Ideologists*. Oxford: Basil Blackwell.

Firth, R. 1967. *The Forest of Symbols: Aspects of Ndembu Ritual*. London/Ithaca: Cornell University Press.

—. 1973. *Symbols: Public and Private*. London: George Allen and Unwin.

Flanagn, O. 1995 (1992). *Consciousness Reconsidered*. Cambridge, Massachusetts: The MIT Press.

Flood, C. G. 2002. *Political Myth*. London and New York: Routledge.

Foucault, M. 1991a. "Politics and the Study of Discourse". In G. Burchel, C. Gordon and P. Miller (eds.). *The Foucault Effect: Studies of Governmentality*. London: Harvester/Wheatsheaf. 53-72.

—. 1982. "The Subject and Power". In H. Dreyfus and P. Rabinow (eds.). *Michel Foucault: Beyond Structuralism and Hermeneutics*. Translated by H. Dreyfus and P. Rabinow. Chicago: University of Chicago Press.

—. 1991b. "Questions of Method". In G. Burchel, C. Gordon and P. Miller (eds.). *The Foucault Effect: Studies of Governmentality*. London: Harvester/Wheatsheaf.

—. 1985 (1969). *The Archaeology of Knowledge*. London: Tavistock.

Fox, R.G. 'Elites: Ethnographic Issues'. *American Anthropologist*. 87 (4): 930-932.

Franco, F. and Kumar, V. 1996. "Dalit Organisations: Reconstituting Reality" in Walter Fernandes (ed.). *The Emerging Dalit Identity: The Re-Assertion of the Subalterns*. New Delhi: Indian Social Institute. 1996.

Frankfort, H. et al. 1949. *Before Philosophy: The Intellectual Adventure of Ancient Man*. Baltimore: Penguin.

Freedman, M. 1979. *Main Trends in Social Anthropology*. London: Holmes and Meier.

Fuller, C.J. 2000 (1996). "Introduction". In Fuller, C.J. (ed.). *Caste Today*. pp. 1-29. Oxford: Oxford University Press.

Fuss, D. 1989. *Essentially Speaking: Feminism, Nature and Difference*. New York: Routledge.

Galanter, M. 1984. *Competing Equalities: Law and the Backward Classes in India*. Berkeley: University of California.

Gardener, K. and Lewis, D. 1996. *Anthropology, Development and the Post-modern Challenge*. London: Pluto Press.

Gardiner, J.K. (ed.). 1995. *Provoking Agents: Gender and Agency in Theory and Practice*. Urbana: University of Illinois Press.

Geertz, C. 1993 (1973). *The Interpretation of Cultures*. London: Hutchinson.

Geetha, V. and Rajadurai, S.V. 1998. *Towards a Non-Brahmin Millennium: From Iyothee Thass to Periyar*. Calcutta: Samya.

Ghurye, G.S. 1963. *The Scheduled Tribes*. Bombay: Popular Prakashan.

—. 1994 (1932). *Caste and Race in India*. Bombay: Popular Prakashan.

Giddens, A. 1984. *The Constitution of Society: Outline of the Theory of Structuration*. Cambridge: Polity Press.

—. 1990. *The Consequences of Modernity*. Cambridge: Polity Press.

—. 1993. *New Rules of Sociological Method*. Cambridge: Polity Press.

Gluckman, M. (1956) 1959. *Custom and Conflict in Africa*. Glencoe Illinois: Free Press.

Goddard, V.A. (ed.) 2000. *Gender, Agency and Change: Anthropological Perspectives*. New York: Routledge.

Goffman, E. 1970. *Strategic Interaction*. Oxford: Basil Blackwell.

—. 1980 (1969). *The Presentation of Self in Everyday Life*. Harmondsworth: Penguin.

—. 2002. "Front and Back Regions of Everyday Life". In Ben Highmore (ed.). *The Everyday Life Reader*. London and New York: Routledge. pp. 50-7.

Gokhale, J. 1993. *From Concessions to Confrontation. The Politics of an Untouchable Community*. Bombay: Popular Prakashan.

Gokhale-Turner, J. 1980. "Bhakti or Vidroha: Continuity and Change". *Dalit Sahitya Journal of Asian and African Studies*. 15. pp. 29-42.

Good, A. 1983. "A Symbolic Type and its Transformations: The Case of South Indian Ponkal". In *Contributions to Indian Sociology* (NS). 17. 223-44.

—. 1991.*The Female Bridegroom. A Comparative Study of Life-Crisis Rituals in South India and Sri Lanka*. Oxford: Clarendon Press.

Gordon, C. 1980. "Afterword". In C. Gordon (ed.). *Power/Knowledge*. New York: Harvester/Wheatsheaf.

Gore, M.S. 1993. *The Social Context of an Ideology: Ambedkar's Political and Social Thought*. New Delhi: Sage.

Gough, K. 1960. "Caste in a Tanjore Village". In E. Leach (eds.). *Aspects of Caste in South India, Ceylon and North-West Pakistan*. pp. 11-60. Cambridge: Cambridge University Press.

—. 1973. "Harijans in Thanjavur". In Gough, K. and H. Sharma (eds.). *Imperialism and Revolution in South Asia*. pp. 222-45. New York: Monthly Review Press.

—. 1989. *Rural Change in South-East India: 1950s to 1980s*. Delhi: Oxford University Press.

—. 1955. "The Social Structure of a Tanjore Village". in McKim Marriot (ed.). *Village India: Studies in the Little Community*. Chicago: University of Chicago Press. pp. 36-52.

Gould, H. 1960. "Castes, Dalits and the Sociology of Stratification". *International Journal of Comparative Sociology*. 1 (1960). pp. 220-38.

Gowthaman, R. 1993. *Dalit Panbadu* (in Tamil) (Dalit Culture: Critical Essays). Puduvai: Gowri Pathipagam.

Grafe, H. 1990. *History of Christianity in India: Tamil Nadu in the Nineteenth and Twentieth Centuries*. Vol. IV. Part 2. Bangalore: Church History Association of India (CHAI).

Gramsci, A. 1971. *Selections from Prison Notebooks*. London: Lawrence and Wishart.

—. 1975. *Selections from the Prison Notebooks*. New York: International Publishers.

Graves, R. 1968. "Introduction". In Guirand, Felix. (ed.). *New Larousse Encyclopedia of Mythology*. Translated by R. Aldington and D. James. London: Hamlyn.

Gunasekaran, K.A. 1995. *Dalit Arankiyal* (Dalit Theatre). Chennai: Keelaikattru Publishers.

Gunasekaran, K.A. 1999. *Dalit Kalai Kalacharam* (Dalit Art and Culture). Chennai: Ragas.

Gupta, D. 1997. *The Context of Ethnicity: Sikh Identity in a Comparative Perspective*. New Delhi: Oxford University Press.

Gupta, S.K. 1985. *The Scheduled Castes in Modern Indian Politics*. Delhi: Munshiram Manoharlal Publishers.

Guru, G. 2001. "The Language of Dalit-Bahujan Political Discourse". In Ghanshyam Shah (eds.). *Dalit Identity and Politics: Cultural Subordination and the Dalit Challenge*. Vol. 2. pp. 74-96. New Delhi: Sage.

Hall, S. 2003. "New Ethnicities". In Linda Martin Alcoff and Eduardo Mendieta (eds.). *Identities. Race, Class, Gender, and Nationality*. Oxford: Blackwell Publishing.

Hardgrave, R.L. 1969. *The Nadars of Tamil Nadu*. Berkeley: University of California Press.

Harper, E. "Ritual Pollution as Integrator of Caste and Religion". *Journal of Asian Studies*. 23 (1964). pp. 179-80.

Harris, G.G. 1989. "Concepts of Individual, Self, and Person in Description and Analysis". In *American Anthropologist*. 91: 599-612.

Harvey, D. 1989. *The Condition of Postmodernity: An Enquiry into the Origins of Cultural Change*. Oxford: Blackwell.

Heeger, G.A. 1974. *The Politics of Underdevelopment.* New York: St. Martin's Press.

Henry, R. "Confronting Ethnographic Holism: Field Site or Field of Sociality". *Canberra Anthropology.* Vol. 22. No. 2. October 1999. pp. 51-61.

Hobsbawm, E. and Ranger, T. 1988 (1983). *The Invention of Tradition.* Cambridge: Cambridge University Press.

Holland, D. et al. 1998. *Identity and Agency in Cultural Worlds.* Cambridge, MA: Harvard University Press.

Hopa, N.K. 1999. "Land and Re-empowerment: 'The Waikato Case'". In Angela Cheater (ed.). *The Anthropology of Power: Empowerment and Disempowerment in Changing Structures.* London: Routledge.

Horowitz, D.L. 2000 (1985). *Ethnic Groups in Conflict.* Berkeley, Los Angeles, London: University of California Press.

Howarth, D. 1998. "Discourse Theory and Political Analysis". In Elinor Scarbrough and Eric Taenbaum (eds.). *Research Strategies in the Social Sciences: A Guide to New Approaches.* Oxford: Oxford University Press.

Howe, L. 2001. *Hinduism and Hierarchy in Bali.* Oxford: James Currey; Santa FE, New Mexico: School of American Research Press.

Hume, R. E. (tr). 1951. *The Thirteen Principal Upanishads.* London.

Hutton, J. 1973 (1946). *Caste in India: Its Nature, Function, and Origins.* Cambridge: Cambridge University Press.

Ilaiah, K. 2001. "Dalitism vs Brahminism: The Epistemological Conflict in History". In Ghanshyam Shah (ed.). *Dalit Identity and Politics: Cultural Subordination and the Dalit Challenge.* Vol. 2. pp. 97-107. New Delhi: Sage.

Ilaiah, K. 1996. "Productive Labour, Consciousness and History: The Dalit-Bahujan Alternative" in Shahid Amin and Dipesh Chakrabarty (eds.). *Subaltern Studies IX: Writings on South Asian History and Society.* New Delhi: Oxford University Press.

Inden, R. 1990. *Imagining India.* Oxford: Blackwell.

Irschick, E. 1969. *Politics and Social Conflict in South India.* Berkeley: University of California.

Jacob, T.G. 2000. *Reflections on the Caste Question. Overview of Tamil Nadu, Karnataka and Kerala.* Bangalore: NESA.

Jaffrelot, C. 1993. *The Hindu Nationalist Movement and Indian Politics 1925 to the 1990s.* London: Hurst and Company.

—. 2003. *India's Silent Revolution: The Rise of the Lowercastes.* London: Hurst and Company.

Jeffrey, R. 1976. "Temple-Entry Movements in Travancore 1860-1940". *Social Scientist.* 4 (1976). pp.3-27.

James, W. 1973. "Anthropologist as reluctant Imperialist". In Talal Asad (ed.). *Anthropology and the Colonial Encounter*. London: Ithaca Press. pp. 41-70.

Jenkins, R. 1992. *Key Sociologists. Pierre Bourdieu*. London: Routledge.

—. 1996. *Social Identity*. London: Routledge.

Juergensmeyer, M. 2000. *Terror in the Mind of God. The Global Rise of Religious Violence*. Berkeley/Los Angeles/London: University of California Press.

Kamble, N.D. 1982. *The Scheduled Castes*. New Delhi: Ashish Publishing House.

Kananaikal, J. (ed.). 1983. *Scheduled Castes and the Struggle Against Inequality: Strategies to Empower the Marginalised*. New Delhi: Indian Social Institute.

Kapadia, K. 1995. *Siva and Her Sisters: Gender, Caste, and Class in Rural South India*. Boulder, Colorado: Westview Press.

Karp, I. 1986. "Agency and Social Theory: A Review of Anthony Giddens". In *American Ethnologist* 13 (1): 13-37.

Kearney, R. 2002. *On Stories*. London and New York: Routledge.

Keer, D. 1964. *Mahatma Jotirao Phooley: Father of Indian Social Revolution*. Bombay: Popular Prakashan.

Kelly, D. and Kaplan, M. 1999. "Discourse and Power: 'Cults' and 'Orientals' in Fiji". *American Anthropologist*. Vol. 26. No. 4. November 1999.

Kesavan, K. 1994. *Samuga Viduthalaiyum Thazhthapattorum*. (Dalits and Social Justice). Villupuram: Saravanabalu Pathipagam.

Khare, R.S. 1984. *The Untouchable as Himself: Ideology, Identity and Pragmatism among the Lucknow Chamars*. Cambridge: Cambridge University Press.

Kripke, S. 1980. *Naming and Necessity*. Oxford: Blackwell.

Krishnan, P.S. 2002. "Untouchability and Atrocities". In Ghanshyam Shah (ed.). *Dalits and the State*. Mussoorie: Centre for Rural Studies.

Kshirsagar, R.K. 1994. *Dalit Movement in India and Its Leaders*. New Delhi: M D Publications.

Kuber, W.N. 1991. *Ambedkar: A Critical Study*. New Delhi: People's Publishing House.

Kumar, D. 1965. *Land and Caste in South India: Agricultural Labour in Madras Presidency in the Nineteenth Century*. Cambridge: Cambridge University Press.

—. 1994. "Caste and Landlessness in Modern India and Pakistan". In Gyan Prakash (ed.). *The World of the Rural Labourer in Colonial India*. Delhi: Oxford University Press.

Kuper, A. 1988. *The Invention of Primitive Societies: Transformation of an Illusion*. London: Routledge.

Kuruvilla, P. 2000. *Idols to Die, Symbols to Live: Dynamic Interaction between Language, Reality and the Divine*. New Delhi: Intercultural Publications.

Laclau, E. (ed.). 1994. *The Making of Political Identities*. London: Verso.

—. 1985. *Hegemony and Social Strategy*. London: Verso.

—. 1993. "Discourse". In Gooding and Pettit (eds.). *The Blackwell Companion to Contemporary Political Philosophy*. 1993. Oxford: Blackwell.

Langer, S.K. 1956 (1942). *Philosophy in a New Key*. New York: Mentor Book.

Lawson, P. 1993. *The East India Company: A History*. Harlow: Longman.

Leach, E. 1967. "Genesis as Myth". In Middleton (ed.). *Myth and Cosmos. Readings in Mythology and Symbolism*. pp.1-14. Garden City, New York: The Natural History Press.

Leach, E. 1976. *Culture and Communication*. Cambridge: Cambridge University Press.

Levi-Strauss, C. 1968. *Structural Anthropology* (Shamanism and Psycho-analysis). New York: Penguin.

—. 1969 (1964). *The Raw and the Cooked: Introduction to a Science of Mythology: I*. New York: Harper and Row.

—. 1973 (1966). *From Honey to Ashes: Introduction to a Science of Mythology: II*. London: Jonathan Cape.

—. 1978. *Myth and Meaning*. London: Routledge and Keegan Paul.

—. 1981 (1971). *The Naked Man: Introduction to a Science of Mythology: IV*. New York: Harper and Row.

—. 1967. "Four Winnebago Myths: A Structural Sketch". In John Middleton (ed.). *Myth and Cosmos. Readings in Mythology and Symbolism*. Garden City, New York: The Natural History Press.

Lincoln, B. 1989. *Discourse and the Construction of Society: Comparative Studies of Myth, Ritual, and Classification*. Oxford: Oxford University Press.

—. 1999. *Theorizing Myth: Narrative, Ideology, and Scholarship*. Chicago and London: The University of Chicago Press.

Lindow, J. 2001. *Norse Mythology: A Guide to the Gods, Heroes, Rituals, and Beliefs*. Oxford: Oxford University Press.

Lobo, L. 2001. "Visions, Illusions and Dilemmas of Dalit Christians". In Shah, G. 2001. (ed.). *Dalit Identity and Politics: Cultural Subordination and the Dalit Challenge*. Vol. 2. pp. 242-57. London: Sage

Ludden, D. 1989. *Peasant History in South India*. Oxford: Oxford University Press.

Lynch, O. 1969. *The Politics of Untouchability: Social Mobility and Social Change in a City of India*. New York: Columbia University Press.

Lyotard, J. F. 1989. *The Postmodern Condition: A Report on Knowledge*. Translated by Geoff Bennington. Manchester: Manchester University Press.

—. 1988. *The Differend: Phrases in Dispute*. Translated by Georges Van Den Abeele. Manchester: Manchester University Press.

Macdonell, A. A. and Keith, A.B. 1912. *Vedic Index of Names and Subjects*. Vol. I. London.

Madan, T.N. et al. "On the Nature of Caste in India: A Review Symposium of Dumont's *Homo Hierarchicus*". *Contributions to Indian Sociology.* NS (1971). 5: 1-81.

Mahar, M.J. 1998. *The Untouchables in Contemporary India*. Jaipur: Rawat Publications.

Malinowski, B. 1974 (1948). *Magic, Science and Religion, and Other Essays*. Glencoe Illinois: Free Press.

Mallar, A.V.K. 1999. *Mallarum Samuga Viduthalaiyum*. Kovai: Saathi Aathikka Ethirppu Munnani.

Manikumar, K.A. "Caste Clashes in South Tamil Nadu". *Economic and Political Weekly.* September 6, 1997.

Marcus, G. E. 1995. "Ethnography in/of the World System: The Emergence of Multi-sited Ethnography". *Annual Review of Anthropology.* (1995) 24: 95-117.

Marcus, G.E. (ed.). 1983. *Elites: Ethnographic Issues*. Albuquerque: University of New Mexico Press.

—. 1998. *Ethnography through Thick and Thin*. Princeton, New Jersey: Princeton University Press.

—. 1999. "What is at Stake – and is not – in the Idea and Practice of Multi-sites Ethnography". *Canberra Anthropology.* Vol. 22. No. 2. October. pp. 6-14.

Marriott, M., and M. Moreno. 1990. "Humoral Transactions in Two Tamil Cults: Murukan and Mariyamman". In McKim Marriott (ed.). *India through Hindu Categories*. Sage: New Delhi. pp. 149-67.

Massey, J. 1991. *Roots: A Concise History of Dalits*. Delhi: ISPCK.

—. 1994. "The Role of the Churches in the Whole Dalit Issue". In *Religion and Society*. Vol. XLI. No. 1. March.

—. 1995. *Dalits in India: Religion as a Source of Bondage or Liberation with Special Reference to Christians.* Delhi: ISPCK.

—. 1997. *Down Trodden. The Struggle of India's Dalits for Identity, Solidarity and Liberation.* Geneva: WCC Publications.

Mathew, J. 1986. *Ideology Protest and Social Mobility.* New Delhi: Inter-India Publications.

Mauss, M. 1999 (1985). "A Category of the Human Mind: The Notion of Person; the Notion of Self". In M. Carrithers et al. (eds.). *The Category of the Person: Anthropology, Philosophy, History,* pp. 1-25. Cambridge: Cambridge University Press.

Mead, G.H. 1970 (1934). *Mind, Self and Society: From the Standpoint of a Social Behaviourist.* Chicago: University of Chicago Press,

Mencher, J. 1974. "The Caste System Upside Down, or the Not-so-Mysterious East". In *Current Anthropology.* 15. pp. 469-93.

Mendelsohn, O. and Vicziany, M. 1998. *The Untouchables: Subordination, Poverty and the State in Modern India.* Cambridge: Cambridge University Press.

Michael, M. 1998. *The Untouchables in Cotemporary India.* Jaipur: Rawat Publications.

Michael, S.M. (ed.). 1999. *Untouchable: Dalits in Modern India.* London: Lynne Rienner Publishers.

Middleton, J. (ed.). 1967. *Myth and Cosmos: Readings in Mythology and Symbolism.* Garden City, New York: The Natural History Press.

Mines, D.P. 1990. "Hindu Periods of Death 'impurity'". In McKim Marriott (ed.). *India through Hindu Categories.* New Delhi: Sage.

Moffatt, M. 1975. "Untouchables and the Caste System: A Tamil Nadu Case Study". In *Contributions to Indian Sociology.* NS 9(1): 111-37.

—. 1979. *An Untouchable Community in South India: Structure and Consensus.* Princeton: Princeton University Press.

Mohanty, S.P. 2000. "The Epistemic Status of Cultural Identity: On *Beloved* and the Postcolonial Condition". In Moya, P.M.L. and Hames-Garcia, M.R. (eds.). *Reclaiming Identity: Realist Theory and the Predicament of Postmodernism.* Berkeley/Los Angeles/London: University of California Press. pp.29-66.

Mosse, D. 1994. "Idioms of Subordination and Styles of Protest among Christian and Hindu Harijan Castes in Tamil Nadu". In *Contributions to Indian Sociology* (NS). 28 (1994). pp. 67-106.

—. 1985. "Caste, Christianity and Hinduism: A Study of Social Organization and Religion in Rural Ramnad". D.Phil Thesis. Oxford University. Institute of Social Anthropology.

—. 2003. *The Rule of Water, Statecraft, Ecology, and Collective Action in South India.* New Delhi: Oxford University Press.

Mouffe, C. 1979. "Hegemony and Ideology in Gramsci". In Mouffe (ed.). *Gramsci and Marxist Theory*. London: Routledge and Kegan Paul. 168-205.

—. 1981. "Hegemony and Integral State in Gramsci: Towards a New Concept of Politics". In Bridges and Brunt (eds.). *Silver Linings: Some Strategies for the Eighties*. London: Lawrence and Wishart. 167-87.

Moya, P.M.L. and Hames-García, M.R. (eds.) 2000. *Reclaiming Identity: Realist Theory and the Predicament of Postmodernism*. Berkeley, Los Angeles and London: University of California Press.

—. 2000. Introduction. "Reclaiming Identity". In Moya, P.M.L. and Hames-García, M.R. (eds.). 2000. *Reclaiming Identity: Realist Theory and the Predicament of Postmodernism*. Berkeley, Los Angeles and London: University of California Press.

Murugkar, L. 1991. *Dalit Panther Movement in Maharashtra: A Sociological Appraisal*. Bombay: Popular Prakashan.

Nader, L. 1968. "Conflict: Anthropological Aspects". In David L. Sills (ed.). *International Encylopedia of the Social Sciences*. Vol. 3. pp. 236-42.

Natesan, G.A. 1911. *The Depressed Classes: An Enquiry into their Conditions and Suggestions for their Uplift*. Madras: Natesan.

Neale, W.C. 1998. "The Marginal Laborer and the Harijan in Rural India". In J. Nordstrom, C. 1997. *A Different Kind of War Story*. Philadelphia: University of Pennsylvania Press.

O'Hanlon, R. 1985. *Caste, Conflict and Ideology: Mahatma Phule and the Low Caste Protest in Nineteenth-Century Western India*. Cambridge: Cambridge University Press.

Oddie, G.A. 1979. *Social Protest in India: British Protestant Missionaries and Social Reform 1850-1900*. New Delhi: Manohar Publishers.

Okely, J. 1992. "Anthropology and Autobiography: Participatory Experience and Embodied Knowledge". In J. Okely and H. Callaway (eds.). *Anthropology and Autobiography*. London: Routledge.

Omvedt, G. 1976. *Cultural Revolt in a Colonial Society: The Non-Brahman Movement in Western India 1873 to 1930*. Pune: Scientific Socialist Education Trust.

—. 1987. "Dalit Literature in Maharashtra: Literature of Social Protest and Revolt in Western India". *South Asia Bulletin*. 7.

—. 1990. *Protest and Change: Studies in Social Movements*. New Delhi: Sage.

—. 1995. *Dalit Visions: The Anti-Caste Movement and the Construction of an Indian Identity*. New Delhi: Orient Longman.

Oommen, T.K. 1984. "Sources of Deprivation and Styles of Protest: The Case of the Dalits in India". *Contributions to Indian Sociology*. NS 18. 1984. pp. 45-61.

Ortner, S.B. 2002. "On Key Symbols". In Michael Lambek (ed.). *A Reader in the Anthropology of Religion*. pp. 158-67. Oxford: Blackwell Publishers

Otte, T.G. 2002. "The Father of All? A Persuasive Vision of Epochal War and State Formation". In *The Times Literary Supplement*. June, 21. No. 5177. pp. 8-10.

Owen, R. 1973. "Imperial Policy and Theories of Social Change". In Talal Asad (ed.). *Anthropology and the Colonial Encounter*. London: Ithaca Press. pp. 223-44.

Pai, S. 2001. "From Harijan to Dalits: Identity Formation, Political Consciousness and Electoral Mobilisation of the Schedule Castes in Uttar Pradesh". In Ghanshyam Shah (ed.). *Dalit Identity and Politics: Cultural Subordination and the Dalit Challenge.* Vol. 2. pp. 258-87. New Delhi: Sage.

Parish, S.M. 1996. *Hierarchy and Its Discontents: Culture and the Politics of Consciousness in Caste Society*. Philadelphia: University of Pennsylvania Press.

Parry, J. 1980. "Ghosts, Greed, and Sin: The Occupational Identity of the Benares Funeral Priests". *Man* (NS). 21 (1980). pp. 453-73.

Patil, P.G. 1991(tr.). *Collected Works of Mahatma Jotirao Phule*. Vol. II. Selections. Bombay: Government of Maharashtra.

Peacock, J.L. 1975. *Consciousness and Change: Symbolic Anthropology in Evolutionary Perspective*. Oxford: Basil Blackwell.

Pels, P. and Salemink, O. (eds.) 2000. *Colonial Subjects. Essays on the Practical History of Anthropology*. Ann Arbor: The University of Michigan Press.

Pérez-Sarduy, P. and Stubbs, J. (eds.) 1995. *No Longer Invisible: Afro-Americans Today*. London: Minority Rights Group Publications.

Perumal, A.K., and Ramachandran, N. 2001. *Thamilaga Nattar Nigalthukalaigal* (in Tamil), (The Folk Arts of Tamil Nadu). Chennai: Tamil Nadu Iyal, Isai and Nadaga Mandram.

Philomen, A. 1999. *Sathi Thiyil Veguthu Thiruchabai* ('the Church is Burnt in Caste Flames'). Chennai: Arulkadal.

Phule, J. 1990. *Samagra Wanghmay*. Bombay: Government of Maharashtra.

Pinto, A. (ed.) 1999. *Dalits: Assertion for Identity*. New Delhi: Indian Social Institute.

Poole, F.J.P. 2000 (1994). "Socialisation, Enculturation and the Development of Personal Identity". In Tim Ingold (ed.). *Companion Encyclopedia of Anthropology: Humanity, Culture and Social Life*. pp. 831-860. London and New York: Routledge.

Pratto, F. and Sidanius, J. 1999. *Social Dominance: Intergroup Theory of Social Hierarchy and Oppression*. Cambridge: Cambridge University Press.

Punalekar, S.P. 1988. "Identities and Consciousness: An Overview of Dalit Literature in Maharashtra". In *Man and Development*. 10(4) (December).

—. 2001. "Dalit Literature and Dalit Identity". In Shah, G. (ed.). 2001. *Dalit Identity and Politics: Cultural Subordination and the Dalit Challenge*. Vol. 2. London: Sage. pp.214-241.

Pushpendra, 2001. "Dalit Assertion through Electoral Politics". In Shah, G. (ed.) 2001. *Dalit Identity and Politics: Cultural Subordination and the Dalit Challenge*. Vol. 2. pp. 311-40. London: Sage.

Quigley, D. 1993. *The Interpretation of Caste*. Oxford: Clarendon Press.

Quinn, N. and Claudia Strauss. 1997. *A Cognitive Theory of Cultural Meaning*. Cambridge: Cambridge University Press. pp. 13-44; 210-252.

Raheja, G.G. 2000. "The Illusion of Consent: Language, Caste, and Colonial Rule in India". In Peter Pels and Oscar Salemink (eds.). *Colonial Subjects: Essays on the Practical History of Anthropology*. Ann Arbor: The University of Michigan Press.

Raj, A. 1992a. *Children of a Lesser God (Dalit Christians)*. Madurai: DCLM.

—. 1992b. *Discrimination against Dalit Christians in Tamil Nadu*. Madurai: IDEAS Centre.

—. 1995. "The Dalit Christian Reality in Tamil Nadu". In Kanjamala, A. (ed.). *Integral Mission Dynamics: A Interdisciplinary Study of the Catholic Church in India*. New Delhi: Intercultural Publications.

Raja, M.A. 2002. "The Configuration and Powers of Dalit Consciousness". In *Satya Nilayam*. February. Vol. 1. pp. 125-33.

Rajadurai, S.V. and Geetha, V. 1993. "Dalits and Non-Brahmin Consciousness in Colonial Tamil Nadu". *Economic and Political Weekly*. September 25. pp. 2091-98.

—. 1993. "Neo-Brahminism: An Intentional Fallacy?". *Economic and Political Weekly*. January 16-23.

Randeria, S. 1989. "Carrion and Corpses: Conflict in Categorising Untouchability in Gujarat". *Archives europeennes de sociologie*. 30 (1989). pp. 171-91.

Rao, C.R.P. 1993. "Dalit Consciousness and Brahminism: A Multiplex Question". In *The Eastern Anthropologist*. 46: 1.

Rao, M.S.A. 1979. *Social Movements and Social Transformation: A Study of Two Backward Classes Movements in India*. Delhi: Macmillan.

Revathi, V. 1997. *Thamilakathin Arasiyal Munnodigal (The Dalit Pioneering Leaders of Tamil Nadu)*. Pondicherry: Navajothi Publishers.

Rex, J. 1981. *Social Conflict: A Conceptual and Theoretical Analysis*. London: Longman.

Ricoeur, P. 1969. *The Symbolism of Evil*. Translated by Emerson Buchanan. Boston: Beacon Press.

—. 1974. *The Conflict of Interpretations*. Evanstone: Northwest University Press.

—. 1986. "Existence and Hermeneutics". In D.E. Klemm. *Hermeneutical Inquiry*. Vol. 1. Atlanta: Scholars Press.

—. 1984-8. *Time and Narrative*. 3 Volumes. Chicago: University of Chicago Press.

Robb, P. (ed.) 1999 (1993). *Dalit Movements and the Meanings of Labour in India*. New Delhi: Oxford University Press.

Rothschild, J. 1993. *Return to Diversity: A Political History of East Central Europe since World War II*. Oxford: Oxford University Press.

Saberwal, S. and Jayaram, N. (eds.). 1996. *Social Conflict*. Delhi: Oxford University Press.

Said, E.S. 1995. *Orientalism: Western Conceptions of the Orient*. London: Penguin Books.

Saradamoni, K. 1980. *Emergence of a Slave Caste: Pulayas of Kerala*. Delhi: People's Publishing House.

Sathianathan, C. 1998. *Dalits and Christianity*. New Delhi: Oxford University Press.

Schröder, I.W. and Schmidt, B.E. 2001. *Anthropology of Violence and Conflict*. London: Routledge.

Scott, J. 1985. *Weapons of the Weak: Everyday Forms of Peasant Resistance*. London: Yale University Press.

—. 1990. *Domination and the Arts of Resistance: Hidden Transcripts*. London: Yale University Press.

Searle-Chatterjee, M. and Sharma, U. (eds.). 1994. *Contexualising Caste: Post-Dumontian Approaches*. Oxford: Blackewell/The Sociological Review.

Selvam, S. 1999. "Representing Hinduism" In S.M. Michael (ed.). *Untouchable: Dalits in Modern India*. London: Lynne Rienner Publishers.

Shah, Ghanshyam (ed.) 2001. *Dalit Identity and Politics. Cultural Subordination and the Dalit Challenge.* Vol.2. London: Sage.

Shah, Ghanshyam. 2001. "Dalit Movements and the Search for Identity". In Shah, G. (ed.) *Dalit Identity and Politics: Cultural Subordination and the Dalit Challenge*. Vol. 2. pp. 195-213. London: Sage

Sharma, U. 1999. *Caste*. Buckingham: Open University Press.

Shetty, V. R. 1987. *Dalit: The Black Untouchables of India*. Atlanta, GA: Clarity Press.

Shils, E. 1975. *Centre and Periphery: Essays in Macro-Sociology*. Selected Papers of Edward Shils. Vol. 2. Chicago: University of Chicago Press.

Shore, C. 2002. Introduction. "Towards an Anthropology of Elites". In C. Shore and S. Nugent (eds.). *Elite Cultures: Anthropological Perspectives*. ASA Monographs. London and New York: Routledge.

Shore, C. and Nugent, S. (eds.) 2002. *Elite Cultures: Anthropological Perspectives*. ASA Monographs. London and New York: Routledge.

Shulman, D. 1985. *The King and the Clown in South Indian Myth and Poetry*. Princeton: Princeton University Press.

Sidanius, J. and Felicia Pratto. 1999. *Social Dominance: An Intergroup Theory of Social Hierarchy and Oppression*. Cambridge: Cambridge University Press.

Sills, D.L. (ed.) 1968. *International Encyclopaedia of the Social Sciences*. Vol. 3. pp.220-42.

Simmel, G. (1908) 1955. *Conflict: The Web of Group Affiliations*. Glencoe Illinois: Free Press.

Simmel, G. 1955. *Conflict*. (tr. Kurt H. Wolff). New York: Free Press.

Singh, J. and Pai, S. "Politicisation of Dalits and Most Backward Castes: Study of Social Conflict and Political Preferences in Four Villages of Meerut District". *Economic and Political Weekly*. June 7. 1997. pp. 1356-61.

Singh, R. 2001. *Social Movements, Old and New: A Post-modernist Critique*. New Delhi: Sage.

Sivakumar, C. and Sivakumar, S.S. 1993. *Peasants and Nabobs: Agrarian Radicalism in Late Eighteenth Century Tamil Country*. Delhi: Hindustan Publishing Corporation.

Skinner, Q. (ed.). 1997. *The Return of Grand Theory in the Human Sciences*. Cambridge: Cambridge University Press.

Smith, A.D. 1999. *Myths and Memories of the Nation*. Oxford: Oxford University Press.

Smith, W.R. 1938. *Nationalism and Reform in India*. London: Yale University Press.

Sonamandan, K. 1999. "Will there be Re-Polls in Chidambaram?". In *Nandan* (Tamil Journal). Sept 16-30. pp. 13-16 and 36-38.

Sperber, Dan. 1995 (first edition 1975). *Rethinking Symbolism*. Cambridge: Cambridge University Press.

Srinivas, M.N. 1952. *Religion and Society among the Coorgs*. Oxford: Clarendon Press.

Stanilaus, L. 1999. *The Liberative Mission of the Church Among Dalit Christians*. Delhi: ISPCK.

Stryker, S. et al. (eds.) 2000. *Self, Identity, and Social Movements*. Minneapolis and London: University of Minnesota Press.

Subrahmanyam, S. 2002. "Violence and Identities in South Asia: Grievance and Memory in Community Formation". In *Puruṣārtha*. Vol. 22. pp.47-70.

Subramanian, N. 1980. *Sangam Polity: The Administrative and Social Life of the Sangam Polity*. Madurai: Ennes Publications.

Suresh, V. 2000 (1996). "The Dalit Movement in India". In T.V. Satyamurthy (ed.) *Region, Religion, Caste, Gender and Culture in Contemporary India*. Delhi: Oxford University Press.

Tambiah, S.J. 1996. *Levelling Crowds. Ethnonationalist Conflicts and Collective Violence in South Asia*. Berkeley, Los Angeles, London: University of California Press.

Taylor, Y. (ed.) 1999. *I Was Born a Slave: An Anthology of Classic Slave Narratives*. Vol. I, Vol. II. Edinburgh: Playback Press.

Thangaraj, M. 1998. *Thamiḻagathil Jāthikkalavarangal* (in Tamil) (Caste Conflicts in Tamil Nadu). Chengalpattu, Tamil Nadu: Legal Resources for Social Action.

Thomson, P. 2000 (1978). *The Voice of the Past: Oral History*. Oxford: Oxford University Press.

Thorat, S.K. "Dalits and the New Economic Policy". *Dalit International Newsletter*. (2): 1, 4. (1996).

Thurston, E. 1975. *Castes and Tribes of Southern India*. Vol. VI. Delhi: Cosmos Publishers.

Tonkin, E. 1995 (1992). *Narrating Our Past: The Social Construction of Oral History*. Cambridge: Cambridge University Press.

Torfing, J. 1999. *The New Theories of Discourse: Laclau, Mouffe and Zizek*. Oxford; Blackewell.

Touraine, A. 1977. *The Self-Production of Society*. Chicago: Chicago University Press.

—. 1981. *The Voice and the Eye*. New York: Cambridge University Press.

—. 1985. "An Introduction to the Study of Social Movements". In *Social Research*. Vol. 52. No. 4. pp. 749-87.

—. 1987. "Social Movements: Participation and Protest". In *Scandinavian Political Studies*. Vol. 10. No. 3. pp. 207-22.

Trautman, T.R. et al. 1985. "The Study of South Indian Inscriptions". In Robert E. Frykenberg and Pauline Kolenda (eds.). *Studies of South India: An Anthology of Recent Research and Scholarship*. Madras: New Era Publications.

Turner, V. 1957. *Schism and Continuity in an African Society*. Manchester: Manchester University Press.

—. 1967. "Themes in the Symbolism of Ndembu Hunting Ritual". In John Middleton (ed.). *Myth and Cosmos: Readings in Mythology and Symbolism*. Garden City, New York: The Natural History Press.

—. 1974. *Dramas, Fields, and Metaphors: Symbolic Action in Human Society*. Ithaca and London: Cornell University Press.

—. 2002. "Liminality and Communitas". In Michael Lambek (ed.) *A Reader in the Anthropology of Religion*. Oxford: Blackwell. pp. 358-74.

Turner, V. and Bruner, E.M. (eds.) 1986. *The Anthropology of Experience*. Urbana and Chicago: University of Illinois Press.

Unnithan-Kumar, M. 1997. *Identity, Gender and Poverty: New Perspectives on Caste and Tribe in Rajasthan*. Providence and Oxford: Berghahn Books.

Vakil, A.K., 1991. *Gandhi Ambedkar Dispute: An Analytical Study*. New Delhi: Ashish Publishing House.

Valarmathi, M. 1999. *Parai: Isaikaruvi oru Aivu* (Parai: Musical Instrument, An Analysis). Chennai: Thirumagal Nilayam.

Vanaik, A. 1997. *The Furies of Indian Communalism, Religion, Modernity and Secularisation*. London: Verso.

Varshney, A. 2002. *Ethnic Conflict and Civic Life: Hindus and Muslims in India*. Delhi: Oxford.

Vidyasagar, R. 1988. *Caste Conflicts in Tamil Nadu*. Bangalore: Vishtar

Vincentnathan, L. 1993. "Untouchable Concepts of Person and Society". In *Contributions to Indian Sociology*. NS 27, 1.

Wagatsuma, H. and G. De Vos. 1967. *Japan's Invisible Race: Caste in Culture and Personality*. Berkeley, CA: University of California Press.

Washbrook, D. 1999. "Land and Labour in Late Eighteenth-Century South India: the Golden Age of Paraiah?" In Peter Robb (ed.). *Dalit Movements and the Meanings of Labour in India*. pp.68-86. New Delhi: Oxford University Press.

—. 1975. "The Development of Caste Organisation in South India, 1880 to 1925". In C.J. Baker and David A. Washbrook (eds.). *South India: Political Institutions and Political Change, 1880-1940*. Delhi: Macmillan.

—. 1993. "Economic Depression and the Making of 'traditional' Society in Colonial India". *Transactions of the Royal Historical Society* 6 (3): 237-63.

Weber, M. 1964. *The Theory of Social and Economic Organisation* (trans. A.M. Henderson and T. Parsons) New York: Free Press.

Webster, J.C.B. 1992. *The Dalit Christians: A History*. Delhi: ISPCK.

Whitehead, H. 1921. *The Village Gods of South India*. Calcutta: Oxford University Press.

Wilfred, F. 1996. "Towards a Subaltern Hermeneutics: Beyond the Contemporary Polarities in the Interpretation of Religious Traditions". In *Voices from the Third World*. Ecumenical Association of Third World Theologians. Vol. 19. No. 2. 1996. 128-48.

—. 2000. "Identity: Suppressed, Alienated, Lost". *Concilium*, 2000/2 pp. 31-38.

Williams, R. and Velody, I. (eds.). *The Politics of Constructionism*. London: Sage.

Williams, R. 1983. *Keywords: A Vocabulary of Culture and Society*. London: Fontana Paperbacks.

Willis, P. 1981. *Learning to Labor: How Working Class Kids Get Working Class Jobs*. New York: Columbia University Press.

Wolf, E.R. 1999. *Envisioning Power: Ideologies of Dominance and Crisis*. Berkeley/Los Angeles/London: University of California Press.

Yadav, K.C. (ed.) 2000. *From Periphery to Centre Stage. Ambedkar, Ambedkarism and Dalit Future*. New Delhi: Manohar.

Yon, D. 1999. "The Discursive Space of Schooling: On the Theories of Power and Empowerment in Multiculturalism and Anti-racism". In Angela Cheater (ed.). *The Anthropology of Power*. ASA Monographs 36. London and New York: Routledge.

Young, R.J.C. 2003. *Postcolonialism: A Very Short Introduction*. Oxford: Oxford University Press.

Zelliot, E. 1998. *From Untouchable to Dalit: Essays on the Ambedkar Movement*. New Delhi: Manohar Publishers.

—. 2001. "The Meaning of Ambedkar". In Ghanshyam Shah (ed.). *Dalit Identity and Politics*. New Delhi: Sage. pp. 129-142.

ž ižek, S. 2002 (2001). *On Belief*. London and New York: Routledge.

Index